B&B
The Australian
BED & BREAKFAST BOOK
2010

"Personal invitations to stay in one of the most Beautiful Countries in the World"

The Original Guide to Wonderful Accommodation

Over 1000 Places to Stay

THE AUSTRALIAN BED & BREAKFAST BOOK 2010
Australia's Best Accommodation Guide

Editor Carl Southern
Design: Nesel Alliance
Layout: Matt Thomas
Maps: The Map Shop
Editing: Ian Southern
Printing: Book Builders, Hong Kong
Paper: Printed on paper produced from Sustainable Growth Forest

Distribution
Australia: Tower Books, Gordon and Gotch
UK and Europe: Vine House Distribution
New Zealand: Moonshine Press
US: Pelican Publishing Company

Published October 2009

Inn Australia Pty Ltd
PO Box 330, Wahroonga, NSW 2076, Australia
Tel: +61 2 8208 5959
Email: info@BBBook.com.au
Web: www.BBBook.com.au

22nd Edition
Copyright © October 2009 Inn Australia Pty Ltd

This book is copyright. Apart from fair dealing for the purpose of private study, research, criticism or review, as permitted under the Copyright Act, no part may be reproduced by any process without the written permission of the publishers.
Every effort has been made to ensure that the information in this book is as up to date as possible at the time of going to press. All Listing Information including contact details, room rates and accommodation facilities has been supplied by the hosts and B&B Association directory information has been verified by the national or state associations. The publishers have provided the listing information in good faith and will not be liable for any errors nor will they accept responsibility arising from reliance on any contents in the book.

Includes Index
ISBN 978-0-9758040-5-6

We welcome your comments and suggestions

Cover Image:
Lakeside Villas At Crittenden

Tell hosts you found them in the Bed & Breakfast Book

B&B

The Australian
BED & BREAKFAST BOOK
2010

Australia's Best
ACCOMMODATION GUIDE

The Original Guide to Wonderful Accommodation
Over 1000 Places to Stay

Including Directory of National and State B&B Associations
Bed and Breakfast Farmstay and Accommodation Australia
Bed & Breakfast and Farmstay NSW & ACT
Bed & Breakfast and Farmstay Queensland
Bed and Breakfast and Farmstay Association of Far North Queensland

SMALL HOTELS   CITY APARTMENTS   COUNTRY COTTAGES
RURAL RETREATS   FAMILY FARMSTAYS   BEACHSIDE HOLIDAYS
ECO FRIENDLY GETAWAYS   PET FRIENDLY STAYS
B&BS FOR GARDEN LOVERS   ROMANTIC GETAWAYS
TRADITIONAL B&BS   STAYS IN WINE REGIONS

BBBook.com.au

Acknowledgements

Each year it seems to get harder to put this guide together than the previous year, but I guess we are more critical of our own efforts and demand more of ourselves. This year, no less than previous years much effort has been expanded by many in preparing this guide. So it is you the readers of The B&B Book, who I would like to thank first, for without you there would be no book. Thank you for purchasing the book, thank you for using the book and thank you for your many kind comments about the book.

The B&B Book contains a great selection of B&Bs and similar styled accommodation held together by a common thread called 'hospitality'. Since we first published The B&B Book in 1989 hosts have trusted the book to promote their accommodation. Being small businesses hosts have to be careful how to market best their properties, so please tell your hosts, "We found you in The B&B Book."

Most properties included in the B&B Book belong to their industry association, which liaises with government and other industry bodies to support their businesses. Look for their logos in the B&B Book. This year, we especially thank Liz and David Prior from Bed & Breakfast Farmstay and Accommodation Australia (BBFAA), Clare Swaan from Bed & Breakfast and Farmstay NSW & ACT (BBFNSWACT), Jodi Behrend from Bed and Breakfast and Farmstay Queensland (BBFQ) and David Nelson Bed and Breakfast and Farmstay Association of Far North Queensland (BBFAFNQ). Thanks to member associations the 2010 B&B Book includes a new directory index to help you locate hundreds of association member properties across Australia.

Editor:	Carl Southern
Editorial Assistant:	Ian Southern
Design:	Julien Lamb (Nesel Alliance)
Production:	Matt Thomas
Website:	Elizabeth Thomas (Moonshine Press)
Maps:	Anthony Stevens and Bernard Hasseloff (The Map Shop)
Accounts:	Peter Davis and Sarah Palmer (Peter Davis Accountants)
Printing:	Adam Crouch and Sarah Hilsden (Bookbuilders)
Distribution:	Tower Books, Gordon and Gotch (Australia), Vine House (UK), Pelican Inc. (US), Moonshine Press (New Zealand)

A Special thank you to the many others who helped in no small way from research to sales: All the team at B-Sealed, Moh Tang Koh, May Koh, Ming Wei Koh, Ming Chuang Koh and Inge-Lise Kurcubic. To Fred Howell, Jan Howell, Sandy Boyd and Gayle Lamb for your support in many ways. To Eva, Alex and Seb I treasure your patience and understanding. James Pierce for your wonderful computer support. Jim Thomas, there are thousands of hosts in Australia and New Zealand and tens of thousands of guests around the world who know B&Bs thanks to you. And to all the wonderful students, parents and staff at St Edmund's School in Wahroonga, thank you. Your generosity of spirit is beyond value. Finally to Joan Southern, your spirit of family is the epitome of true hospitality.

Carl Southern

Contents

THE AUSTRALIAN BED & BREAKFAST BOOK 2010
Australia's Best Accommodation Guide

Acknowledgements	4
Quick Guide	7
The Website	10
Book Orders	10
Quality Assurance	11

Entries

Australian Capital Territory	12
New South Wales	17
Northern Territory	122
Queensland	130
South Australia	163
Tasmania	185
Victoria	198
Western Australia	251
Index by Name of Accommodation	274

Why Do You Need An Accommodation Guide?

The B&B Book is distributed through newsagents, bookstores, the internet, visitor centres and travel and food and wine shows. We enjoy the shows most of all for the opportunity to share with visitors the varied accommodation styles that make up B&Bs. Many share their stories of recent stays, the welcoming drinks on arrival, the fresh flowers in the room or the amiable host who drove them to the restaurant for dinner. A few suggest books are passé and exclaim, "It's the 21st century, why do you need an accommodation guides when you can use the internet?"

Are they right? We can order groceries on the internet, book theatre tickets, book travel and make appointments. So do we need books? When videos appeared many claimed they would see the demise of cinemas like computers heralded the 'paperless' office? Yes, the internet is wonderful and most of us use it all the time. But there is a quality to a book that the internet can never match. We would like you to consider The B&B Book like your corner shop, a friendly face, a welcoming smile, full of information about the best places to stay and offering great value. Welcome to the 22nd Edition of The Australian Bed & Breakfast Book.

Take a look at the shelves or the racks in bookstores or newsagents today you will see increasingly more wonderful books, with bright covers and stunning designs enticing you to travel. You seem to be 'spoilt for choice.' Well we think not, especially when it comes to that unique accommodation sector widely known as Bed & Breakfast. This niche accommodation sector is special in more ways than many realise and the B&B Book has been promoting the wonders of B&Bs and similar styled accommodation for over 21 years. Within the pages of The B&B Book we bring to you experiences of Australian entrepreneurs, small home based businesses, committed to sharing their passion for the country through personal service, local knowledge and wonderful hospitality.

Geoffrey Chaucer penned a great tale many centuries before there were B&Bs . . . but hospitality-like the 'warm welcome' Harry Bailey from The Tabard Inn shared with his guests - is timeless.

Our host gave each and all a warm welcome,
And set us down to supper there and then.
The eatables he served were of the best;
Strong was the wine; we matched it with our thirst
A handsome man our host, handsome indeed,
And a fit master of ceremonies.
Also a proper man in every way.
And moreover he was a right good sort,
And after supper he began to joke,
And, when we had all paid our reckonings,
He spoke of pleasure, among other things:
'Truly,' said he, 'ladies and gentlemen,
Here you are all most heartily welcome.
Upon my word - I'm telling you no lie -
All year I've seen no jollier company
At one time in this inn than I have now.

Geoffrey Chaucer
Canterbury Tales

"B&B Book hosts treat you as a special guest from the moment you arrive until the moment you leave."

Carl Southern 2009

A Quick Guide

This guide will help you to get the most from the B&B Book. Over 300 accommodation choices are featured with full colour photographs and detailed entries to help you choose your next place to stay. The book is divided into chapters, one for each state or territory in Australia. Maps are located at the beginning of each chapter with the town, city or region indicated where the accommodation is featured in the book.

A 'Locator Directory' of over 1000 properties is included at the end of each chapter. The directory includes all the accommodation included in the chapter together with members of national or state B&B & Farmstay associations. Some properties are featured under a region others under a town or city. To locate a particular accommodation you might need to search first under the town then the region according to how 'well known' they are.

Each entry in the guide has been written by the hosts themselves and you will discover the special features of the accommodation through their description.

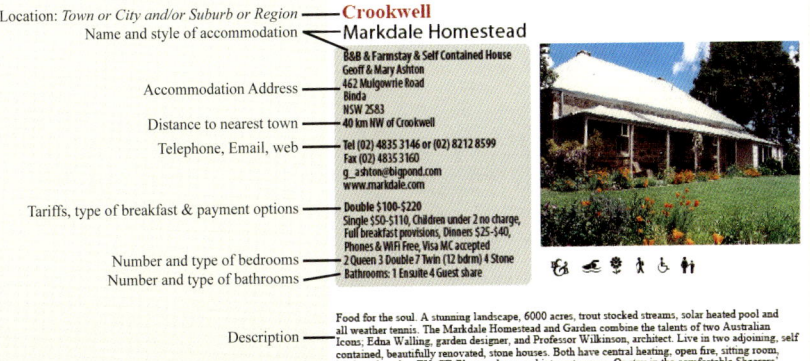

- Location: Town or City and/or Suburb or Region — **Crookwell**
- Name and style of accommodation — **Markdale Homestead**
  B&B & Farmstay & Self Contained House
  Geoff & Mary Ashton
- Accommodation Address — 462 Mulgowrie Road
  Binda
  NSW 2583
- Distance to nearest town — 40 km NW of Crookwell
- Telephone, Email, web — Tel (02) 4835 3146 or (02) 8212 8599
  Fax (02) 4835 3160
  g_ashton@bigpond.com
  www.markdale.com
- Tariffs, type of breakfast & payment options — Double $100-$220
  Single $50-$110, Children under 2 no charge,
  Full breakfast provisions, Dinners $25-$40,
  Phones & WiFi Free, Visa MC accepted
- Number and type of bedrooms — 2 Queen 3 Double 7 Twin (12 bdrm) 4 Stone
- Number and type of bathrooms — Bathrooms: 1 Ensuite 4 Guest share
- Description — Food for the soul. A stunning landscape, 6000 acres, trout stocked streams, solar heated pool and all weather tennis. The Markdale Homestead and Garden combine the talents of two Australian Icons, Edna Walling, garden designer, and Professor Wilkinson, architect. Live in two adjoining, self contained, beautifully renovated, stone houses. Both have central heating, open fire, sitting room, kitchen, laundry, TV, CD Player, phone and internet access. Or stay in the comfortable Shearers' Quarters at cheaper rates.

ACCOMMODATION

B&B Accommodation now covers a range of styles, each with uniquely different characteristics. The common feature for Accommodation included in the B&B Book is 'generous hospitality'. Some properties offer grand suites or luxurious self contained facilities others offer simple and homely B&B accommodation,

You will have your own comfortable and private bedroom, usually with a private or ensuite bathroom. Breakfast is usually included in your room rate unless otherwise indicated.

STYLES

Homestay: Guests may share some areas with hosts such as living or dining rooms.
Bed & Breakfast: Guests do not share any areas with hosts.
Separate Suite: Private accommodation. May include your personal living and dining areas.
Self-Contained: Separate accommodation with kitchen, living and dining areas.
Farmstay: Accommodation on a working farm with farm activities.
Guesthouse or Small Hotel: Accommodation with a restaurant and the warm hospitality found in B&Bs.
Luxury: Higher quality accommodation, often including quality furnishings, bed linen and toiletries.

COMMENT FROM A GUEST
"We received the greatest hospitality, slept in the most wonderful bed and enjoyed the best breakfast in a long, long time. We will return!"
From one of our guests.

ACCOMMODATION DESCRIPTION
Each listing entry and photograph in the guide has been provided by the hosts themselves through which you will discover the uniqueness of the accommodation. Entries are arranged alphabetically by states, then city or region.

ICONS

 **Swimming Pool:** Great for a cool swim on a hot day

 Accommodation with Outstanding Gardens or Unique Location: For garden lovers

 Winery or Wine Activities: Accommodation at a vineyard or where wine activities are possible

 Restaurant: Accommodation next to or adjoining a restaurant

 Eco Tourism: Accommodation complying with or supporting Eco tourism

 Accommodation with Onsite Activities: Maybe horse riding, farm activities or tennis

 Easy Access: Suitable for less able or non ambulant guests. Check details with hosts

 Children Welcome: Check details with hosts

 Accommodation for Couples: Some accommodation is designed for couples or romantic getaways. Other properties may be unsuitable for children due to hazards such as unfenced water

 Pets Welcome: Check details with hosts

 No Smoking on Property: All properties are non smoking inside

 Member of National or State B&B Association

 AAA Tourism Assessed: The stars! Complying with AAA Tourism at time of publication

 Tourism Accredited: The green tick issued by Australian Tourism Accreditation Association

BREAKFAST
One of the delights of staying away is a great breakfast and you can be sure your B&B host will prepare a generous meal, whether it is a traditional country breakfast of country bacon and farm fresh eggs or a platter of seasonal fruits, home made bread and preserves. Some hosts cater for special diets. Your breakfast is included unless otherwise indicated.

Continental or Light: Usually includes cereals, bread or toast, fruit or fruit juice, tea or coffee.
Full: A light breakfast plus a cooked course.
Special: Some hosts offer varied options for B&B or Self Contained Accommodation. Some hosts offer gourmet breakfast. Ask for details.
Breakfast Provisions: Breakfast supplies or Welcome Basket provided. ie Supplies sufficient for a Continental Breakfast, Full Breakfast or sufficient for the first night only.
Accommodation Only: Some Self Contained Accommodation does not provide breakfast offers breakfast for a small addition charge.

ADDITIONAL MEALS
Some rural stays, farmstays or guesthouses offer additional meals. Others offer barbecue packages or picnic hampers. You may need to request meals in advance or by arrangement (B/A).

BEDS AND BEDROOMS
Entries show the number and size of beds, bedrooms and guests that can stay.
Beds for 1 person
Single (1 bed)
Twin (2 single beds)
King twin (2 large single beds).

Beds for 2 persons
Double (small)
Queen (large)
King (very large).

BATHROOMS
Most accommodation provides ensuite or private bathrooms for your exclusive use. Older or historic places may offer private bathrooms for your exclusive use but off the hallway. Some accommodation offer luxurious bathrooms - some with spas.
Ensuite: Exclusive use from your bedroom
Private: Exclusive use, usually off the hallway
Shared: Shared with other guests.

RESERVATIONS
We recommend that you book well in advance to confirm your accommodation. Book directly with your host by email or telephone or mail. Advise dates of arrival and departure, time of arrival, the room/s you require, how many guests in your party, if you are travelling with children or pets or any special requirements. Some accommodation has minimum stays during peak periods. You may need to pay a deposit in advance. Ask how much is due, when full payment is required and the cancellation policy. A travel insurance policy can cover you for unforeseen cancellations. Most hosts accept credit cards.

TARIFFS
Accommodation included in the B&B Book offers great value accommodation, particularly as your breakfast is included in most places. Rates shown include GST and are valid for the current year but are subject to change. They are for two persons (double) or 1 person (single) and vary according to the quality of the accommodation, the location, the facilities offered and seasonal variations. Low season or midweek bookings can offer good value particularly in popular tourism destinations. Confirm rates when booking. Some hosts offer discounts for extended stays. Some can put another bed in the room, for an extra person for a small additional charge.

CHECK-IN
Hosts are usually flexible with check-in and check-out times. Check-in times are usually between 1.00 to 3.00 in the afternoon with check-out between 10.00 to 12.00 in the morning.

CONDITIONS OF STAY
Hosts welcoming guests to stay at their accommodation aim to provide not only you but subsequent guests similar experiences of wonderful accommodation and great hospitality. Most hosts keep their terms and conditions to a minimum; some may invite you to 'sign-in' on arrival and agree to their 'Conditions of Stay'. This could cover you as well as the host in case of an unforeseen incident. Moreover it guarantees all guests that the accommodation will always offer the finest standards.

PLEASE MENTION THE BED & BREAKFAST BOOK
Today many people use a variety of sources to locate their accommodation. We hope that The Bed & Breakfast Book helps you in finding the right accommodation to suit your needs. Whether you telephone, use our website or book through another website, if you found your accommodation through the B&B Book, please tell your hosts, "We found you in The B&B Book."

"The difference between a hotel and a B&B . . . you don't hug the hotel staff when you leave."

The Website - www.BBBook.com.au

Some guests prefer books – some the web. We like books but acknowledge the role of the web, which is why you can find all entries included in the Bed & Breakfast book on our comprehensive website at www.BBBook.com.au. You will find more information on each property, more photographs and direct links to each B&B hosts own website.

Tell Your Hosts, "I Found You In The B&B Book!"

Book Orders

Order a copy of The Australian Bed & Breakfast Book or The New Zealand Bed & Breakfast Book as a gift for a friend or relative. Only $19.95. Free postage Australia. Add $10 for international postage.

You can buy books from bookstores or newsagents or order directly from:

The Bed & Breakfast Book
PO Box 330
Wahroonga
NSW 2076
Info@BBBook.com.au
(02) 8208 5959

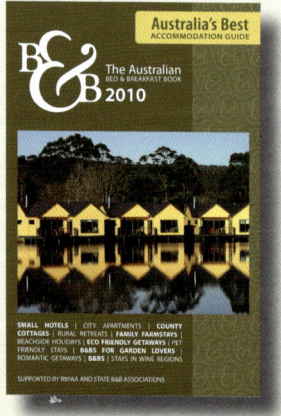

Quality Assurance

Properties included in The Australian Bed & Breakfast Book offer a Commitment to Generous Hospitality. Below are details of the minimum standards you can expect from any of the properties featured in The B&B Book. Or, in simple terms it means ...
"The only surprises you will experience will be Pleasant Surprises!"

HOUSEKEEPING
The Property is well maintained internally and externally with absolute cleanliness in all guest areas, kitchen, refrigerator and food storage areas. All inside rooms are non-smoking.

HOSPITALITY
Hosts are present to welcome and farewell guests (unless advised in self-contained accommodation) Guests are treated with courtesy and respect, and are offered hosts' contact details if hosts leave the premises. Room rates, booking and cancellation policy are advised to guests. Local tourism and transport information is available.

BEDROOMS
Bedrooms solely dedicated to guests, with:
Quality, clean and in sound condition floor coverings, linen, bedding, pillows and furnishings
Bedroom heating and cooling appropriate to the climate
Fans and heating (or reverse cycle air-conditioning)
Bedding and pillows appropriate to the climate, with extra available
Bedside lighting for each guest
Blinds or curtains on all windows where appropriate
Night light or torch in case of power failures
Adequate storage space including wardrobe space with selection of hangers
Adequate sized mirror
power points, alarm clock, waste bin, drinking glasses

BATHROOMS
Sufficient bathroom and toilet facilities for all guests:
Bath or shower, hand basin and mirror
Waste bin in bathroom
Adequate supplies of essential toiletries and towelling: soap, towels, bathmat, facecloths, for each guest
Towels changed or dried daily for guests staying more than one night
Towel rail/hook per guest in the bathroom or bedroom
Privacy lock on bathroom and toilet doors
Power point

MEALS
Breakfast: A generous breakfast is provided (unless advised otherwise in self-contained accommodation)
Meals: Available for guests for additional charge in remote or isolated properties
Drinks: water, tea and coffee offered or available

GENERAL
Roadside identification of property
An honest and accurate description of listing details and facilities
Hosts accept responsibility to comply with government regulations including operational Smoke Alarms
Description includes if hosts' pets and young children are sharing a common area with guests
Adequate Public and Product Liability under a B&B Insurance Policy

OPTIONAL EXTRAS
Most accommodation also provides a number of additional extras including:
Lock on guest rooms or secure storage facilities available, air-conditioning, particularly in hotter areas
laundry facilities, television, DVD, radio, broadband internet services, fresh flowers, magazines, books, fresh fruit and complimentary drinks.
Some are members of National and State B&B Associations, are independently inspected by AAA Tourism or are members of Accredited Tourism Business (Green Tick).

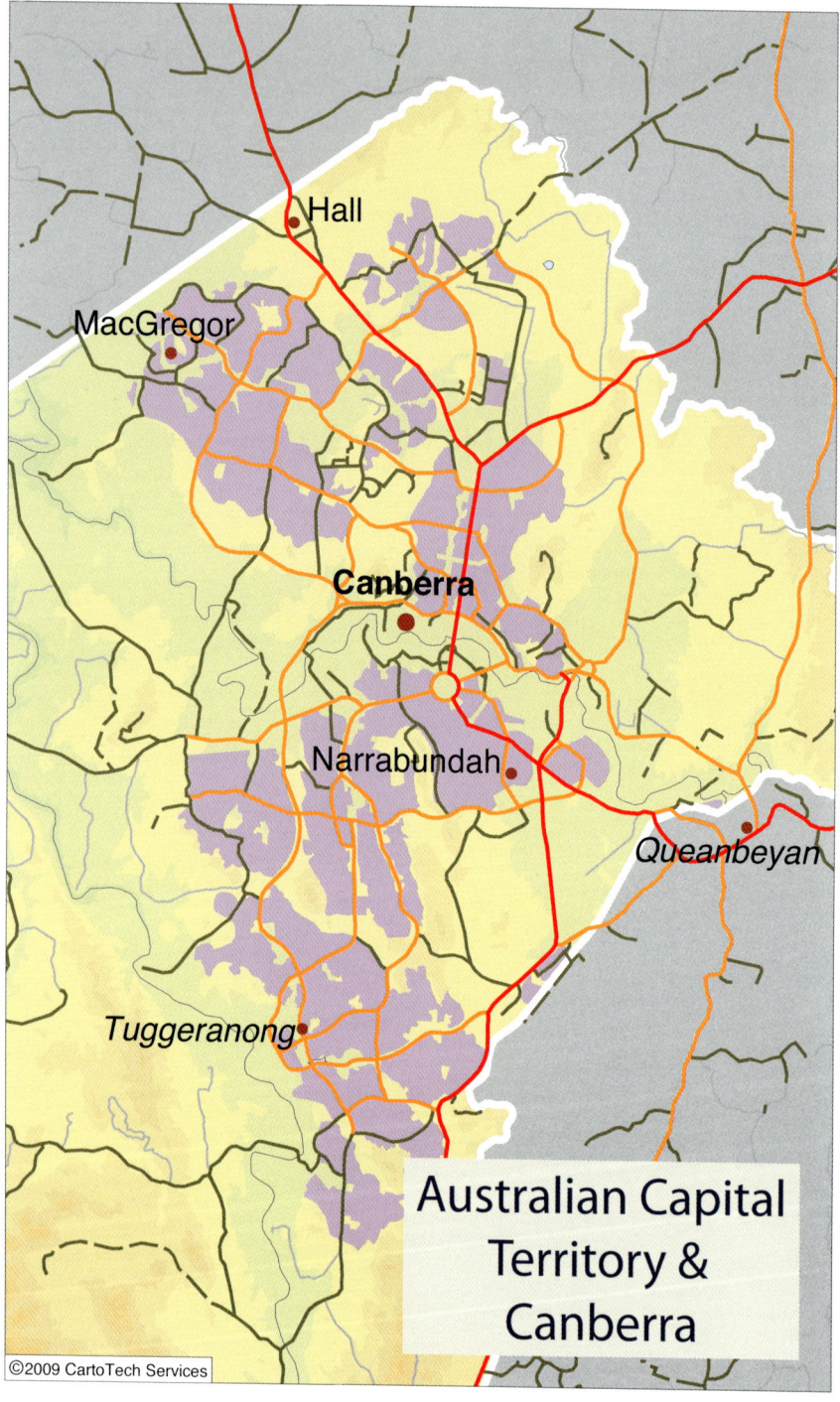

Australian Capital Territory

Canberra - Hall
Surveyor's Hill Winery and B&B

B&B & Farmstay in S/C Historic Cottage & Luxury Studio Apartments
Leigh Hobba
215 Brooklands Road, Wallaroo (near Hall), NSW 2618
25 km N of Canberra

Tel (02) 6230 2046 or 0400 564 030
survhill@westnet.com.au   www.survhill.com.au

Double $150
Single $100, Children from $10,
Full breakfast, Dinner $65 for 3 courses including wine,
Self catering & long stay discounts (double from $130),
Visa MC accepted
Cottage 2 Queen, Studio (A) 1 Queen 1 Double,
Sudio (B) 1 Queen, Cottage 1 Private, Studios both en-suite

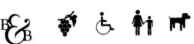

B&B and Farmstay, in 1930 historic farmstead, 230 acre property with vineyards & olives, overlooking Murrumbidgee River, Brindabella Ranges. Easy drive to central Canberra.

Guests enjoy exclusive use of the cottage, fully private, self contained, separate from hosts' residence. Open fire in loungeroom, electric heaters in all rooms ensure cosy warmth. Gourmet meals featuring farm and local produce and premium wines provided in cottage dining room. Excellent kitchen enables self catering.

Generously discounted long stay and self catering rates are negotiable.

New Studio Apartments now also available in modern luxuriously appointed architecturally stunning building, fully private and self-contained including full kitchen facilities. See our website for details.

Australian Capital Territory

Canberra – Hall

The Hills of Hall lie only twenty minutes drive from Canberra. In a strikingly beautiful landscape of rolling hills formed from long-dormant volcanoes, vineyards and olive groves slope down to the valley of the Murrumbidgee River. Of the Canberra District's 40 plus vineyards and cellar doors, four of the best are located here, all within easy walking distance from one another.
Leigh Hobba, Surveyor's Hill Winery and B&B

Canberra

As a young city, and a small one, Canberra offers many special cultural experiences as well as a sense of the vastness of rural Australia. It's easy to fill several days being a tourist, and your entry to many tourist attractions is free.
Merrill Moore, Grevillea Lodge

Australian Capital Territory

Canberra - MacGregor
Grevillea Lodge

B&B & Self-contained unit
Merrill Moore
1 Florey Drive
Macgregor
ACT 2615
11.9 km NW of Canberra GPO

Tel (02) 6161 7646 or 0414 418 374
Fax (02) 6161 7646
merrill@grevillealodge.com
www.grevillealodge.com

Double $100-$140
Single $80-$110, Children 5-12 $10-$20 pn,
Full breakfast, Discounted weekly & self-catered rates on application, Visa MC Diners Eftpos accepted. 2 Queen 1 Single (2 bdrm)
Bathrooms: 2 Ensuite

Grevillea Lodge offers informal country hospitality in suburban Canberra. Very comfortable accommodation in new energy-efficient guest wing with living room, kitchenette, private courtyard, access to large deck and native gardens. Selection of teas, coffee, delicious treats always available. Generous breakfast includes hot dishes, fruit platter, & homemade preserves. Quality bedding, ducted heating, internet (connection in rooms, access in living area), BBQ. Nature reserve, walking/bike tracks 80m. Bus stop 50m. Short drive to all Canberra attractions. Well-behaved pets very welcome inside.

Canberra - Narrabundah
Narrabundah B&B

B&B & Homestay
John & Esther Davies
5 Mosman Place
Narrabundah
ACT 2604
3 km SE of Parliament House

Tel (02) 6295 2837 or 0419 276 231
info@narbb.com
www.narbb.com

Double $130
Single $110, Continental breakfast
Discounts for stays of 4 days or more
Visa MC accepted
1 King (1 bdrm)
Bathrooms: 1 Ensuite

Comfortable, renovated home in quiet street. Conveniently located in relation to Canberra's main tourist attractions, such as Parliament House, National Gallery and War Memorial. Short drive to restaurants in Manuka. Close to public transport and to train station and airport. Air-conditioned (heating and cooling). Hosts are semi-retired and interests include history, genealogy, computing, music, gardening and embroidery. Miniature poodle in residence.

Australian Capital Territory

Recommended Accommodation - Australian Capital Territory

Properties included below with a page reference are included in this chapter and with further details. We have also included recommended accommodation with information supplied by BFNSWACT. Contact the hosts by telephone number for further details and tell them, *"We found you in The B&B Book."*

Canberra - Curtin	Birch Corner	31 Parker St	Curtin	02 6281 4421	
Canberra - Hall	**Surveyor's Hill Winery and B&B**	**215 Brooklands Rd**	**Wallaroo**	**02 6230 2046**	*Page 13*
Canberra - Kambah	Edwil House B&B	6 Rudder Place	Kambah	02 6231 4001	
Canberra - MacGregor	**Grevillea Lodge**	**1 Florey Dv**	**MacGregor**	**02 6161 7646**	*Page 15*
Canberra - Murrumbateman	Redbrow Garden B&B	1143 Nanima Rd	Murrumbateman	02 6226 8166	
Canberra - Narrabundah	**Narrabundah B&B**	**5 Mosman Place**	**Narrabundah**	**02 6295 2837**	*Page 15*
Queanbeyan	Guy's Cross Farm Cottage	419 Captain's Flat Rd	Queanbeyan	02 6297 3440	

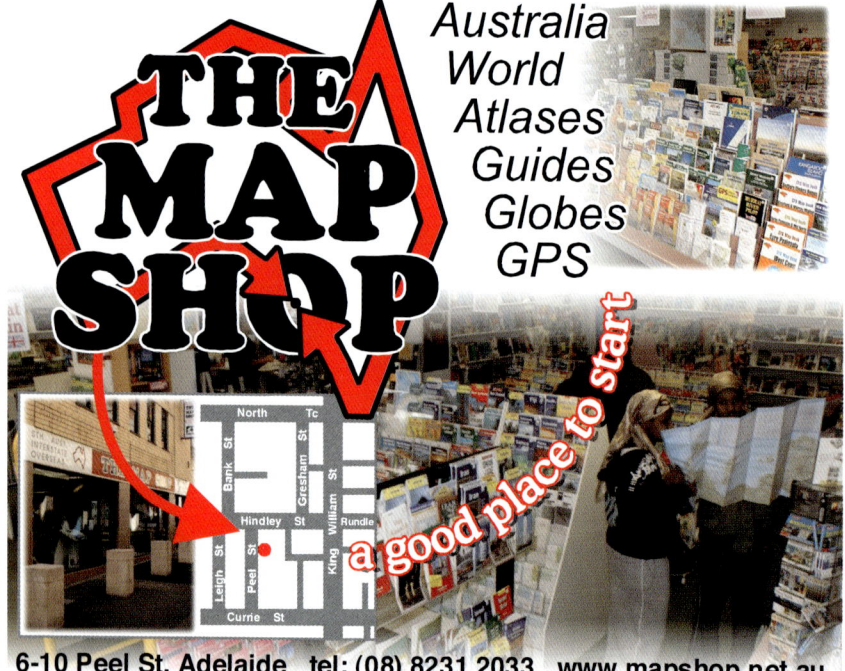

Tell hosts you found them in the Bed & Breakfast Book

Adaminaby - Snowy Mountains
Reynella Homestead

Riding through the wildflowers

Farmstay & Ski Lodge, Homestead
Horse Treks November until end of April. Special Homestead Horse riding 3 day 4 nights October School Holidays
Roslyn & John Rudd
669 Kingston Road, Reynella, Adaminaby, NSW 2629
9 km E of Adaminaby

Tel (02) 6454 2386 or 1800 029 909
Fax (02) 6454 2530   reynella@activ8.net.au
www.reynellarides.com.au

Single $115
Children on application, Full breakfast, Full 3 course dinner included, $115pp (Lodge), Homestead horse riding $95pp, Visa MC Amex Eftpos accepted. 2 King 1 Queen 4 Double 10 Twin 23 Single (19 bdrm).   Bathrooms: 5 Guest share

Lodge accommodation on working sheep and cattle property - opportunities for some involvement.

Largest horse trekking operation in Kosciuszko National Park. 3 day/4 night or 5 day/6 night Safaris. First and last night at the Homestead. With 2 two nights out camping or 4 nights out camping in the Kosciuszko National Park. Operating from October to May.

Stay at The Homestead $115 per night, horse riding an extra $95 per day. We require 4 people riding to take rides.

Stay at the Ski Lodge in the winter only $115 per adult, discount for families, includes 3 course dinner. Ideal base for Skiing Accommodation. Discounts for direct bookings on ski accommodation. Also cottage available for Hire, sleeps 12.

Superb food. BYO. Local fishing, bush walking, riding instruction. (Summer). Original operators - 38 years. Visit our website for dates and rates for trekks.

New South Wales

Adaminaby - Selwyn Snowfields

Selwyn is the perfect place to learn to ski or snowboard with it's gentle, progressing terrain and caring mountain staff. Our family friendly atmosphere will make you and your family feel right at home. In summer you can go horse trekking in the Kosciuszko National Park.
Roslyn Rudd, Reynella Homestead

Albury
Elizabeth's Manor

Luxury B&B & Self Contained House
Larry & Betty Kendall
531 Lyne Street
Lavington, North Albury
NSW 2641
1.5 km W of North Albury PO

Tel (02) 6040 4412
Fax (02) 6040 5166
bookins@elizabethsmanor.com.au
www.elizabethsmanor.com.au

Double $170-$180
Single $140-$150, Children $25
Full breakfast, Dinner $44-$55
Visa MC Diners Amex Eftpos accepted
3 Queen 1 Double (3 bdrm)
Bathrooms: 3 Ensuite

AAA Tourism
★★★★★

Elizabeth's Manor would have to be the most luxurious and romantic adults only accommodation in Australia. On arrival guests will be presented with complimentary sparkling wine and chocolates. A gourmet breakfast can be served in your suite or the Gallery. Although we have a 'No Smoking' policy in the house, smoking is permitted anywhere outside. We also have a late check-out, twelve PM, a good excuse to try our new outside 'Therapeutic' heated spa.

Alstonville - Ballina

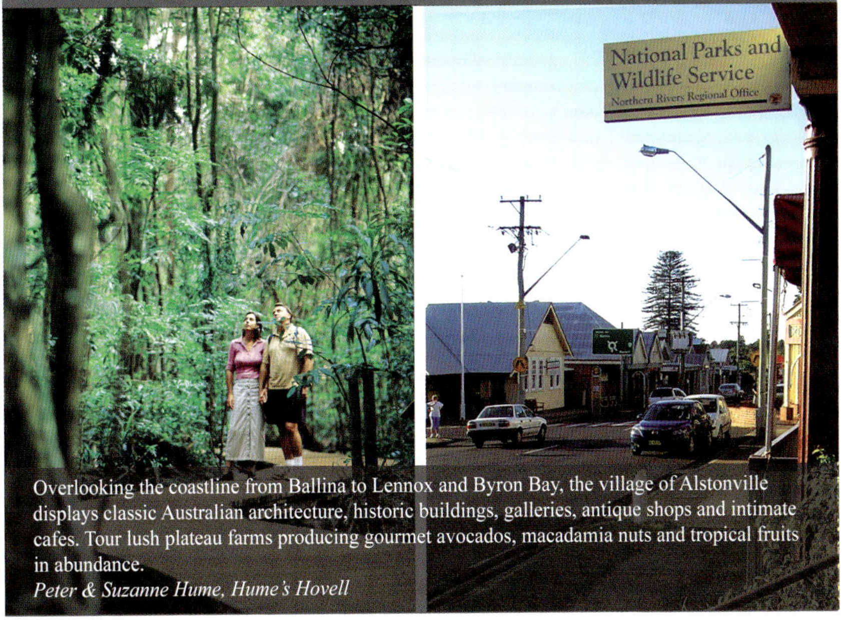
National Parks and
Wildlife Service
Northern Rivers Regional Office

Overlooking the coastline from Ballina to Lennox and Byron Bay, the village of Alstonville displays classic Australian architecture, historic buildings, galleries, antique shops and intimate cafes. Tour lush plateau farms producing gourmet avocados, macadamia nuts and tropical fruits in abundance.

Peter & Suzanne Hume, Hume's Hovell

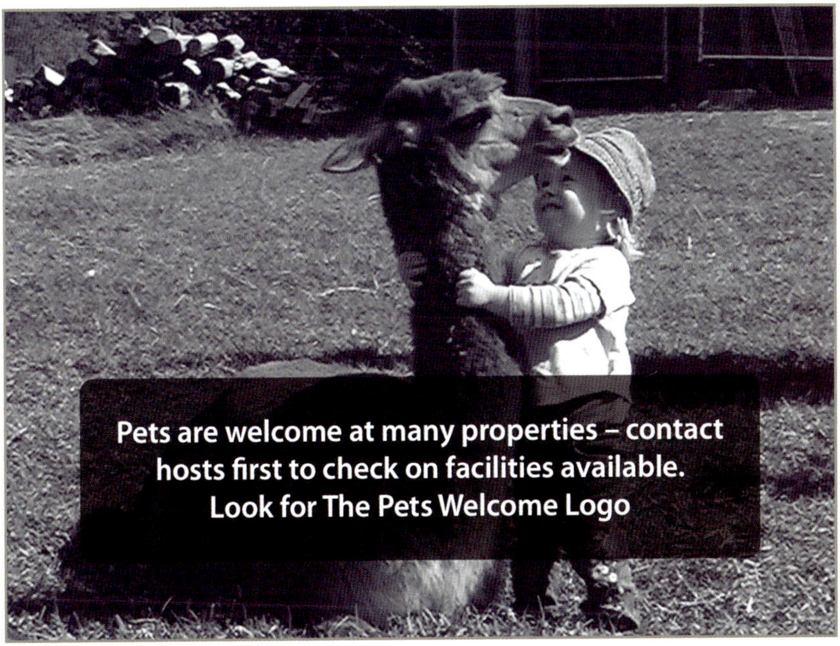
Pets are welcome at many properties – contact
hosts first to check on facilities available.
Look for The Pets Welcome Logo

New South Wales
Alstonville - Ballina
Hume's Hovell

Luxury B&B & Farmstay with Separate Suites
Peter & Suzanne Hume
333 Dalwood Road, Alstonville, NSW 2477
8 km S of Alstonville

Tel (02) 6629 5371
Fax (02) 6629 5471
stay@humes-hovell.com
www.bed-and-breakfast.com.au

Double $205-$370
Single $135-$225, Children $25, Full breakfast,
Dinner $35-$55, Visa MC accepted
2 King/Twin 2 King 3 Single (3 bdrm) Spacious Air conditioned
Luxury with King Beds. Bathrooms: 3 Ensuite 1 Private

AAA Tourism
★★★★☆

**4.5 STAR RATED: AAA TOURISM REVIEWED:
'ONE OF THE STATES BEST'**
Set on our Award Winning macadamia plantation this absolutely fabulous B&B is found amid the rolling green hills & rainforests of the spectacular Ballina/Byron region. It's an oasis of luxury 4.5 star accommodation with friendly hosts to help you. Explore villages, country lanes, nearby World Heritage National Parks, see echidnas, baby kangaroos & koalas. Relax under night skies lit by sparkling stars; wake to the calls of magpies kookaburras, & multi coloured eastern rosellas.
Breathe fresh country air yet magically be only minutes to some of the best beaches in the world. Spacious Suites, Large Pool, Tennis Court, BBQ Dining Pavilion, Free Wireless Internet, hot gourmet breakfasts, evening drinks, savouries & chocolate macadamias all combine for a very special experience you'll remember. If your flying here we're also wholesale agents for Europcar and Pre-booked wholesale rates are available to guests. Phone us or Book Online from our website.

New South Wales

Armidale

Needing a holiday to expand your horizons . . . look no further than New England . . . "where the stars seem to touch the earth". This area, unique in Australia, claims a bracing mountain altitude of about 1000 metres and provides four very distinct seasons with warm Summers, fantastically colourful Autumns, cold frosty Winters sometimes even snow, and magical Springs.
Anne Thackway, Cruickshanks Farmstay and B&B

Armidale
Armidale Boutique Accommodation

Self Contained Cottages (2)
Tracy & David Everett
c/- 134 Brown Street
Armidale
NSW 2350
0.5 km S of Town Centre

Tel (02) 6772 5276 or 0402 058 504
Tracy@ArmidaleBnB.com.au
www.ArmidaleBnB.com.au

Double $130-$140
Breakfast provisions first night
$55 per extra person per night
Visa MC accepted
2 Queen 1 Double (3 bdrm)
Camellia Court: 2B/R; The Elms: 1B/R
Bathrooms: 1 Private One in each cottage

AAA Tourism ★★★★

Two unique and very stylish self-contained properties, situated in the heart of Armidale. The cottages are provided with reverse-cycle air conditioning. Each kitchen is exceptionally well equipped and includes a quiet dishwasher. "Camellia Court" is contemporary in design and style, complete with leather lounges and a fabulous north-facing deck - wheelchair friendly too. "The Elms" is charmingly private with its own small garden protected from the elements, and is perfect for a single or couple.

BBBook.com.au

New South Wales

Armidale - Uralla

Uralla steeped in history . . . bushranger "Thunderbolt" and Rocky River gold diggings. New England is renowned worldwide for its spectacular National Parks, with pristine wilderness, rainforests and waterfalls. Geologically unique World Heritage National Parks, magnificent bushwalking & scenery.
Anne Thackway, Cruickshanks Farmstay and B&B

Armidale - Uralla
Cruickshanks Farmstay B&B

Farmstay. Hosted B&B in Homestead. Self Contained Cottage
Anne & Mike Thackway
313 Mihi Rd, Tourist Drive 19, Uralla, NSW 2358
20 km E of Uralla

Tel (02) 6778 2148 or 0438 333 410
anne@cruickshanks.com.au
www.cruickshanks.com.au

Double $130
Single $95, Children in own cot free,
Under 3 $25, Under 15 $45, Dinner by prior arrangement from $25-$45 pp, Breakfast Extra: Continental $10 pp Full English $20 pp
Visa MC Amex JCB accepted
2 Queen 1 Double 1 Twin 4 Single (5 bdrm)
Bathrooms: 1 Ensuite 1 Guest share 1 Private

Try life in the slow lane, you deserve to Relax in complete comfort, enjoy good local food & premium wines, cosy log-fires for our crispy winter nights, or to participate in exciting outdoor activities. Options are 'Cottage' or 'Homestead' B&B or Self-contained. SMH journalist said 'A glimpse into a working property, fantastic for children and those seeking a break from the big smoke. This New England B&B graduates with honours.'. We say .. 'Simply pack expectations of a great holiday and take home wonderful memories'.

Ballina
Landfall

B&B & Homestay
Gaye & Roger Ibbotson
109 Links Avenue
East Ballina
NSW 2478
3 km NE of Ballina Township

Tel (02) 6686 7555 or 0428 642 077
Fax (02) 6686 7377
landfall@tpg.com.au
www.bbbook.com.au/landfall.html

Double $120
Single $80
Continental breakfast
1 Queen 2 Single (2 bdrm)
Bathrooms: 1 Guest share

This home was the residence of Captain Tom Martin and his wife, Marjorie; he named this home "Landfall" when he retired to Ballina after many years at sea. "Landfall" is situated in East Ballina overlooking the golf course. You are invited to relax in our courtyard with its indoor solar heated pool and spa. "Landfall" is a "non smoking" home. We offer you friendly hospitality. The main part of our home is air conditioned as is the Queen Bedroom. Your hosts Gaye and Roger Ibbotson.

Batemans Bay
Chalet Swisse Spa

B&B & Guest House & Self Contained
Herbert & Elizabeth Mayer
676 The Ridge Road
Surf Beach, Batemans Bay, NSW 2536
10 km S of Batemans Bay

Tel (02) 4471 3671
Fax (02) 4471 1671
info@chaletswissespa.com.au
www.chaletswissespa.com.au

Double $120-$295
Single $90-$255, Children $40
Continental breakfast
S/C cabins incl. linen $140-$230
Visa MC Diners Amex Eftpos accepted
2 King 6 Queen 9 Double 2 Twin
9 Single (17 bdrm) Bathrooms: 17 Ensuite

AAA Tourism ★★★★☆

Situated on top of 'Hero's Hill' above Surf Beach our 85 ac Retreat & Health Spa offers you:- our own mineral spring water, fresh clean air, tranquillity, 120 degree ocean views from our Cafe-verandah, visits by birds and wallabies. Facilities: Indoor heated pool (26 degrees C), Day Spa, revitalising therapies and massages, rainforest walks, tennis, table tennis, archery. Guest lounge with large open fireplace, games corner. Friendly, widely travelled hosts. A place for you to relax, wind down and get pampered.

New South Wales
Bawley Point
Interludes at Bawley

Luxury self contained cottages & B&B
Sandra Worth & Ken Purves
103 Forster Drive
Bawley Point
NSW 2539
26 km S of Ulladulla

Tel (02) 4457 1494 or 0418 665 735
interludes@bigblue.net.au
www.interludes.com.au

Double $160-$230
Full breakfast
Kitchen facilities available in B&B
Visa MC accepted
10 Queen (10 bdrm) 7 in cottages, 3 in B&B
Bathrooms: 7 Ensuite 1 Private
2 x 1 bedroom cottages have spas

Set in 26 acres of coastal bushland, Interludes boasts magnificent panoramic ocean views. Be lulled to sleep by the murmur of the sea and waken to a dazzling ocean sunrise, morning birdsong and the rustle of leaves in the trees. Enjoy the unsurpassed beauty of local beaches. Swimming, surfing, snorkelling, fishing and boating are all activities available to the energetic. Our new luxury cottages are fully self contained and self catering (breakfast not included) while a sumptuous, cooked breakfast is served in the B&B.

Bega Valley - Bemboka
Giba Gunyah Country Cottages

B&B & Farmstay & Self Contained Cottages
John and Ros Raward
224 Polacks Flat Road
Bemboka
NSW 2550
20 km E of Bega

Tel (02) 6492 8404 or 0438 674 449
Fax (02) 6492 8404   ggunyah@yahoo.com.au
www.gibagunyah.com.au

Double $150-$180
Family with 3 children $170
Breakfast provisions first night
2 course dinner + wine on request $40 pp
Extra adult $35-$40
1 King/Twin 1 Queen 1 Twin (2 bdrm)
Bathrooms: 2 Private

AAA Tourism ★★★☆

Giba Gunyah cottages are perfect for that romantic weekend escape for two or for a longer, more relaxed family break. Set in more than thirty hectares of bush and rolling dairy farmland are two charming cottages furnished in country style. Cottages have 2 bedrooms, large bathroom, country kitchen, wheel-chair access, log fires, secluded fenced gardens, stunning views and prolific bird life. All linen is supplied and special little touches are provided to delight you. Your canine guests will love exploring new spaces, smells, and river.

Bellingen
Rivendell

B&B
Janet Hosking
10 -12 Hyde Street
Bellingen
NSW 2454
0.1 km E of Bellingen

Tel (02) 6655 0060 or 0403 238 409
rivendell@wirefree.net.au
www.rivendellguesthouse.com.au

Double $140-$155
Single $115-$155
Full breakfast
Visa MC Eftpos accepted
3 Queen 2 Twin (4 bdrm)
Bathrooms: 3 Ensuite 1 Private

AAA Tourism ★★★★

In the heart of historic Bellingen, Rivendell is a beautifully decorated Federation home. Luxurious rooms furnished with antiques, fluffy bathrobes, open to shady verandahs and picturesque gardens. Take a refreshing dip in the freshwater pool, or in winter, relax by the log fire. After dinner enjoy complimentary port and chocolates. TV, stereo, books, games, magazines and tea/coffee making is provided in the guest lounge. "Lovely stay, fab food and cosy accommodation -we will be back! Thank you" Justin & Caroline UK.

Bellingen
Bellingen Heritage Cottages

2 Luxury Self Contained Cottages
Gail & Gus Raymond
7 - 9 William Street
Bellingen
NSW 2454
0.25 km W of PO

Tel (02) 6655 1311 or 0428 551 311
Fax (02) 6655 1311
graymond@bigpond.net.au
www.auntylils.com.au

Double $160
Single $120, Extra person $30
Continental provisions
Apply for rates during festivals
1 King/Twin 2 Queen (3 bdrm)
Bathrooms: 1 Private

AAA Tourism ★★★★

'Aunty Lil's' and 'Aunty Rene's' Cottages nestle beside each other. Built by the Raymond family circa 1910 and lovingly restored to the period with all comforts of home and beyond.Fascinating family memorabilia. Lots of pillows and feather doonas, warm cosy atmosphere. In heart of Bellingen in quiet street. Self contained - lounge, dining, full kitchen, 3 bedrooms, bathroom, laundry and verandahs front and back. TV, DVD,sound system. Cottage garden/off street parking. Minutes walking distance to Heritage and craft shops, restaurants, Bellinger River, Markets, and attractions.

BBBook.com.au

New South Wales

Berry - Kangaroo Valley
Barefoot Springs

B&B & Homestay & Cottage, no kitchen
Tim & Kay
155 Carrington Road
Beaumont
NSW 2577
9.5 km SE of Kangaroo Valley

Tel (02) 4446 0509
Fax (02) 4446 0530
info@barefootsprings.com.au
www.barefootsprings.com.au

Double $185-$285
Single $175-$275, Full breakfast
Dinner $55 BYO 3 courses, $45 BYO 2 courses
Awarded AAAT Green Star
Visa MC Eftpos accepted
1 King 3 Queen (4 bdrm) Bathrooms: 4 Ensuite

      AAA Tourism ★★★★☆

Barefoot Springs rests high on Cambewarra Mountain; between Berry, Kangaroo Valley and the Shoalhaven coast. Enjoy our mountain and coastline views, while strolling through 5 acres of beautiful gardens. Many tourist destinations within a 20-30 minute drive. Accommodation within our homestead is a Queen bedroom with en-suite, or three separate studio cottages, each with double spa, wood fire, TV/DVD, air con. and kitchenette. Full breakfast is served overlooking panoramic views. Our 37 acre property boasts waterfalls, creeks and natural rainforest, with abundant native wildlife.

Berry - Kangaroo Valley
Wombat Hill B&B

Luxury B&B & Farmstay
& Self contained cottage
Trish and Ken Jessop
1010 Kangaroo Valley Road
Bellawongarah
NSW 2535
10 km W of Berry

Tel (02) 4464 1924
trishandken@wombathillbandb.com
www.wombathillbandb.com

Double $205-$225
Pre school child $30 per night, school age $45,
Full breakfast, Extra $25 for 1 night only,
Extra adult $70 per night, Pets $25,
Visa MC accepted
2 Queen (2 bdrm) Bathrooms: 2 Ensuite

Enjoy luxury, perfect peace and quiet, expansive mountain views, acres of glorious gardens, friendly farm animals, great wildlife, scrumptious breakfasts. Close to Berry and Kangaroo Valley, 2 hours from Sydney, 2.5 hours from Canberra. We can recommend local activities and venues for your enjoyment. Everyone welcome, including children and pets. Each unit has comfortable, modern amenities. Wombat Cottage: Q/S bedroom, living room, kitchen, bathroom and sofa bed. The Bower: Q/S bedroom, living room, bathroom, sofa bed, microwave and fridge. Both units also include, air conditioning, fans, electric blankets, books, magazines, TV/VCR/DVD player, CD player, private deck and separate entry.

Blue Mountains - Blackheath
Amani B&B

B&B
Rosemary & Bill Chapple
31 Days Crescent
Blackheath
NSW 2785
2 km N of Blackheath

Tel (02) 4787 8610 or 0411 111 391
Fax (02) 4787 8894
amanicottage@optusnet.com.au
www.bbbook.com.au/amanibb.html

Double $120-$140
Single $80, Children $40
Full breakfast
1 King/Twin 1 Queen (2 bdrm)
Both bedrooms have wonderful views
Bathrooms: 2 Ensuite

Our home is surrounded by lovely gardens on the edge of the National Park, overlooking the spectacular cliffs that tower above the Grose Valley. We enjoy sharing the wonderful views from our home and the many scenic bush walks that begin nearby. Our guest rooms, with private entrance, are upstairs. Two bedrooms, each with an ensuite and a guests lounge. There is central heating, TV, CD, fridge, microwave oven and tea and coffee making facilities. Blackheath is two hours by road or rail from Sydney.

Blue Mountains - Blackheath
Jemby-Rinjah Eco Lodge

Eco Lodges and Cabins
Christine Le Marseny
336 Evans Lookout Road, Blackheath, NSW 2785
4 km SE of Blackheath

Tel 02 4787 7622
Fax 02 4787 6230
info@jemby.com.au
www.jemby.com.au

Double $170-$219
Single Midweek – Weekend $95-$135
Minimum 2 night weekend stay
Full breakfast
Visa MC Diners Amex Eftpos accepted
3 Eco Lodges, 10 Cabins
Queen Beds and Single Beds (32 bdrm)
Private and Share Bathrooms

AAA Tourism ★★★☆

Jemby-Rinjah Eco Lodge is a unique Eco-tourisn escape in the heart of the beautiful Blue Mountains. The surrounding bush comes up to, between and around the entire complex which consists of a conference centre; fully licensed restaurant with sunken lounge around a roaring open fire; ten private self contained cabins for couples and families; and three large eco-lodges ideal for group bookings. We are just minutes from World Heritage-listed Blue Mountains National Park, walking tracks and breathtaking lookouts providing the ideal location to unwind and breathe.

New South Wales

Blue Mountains - Hampton

Historic rural Hampton is on the ridge west of the Kanimbla Valley. The once larger community still has a small school and sandstone church and a pub. The district is home to cockatoos, eagles. At the right time the pine forests are famous for their mushrooms and snow falls are possible.
Deb & Richard, Hampton Homestead

Blue Mountains - Hampton - Jenolan Caves
Hampton Homestead

B&B
Deb and Richard
1991 Jenolan Caves Road
Hampton
NSW 2790
28 km NE of Jenolan Caves

Tel (02) 6359 3337
hhomestead@ozemail.com.au
www.hamptonhomestead.com.au

Double $200-$250
Single $170-$220, Full breakfast
Dinner BYO from $35
Tea/coffee, TV/DV, clock radio, electric blankets
1 King/Twin 2 Queen (3 bdrm)
King/twin has extra bed, fridge & external door
Bathrooms: 3 Ensuite each with a deep bath

In a country setting with glorious 180 degree views and only 20mins from Jenolan Caves, Mt Victoria or Oberon the centrally-heated Homestead is a great place to relax after a day exploring in the fresh air. Sit in front of the s/c fire in the guest lounge watching the sunset-lit escarpments before having a delicious candlelit dinner there in the 1920's lead-lighted B&B wing or in the 19th Century stone cottage with its open fire, and then choose from the extensive DVD library before retiring.

Blue Mountains - Katoomba
Melba House

Luxury B&B
Marion & Trevor Hall
98 Waratah Street
Katoomba
NSW 2780
0.5 km E of Katoomba

Tel (02) 4782 4141 or 0403 021 074
stay@melbahouse.com
www.melbahouse.com

Double $220-$269
Single $210-$259
Full breakfast
Visa MC Eftpos accepted
1 King/Twin 1 King 2 Queen (3 bdrm)
2 Spa Ensuites and 1 Shower Ensuite

  AAA Tourism ★★★★☆

Imagine your own log fire and spa, central-heating, electric blankets, large comfortable suites with own sitting and dining areas, sumptuous breakfasts, that's historical 4.5* Melba House. Quiet and secluded yet close to many restaurants, galleries, antique and craft shops and walking tracks. Also, close to the best-loved attractions of Katoomba and Leura. See our website www.melbahouse.com. "Of the B&Bs around the world we have stayed, this is our best experience, it's exquisite." (W. Dallas Texas). Stay 3 consecutive nights Midweek and only pay for 2.

Blue Mountains - Leura
Broomelea

B&B
Bryan & Denise Keith
273 Leura Mall
Leura
NSW 2780
0.5 km S of Leura

Tel (02) 4784 2940 or 0419 478 400
Fax (02) 4784 2611
info@broomelea.com.au
www.broomelea.com.au

Double $165-$215
Single $130-$190
Full breakfast
Visa MC Diners Amex Eftpos JCB accepted
1 King/Twin 3 Queen 2 Single (4 bdrm)
Bathrooms: 4 Ensuite

 AAA Tourism ★★★★☆

A beautiful 1909 mountain home for guests who would like more than simply a bed and a breakfast. We offer spacious ensuite rooms with 4 poster beds, open fires, lounges, TV, Video, CD Players, a freshly prepared gourmet breakfast each morning and most importantly local knowledge. Broomelea is perfectly located in the Living Heritage precinct of Leura just a 10 minute stroll to famous cliff top walks with great views or our beautiful village with numerous restaurants and galleries.

New South Wales
Blue Mountains - Leura
Leura's Magical Manderley

Luxury Self Contained Spa Apartments
Robyn Piddington
157 Megalong Street
Leura
NSW 2780
0.3 km E of Leura

Tel (02) 4784 3252 or 0417 286 333
Fax (0)2 4784 1603   manderleys@bigpond.com
www.manderley.com.au

Double $170-$240
Single $150-$180, Full breakfast provisions
Stay 4 nights midweek, pay 3, Visa MC Eftpos accepted
1 King 1 Queen (2 bdrm)
Bathrooms: 2 Private 2 double hydro spas and showers

Experience the Magic of Manderley - Peace, Privacy and Luxury - right in the heart of historic Leura. Two stunning, self-contained and elegant garden apartments - Treetops and The Terrace - each accommodate one couple in ultimate luxury.

Guests enjoy the idyllic and secluded setting just a stroll to popular Leura village, with its famous restaurants, galleries and tea rooms. Exquisite furnishings and decor create that unique and special ambience. After a day exploring, pour a glass of champagne, relax and rejuvenate the body and mind in your private, double 36 jet Hydro Spa.

Tariffs include generous breakfast provisions, aperitifs, champagne, chocolates, Molton Brown English toiletries and spa products. Book 4 Nights Midweek - Pay For 3.

Blue Mountains - Leura
Bethany Manor Bed & Breakfast

B&B
Greg & Jill Haigh
8 East View Avenue
Leura
NSW 2780
0.8 km NW of Leura

Tel (02) 4782 9215
Fax (02) 4782 1962
bmanor@optusnet.com.au
www.bethanymanor.com.au

Double $135-$205
Single $115-$185
Full breakfast
Visa MC accepted
3 Queen (3 bdrm)
Bathrooms: 3 Ensuite

   AAA Tourism ★★★★☆

Looking for a welcoming place to call home when visiting the World Heritage Blue Mountains? Bethany Manor is a Federation style home set on over an acre of parklike grounds, with tennis court. Your ensuite bedroom incorporates a spa-bath and verandah access while the Garden View room provides the perfect setting for enjoying a sumptuous breakfast in any season. Centrally heated with a wood fire in the guest's lounge. We're an easy walk to Leura village with its speciality shops, restaurants and railway station.

Blue Mountains - Leura
The Greens of Leura

B&B
Hayley & Richard Clifton
24-26 Grose Street
Leura
NSW 2780
0.1 km E of Leura

Tel (02) 4784 3241
Admin@TheGreensLeura.com.au
www.TheGreensLeura.com.au

Double $145-$195
Single $125-$185
Full breakfast
Visa MC Eftpos accepted
1 King 3 Queen 1 Twin (5 bdrm)
Bathrooms: 5 Ensuite

 AAA Tourism
★★★★☆

Accommodation, Location and Value, The Greens offers the best combination in Leura and the Blue Mountains. Set in the heart of Leura just a minutes walk from the chic shops and restaurants, The Greens enjoys a tranquil yet convenient setting. Enjoy the full size snooker table and extensive range of books from the library before retiring to one of our comfortable rooms for a good nights sleep. Awake to our generous full cooked breakfast that will set you up for a days' exploring!

New South Wales

Blue Mountains - Leura
Argyll House

B&B & Guest House
Cherril & Jane Canfield
11A Craigend Street
Leura
NSW 2780
0.3 km S of Leura

Tel (02) 4784 1555 or 0402 980 311
Fax (02) 4784 1566
stay@argyll.com.au
www.argyll.com.au

Double $130 midweek to $220 weekend
Single $110-$165
Special 4 course English or Scottish breakfast
Visa MC Eftpos accepted
Spa suite, ensuite & traditional two rooms

Visit Argyll House and step back in time. This lovely old 1918 California Bungalow is in a quiet spot 300m from Leura, the premier Blue Mountains village. Two private suites with ensuite bathrooms (one with 2 person corner spa and 4 poster bed). Both have private sun rooms with tv, dvd, cd. Two traditional rooms with share bathroom, perfect for family and friends or the budget conscious. The spacious rooms include a sunny breakfast room with continuous tea/coffee and a large lounge with a selection of dvds, cds. Wood burning fires in season and central heating/air conditioning. Four course hot English or Scottish breakfast. Situated in the garden is the studio of award winning artist Jane Canfield and visitors are welcome to view her work by appointment.

Blue Mountains - Lithgow - Hartley
Majic Views B&B

B&B & Self Contained Apartment
Allan & Jeanie Cupitt
157 McKanes Falls Road
Lithgow
NSW 2790
6 km E of Lithgow

Tel (02) 6353 1094 or 0409 244 791
0421 647 898   Fax (02) 6353 1094
relax@majicviews.com.au
www.majicviews.com.au

Double $165
Children $20, Dinner B/A
Continental breakfast, Full breakfast B/A
Visa MC Eftpos accepted
2 King/Twin 3 Queen 3 Single (4 bdrm)
Bathrooms: 2 Private, Ensuite by arrangement

Quiet, private rural setting on 5 acres with 'Majic Views' across the valley to the Blue Mountains Escarpment. Contemporary styled home, with the main accommodation offering 1 Queen and 1 Kingtwin bedroom, living area with CD, TV, VCR, DVD, kitchenette, luxury three way bathroom with spa and a private barbecue area. Suitable to families with additional bedding available. Private access. Central to Jenolan Caves, the Zig Zag Railway and Blue Mountains attractions.

Blue Mountains - Mount Tomah

Discover remnant rainforest and themed plant displays that highlight biodiversity and adaptation at Mount Tomah Botanic Garden. Showcasing both native and exotic plants from around the world, with over 40,000 plants, and is set against the stunning backdrop of breathtaking views.
Bill & Gai Johns, Tomah Mountain Lodge

Blue Mountains - Mount Tomah - Bells Line of Road
Tomah Mountain Lodge

B&B & Homestay
Bill & Gai Johns
25 Skyline Road
Mount Tomah via Bilpin
NSW 2758
14 km W of Bilpin

Tel (02) 4567 2111 or 0419 908 724
tomahlodge@ozemail.com.au
www.tomahmountainlodge.com.au

Double $220-$250
Single $190-$220, Full breakfast
Gourmet three course candlelit dinners by arrangement BYO alcohol
Visa MC Eftpos accepted
2 King/Twin 1 Queen (3 bdrm)
Bathrooms: 3 Ensuite

AAA Tourism
★★★★☆

Tomah Mountain Lodge is situated in the World Heritage Blue Mountains National Park and offers comfortable, executive style accommodation. Mount Tomah is over 1000 metres above sea level, with mountain views. This secluded setting is only two minutes drive to Mount Tomah Botanic Garden, and a short drive to the historic gardens at Mount Wilson. The lodge offers spacious & comfortable lounge rooms with log fires. Gourmet three course candlelit dinners are a speciality.

New South Wales
Blue Mountains - Springwood - Faulconbridge
Mountain Jewel B&B

**Self Contained Suites
& Self Contained Cottage**
Betty & Warwick Reynolds
51 Summer Road
Faulconbridge
NSW 2776
4 km W of Springwood

Tel (02) 4751 9270 or 0418 431 341
Fax (02) 4751 1186   jewel@pnc.com.au
www.bluemts.com.au/jewel

Double $225-$450
Children 1 small in suites, up to 4 in cottage
Full breakfast, Dinner by arrangement
Visa MC Amex Eftpos JCB accepted
3 King 2 Queen (5 bdrm)
Bathrooms: 3 Ensuite

AAA Tourism ★★★★★

Spectacular 13 acre property adjoining the World Heritage National Park. Breathtaking views of the valley and mountains with spacious gardens and swimming pool. Many vegetables and fruit grown in our gardens. Superb gourmet breakfasts! Suites are very private with separate entrances, reverse cycle air conditioning, TV, DVD, bathrobes, hairdryers, irons and ironing boards. Some include kitchenettes, the Honeymoon Suite has a separate lounge with log fire. Complimentary flowers, chocolates, teas, coffees, fruit drinks and cheese platter on arrival. Just over one hour from Sydney. Friendly hosts who will assist you to make your stay a memorable one.

Blue Mountains - Wentworth Falls
Blue Mountains Lakeside

B&B & Self Contained Apartment
Michaela Russell
30 Bellevue Road
Wentworth Falls
NSW 2782
1 km N of Wentworth Falls train station

Tel (02) 4757 3777 or 0410 443 322
stay@lakesidebandb.com.au
www.lakesidebandb.com.au

Double $180-$240
Single $135-$190, Children 12 years plus $30
Full breakfast, Dinner by prior arrangement
Mid-week specials for longer stays
Visa MC accepted
2 Queen 1 Double 2 Single (2 bdrm)
Bathrooms: 2 Ensuite

Blue Mountains' only Waterfront Bed & Breakfast. "At the edge of the Lake in the Heart of the Mountains." Looking for somewhere unique, secluded, plus log fire and spa? Lake Suite with delicious country cooked breakfasts home grown produce or the new self contained Reflections Spa Suite with living room, kitchenette, verandah - both with tranquil Lake views. Try a soothing in-house massage. Complimentary boats, trout fishing. Birdwatchers paradise. Minutes to Three Sisters Katoomba. "An amazing piece of paradise." Michael and Ashley (Visitors' Book).

Blue Mountains - Woodford
Braeside

B&B
Robyn Wilkinson & Rex Fardon
97 Bedford Road
Woodford
NSW 2778
19 km E of Katoomba

Tel **(02) 4758 6279** or **0414 542 860**
Fax (02) 4758 8210
Braeside.BandB@bigpond.com
www.bluemts.com.au/braeside

Double $130-$150
Single $90-$100, Children from $20,
Full breakfast, Dinner available $20-$35 pp,
Visa MC Diners Amex accepted
1 King/Twin 1 Queen 1 Double (3 bdrm)
Bathrooms: 2 Ensuite 1 Private

AAA Tourism

Braeside offers a quiet escape as well as being central to the attractions of the upper and lower Blue Mountains. Three bedrooms are available to suit a variety of needs including singles sharing, family groups with children and couples looking for a quiet escape. Flexible arrangements include providing an evening meal with a little notice. The guests lounge has an open log fire for cooler weather. Set in large parklike gardens Braeside offers a home away from home. No smoking inside.

Byron Bay
Victoria's Byron Bay

Luxury Guest House
Victoria McEwen
Marine Parade & McGettigans Lane
Byron Bay
NSW 2481
2 km E of Byron Bay

Tel **(02) 6684 7047** or **(02) 6685 5388**
Fax (02) 6684 7687
indulge@victorias.net.au
www.victorias.net.au

Double $250-$899
Full breakfast
Visa MC Diners Amex Eftpos JCB accepted
5 King 5 Queen (10 bdrm)
Bathrooms: 10 Ensuite

"Victoria's At Ewingsdale", a stately country manor, situated on 4 acres of landscaped gardens and features panoramic ocean, mountain and rural views. "Victoria's at Wategos", a stunning Tuscan style guesthouse, nestled in an exclusive ocean front valley at beautiful Wategos beach, just under the famous Cape Byron lighthouse. Both properties feature a salt-water swimming pool, open fireplaces, air-conditioning, rooms with spas and balconies. Experience personalised service in our small and exclusive boutique retreats, dedicated to providing the best in first class hospitality, quality and style.

New South Wales

Byron Bay Hinterland

The hinterland of Byron Bay is an area of stunningly beautiful countryside, combining rolling hills and luscious pockets of rainforest with neat macadamia and coffee plantations. It is laced with winding country lanes that just beg to be explored!
Susie Briscoe, Green Mango Hideaway

Byron Bay Hinterland
Green Mango Hideaway

B&B
Susie Briscoe
Lofts Road, off Coolamon Scenic Drive
Coorabell
NSW 2479
12 km W of Byron Bay

Tel (02) 6684 7171
relax@greenmango.com.au
www.greenmango.com.au

Double $165-$250
Single $150-$220
Full breakfast
Visa MC Eftpos accepted
2 King 2 Queen (4 bdrm)
Bathrooms: 4 Ensuite

From the moment you walk down its leafy path, you'll be captivated by the tropical atmosphere of this peaceful B&B set in Byron's spectacular hinterland. With just four guestrooms, each with ensuite & verandah, you'll be escaping the crowds and yet be within 10 minutes of fabulous shops & cafes and glorious beaches. The muslin-draped beds & Oriental decor, the sparkling palm-fringed pool & lush gardens with abundant birdlife, and the wonderful breakfasts all guarantee you a relaxing and memorable stay.

New South Wales

Camden - Southern Highlands
Botanica Lodge

B&B & Self Contained Cottage
Margaret & Roger Roberts
70 Wattle Creek Drive
Theresa Park, Camden
NSW 2570
10 km W of Camden

Tel (02) 4648 1320 or 0402 073 960
Fax (02) 4648 1319
booking@botanicalodge.com
www.botanicalodge.com

Double $220-$250
Single $100-$120
Full breakfast provisions
Visa MC Eftpos accepted
1 King 1 Queen (2 bdrm) Spacious bedrooms
Bathrooms: 1 Private

Relax and unwind amongst 6 acres of private landscaped gardens. Heaps of attractions and things to do in and around historic Camden and surrounding areas eg hot air ballooning, vineries and first class golf courses. Luxurious suites, feather doonas and pillows, fresh towels daily. Reverse cycle airconditioning, foxtel, DVD books and games. Fully equipped kitchen enables self catering. Cappuccino machine and icemaker, BBQ facilities. Saltwater pool, spacious decks and Bali hut. Bubbly and chocolates upon arrival.

Candelo - Bega Valley
Bumblebrook Farm Motel

Farmstay & Self Contained Apartment
Alan & Wendy Cross
Kemps Lane
Candelo, NSW 2550
20 km SW of Bega

Tel (02) 6493 2238
Fax (02) 6493 2299
stay@bumblebrook.com.au
www.bumblebrook.com.au

Double $110-$125
Single $90-$125, Children under 13 free,
Full breakfast provisions,
Mid week specials & long stay specials,
Visa MC Eftpos accepted
1 King/Twin1 King 1 Queen 2 Double
4 Single (4 bdrm)   Bathrooms: 4 Ensuite

AAA Tourism
★★★☆

A 100 acre beef property with magnificent views and lovely bush walks, fronting Tantawangalo Creek. We have four well equipped self-contained units. Breakfast is a "cook-your-own" from our fresh farm ingredients. Children are welcome and can often help feed the farm animals. BBQs are provided by the creek and in the playground near the units. Beaches and National Parks nearby. Pets welcome with prior arrangement. Relaxation massages available by your host Wendy.

BBBook.com.au

New South Wales

Central Coast – Terrigal

The Central Coast is a holiday playground with trendy markets, al fresco cafes and classy boutique shops. Splash Out in Terrigal - a dazzling seaside vista with sweeping curves of brilliant blue ocean and soft golden sand. Take a scenic drive through the lush valleys and feel the natural beauty of the hinterlands or see the pelican feeding daily at The Entrance.
Gaby Schaudinn AnDaCer Boutique B&B and Elizabeth & John Fairweather, Greenacres B&B

Central Coast - Terrigal
AnDaCer Boutique B&B

Luxury B&B
Gaby Schaudinn
28 Serpentine Road
Terrigal
NSW 2260
4 km W of Terrigal

Tel (02) 4367 8368
Fax (02) 4367 8368
stay@terrigalretreat.com.au
www.terrigalretreat.com.au

Double $140-$350
Single $120-$140, Full breakfast
Book ahead for Light dinner - Seafood Platter,
Romantic Weekend Accommodation Package
from $330 per night, Visa MC accepted
3 Queen (3 bdrm)   Bathrooms: 3 Ensuite

   AAA Tourism ★★★★

If you are looking for a romantic getaway close to Sydney, An'da'cer House Retreat provides the perfect destination with luxury boutique B&B accommodation. Stay in a secluded and relaxing resort-style atmosphere set in beautiful gardens surrounded by tranquil coastal acreages. An'Da'Cer House Retreat offers three individual luxury Suites - two with direct access into the garden and pool area via private gardens. The breakfast conservatory, with its casual and inviting appeal, overlooks the pool and garden and is a delightful spot to sit while indulging yourself with the fabulous breakfasts served each morning.

Central Coast - Tuggerah
Greenacres B&B

Self Contained Suites
Elizabeth & John Fairweather
8 Carpenters Lane
Mardi
NSW 2259
1 km W of Tuggerah

Tel (02) 4353 0643 or (02) 4353 0309
greenacres-bb@tpg.com.au
www.greenacres-bb.com

Double $125-$160
Single $110-$145
Children $20 each per night over 4 years old
Full breakfast provisions
2 Queen (2 bdrm)
Lounge has folding double bed
Bathrooms: 2 Ensuite

Greenacres B&B is a tranquil private retreat set on 3.5 evergreen acres, only 4 minutes to Westfield Tuggerah and a short drive to Tuggerah Lakes, Gosford, The Entrance and Shelly Beach. Two fully self contained air-conditioned suites with luxury queen beds, sofa beds, TV and DVD. Guests have use of the games room and home movie theatre, free in house movies, 14 metre swimming pool, Bali style gazebos, extensive landscaped gardens with ponds, fountains, waterfalls, bushwalking trails, dam. Enjoy hand feeding our Silver Perch fish. Pets by arrangement..

Central Tilba - Tilba Tilba - Narooma
The Two Story B&B

B&B
Ken & Linda Jamieson
Bate Street
Central Tilba
NSW 2546
In Central Tilba

Tel (02) 4473 7290 or 1800 355 850
Fax (02) 4473 7992
stay@tilbatwostory.com
www.tilbatwostory.com

Double $140
Single $120
Full breakfast
Visa MC Eftpos accepted
2 Queen 1 Double 1 Single (3 bdrm)
Bathrooms: 3 Ensuite

A warm welcome awaits you at the Two Story B&B in the National Trust Village of Central Tilba. Our building is 115 years old built in 1894 and was originally the Post Office and residence, it has great character and views overlooking a superb valley of rolling hills and lush greenness. Enjoy the atmosphere, warmth in front of our log fire. Our weather is temperate and beaches are close by. We offer our guests off street parking, a choice of continental and full cooked breakfasts with tea/coffee facilities, in a totally relaxed atmosphere of pleasant old world charm.

BBBook.com.au

New South Wales
Coffs Harbour
Boambee Palms B&B

Luxury B&B
Colleen & Marcus Blackwell
5 Kasch Road, Coffs Harbour, NSW 2450
6 km S of Coffs Harbour

Tel (02) 6658 4545 or 0417 787 790
Fax (02) 6658 4545
info@boambeepalms.com.au
www.boambeepalms.com.au

Double $160-$250
Single $130-$250, Full breakfast,
Visa MC Amex accepted
1 King/Twin 2 King 1 Queen (4 bdrm)
Super King with Double Spa and separate shower
Bathrooms: 4 Ensuite, 2 with luxurious Double Spas

AAA Tourism
★★★★☆

The perfect adults only escape. Everything a guest could wish for is here, 4 acres of lush landscaped gardens abundant with bird life. Facilities include floodlit tennis court, large sub tropical pool with BBQ area. There are four well appointed King and Queen ensuite rooms some with double spas. All rooms have private entrances, outside seating areas, air conditioning flat screen TVs, CD, DVD, wireless internet, mini fridges, bathrobes, tea/plunger coffee, hair dryers.

Breakfast is a lazy 3 course gourmet affair served on the balcony overlooking the landscaped gardens on individual tables. Start with fresh juices, seasonal tropical fruits, a choice of cooked breakfasts - maybe potato pancakes topped with smoked salmon and dill and sour cream sauce whets your appetite or Turkish bread with avocado, bacon and topped with a poached egg or perhaps a traditional English breakfast followed by muffins and toast good coffee and a selection of teas. Of course the rainbow lorikeets are on hand to keep you entertained.

We can also offer a range of meal options if you don't want to go out in the evening such as a cold local seafood platter.

New South Wales

Coffs Harbour – Woolgoolga

Woolgoolga is one of the very few places in the world where you can sit in the comfort of your car and watch pods of migrating humpback whales as they make their way up and down the beautiful Mid-North Coast between May and November. It's a spectacle you cannot afford to miss.
Denise Hannaford, Solitary Islands Lodge

Coffs Harbour - Woolgoolga
Solitary Islands Lodge

B&B
Denise & John Hannaford
3 Arthur Street
Woolgoolga
NSW 2456
25 km N of Coffs Harbour

Tel (02) 6654 1335 or 0419 248 081
denise@solitaryislandslodge.com.au
www.solitaryislandslodge.com.au

Double $140-$180
Continental breakfast
Visa MC accepted
3 King/Twin (3 bdrm)
King size beds or long singles
Bathrooms: 3 Ensuite 1 room has bath

Solitary Islands Lodge is the perfect accommodation to embrace all that the area has to offer being two minutes stroll to the beach and village. Nestled just 25km north of Coffs Harbour in the seaside village of Woolgoolga, Solitary Islands Lodge overlooks the Pacific Ocean with spectacular northerly views of the ocean, mountains and Solitary Islands Marine Park. Three unique rooms provide ample space and comfort with king beds, ensuite bathrooms, television, DVD, radio, bar fridge also tea/coffee facilities. A large deck with ocean views and barbeque is also available for guests. Airport transfers from Coffs Harbour can be arranged.

BBBook.com.au

New South Wales
Coffs Harbour Northern Beaches
Headlands Beach Guest House

B&B & Guest House
Valerie & Terry Swan
17 Headland Road
Arrawarra Headland
NSW 2456
5 km N of Woolgoolga

Tel (02) 6654 0364 or 0417 240 440
0417 249 500
Fax (02) 6654 0308
info@headlandsbeach.com.au
www.headlandsbeach.com.au

Double $145-$170
Single $125-$140, Full breakfast,
Refreshments on arrival, Visa MC accepted
3 Queen (3 bdrm)
Bathrooms: 3 Ensuite

   AAA Tourism ★★★★☆

Enjoy absolute beach frontage with warm hospitality at Headlands Beach Guest House located 20 mins north of Coffs Harbour on the Solitary Islands Marine National Park & 5km from Woolgoolga. A fully equipped kitchen is available for guests to use along with the BBQ poolside. Guest lounge & dining room overlook the pool, Mullawarra Beach & Arrawarra Headland. Complimentary refreshments on arrival.

**Many properties offer activities onsite such as horse riding.
Look for The Onsite Activities Logo**

Cowra - Mandurama
Millamolong

Farmstay & Homestead, Farmhouse and Cottages
James and Sue Ashton
Millamolong Station, Mandurama, NSW 2792
16 km W of Mandurama

Tel (02) 6367 5241 or 0429 635 155
Fax (02) 6367 5120
millamolonghs@bigpond.com
www.millamolong.com.au

Double $160-$240
Single $45-$150, Children $0-$80,
Full breakfast, Visa MC Eftpos accepted
8 Queen 8 Double (8 bdrm)
Bathrooms: 3 Ensuite 3 Family share

Millamolong is a large working station in the central west of NSW famous for its leisurely and relaxing atmosphere. It has thousands of sheep and cattle and hundreds of horses. Millamolong offers luxury accommodation at the homestead and budget accommodation at the historic slab farmhouse.

Enjoy country cuisine in our fully licensed restaurant with a wide range of local wines. Horse riding, children, polo are all a feature. A tennis court and swimming pool are available and guests can fish in the beautiful Belubula River.

BBBook.com.au

New South Wales

Crookwell

Crookwell experiences the seasons in all their glory. Autumn is a blaze of colour - winter sees rolling hills blanketed in white powdery snow. Masses of exquisite blossoms, bulbs and flowers herald spring and a gentle summer allows you to escape the harsh heat and humidity of coastal regions. Nestled on top of the Great Dividing Range, an hour from Canberra, great for Abercrombie and Wombeyan Caves.
Mary and Geoff Ashton, Markdale Homestead

Crookwell
Markdale Homestead

B&B & Farmstay & Self Contained House
Geoff & Mary Ashton
462 Mulgowrie Road
Binda
NSW 2583
40 km NW of Crookwell

Tel (02) 4835 3146 or (02) 8212 8599
Fax (02) 4835 3160
g_ashton@bigpond.com
www.markdale.com

Double $100-$220
Single $50-$110, Children under 2 no charge,
Full breakfast provisions, Dinners $25-$40,
Phones & WiFi Free, Visa MC accepted
2 Queen 3 Double 7 Twin (12 bdrm)
Bathrooms: 1 Ensuite 4 Guest share

Food for the soul. A stunning landscape, 6000 acres, trout stocked streams, solar heated pool and all weather tennis. The Markdale Homestead and Garden combine the talents of two Australian Icons; Edna Walling, garden designer, and Professor Wilkinson, architect. Live in two adjoining, self contained, beautifully renovated, stone houses. Both have central heating, open fire, sitting room, kitchen, laundry, TV, CD Player, phone and internet access. Or stay in the comfortable Shearers' Quarters at cheaper rates.

Dorrigo - Coffs Harbour Hinterland
Fernbrook Lodge

B&B
Craig & Glennis
4705 Waterfall Way
Dorrigo
NSW 2453
6 km W of Dorrigo

Tel (02) 6657 2573 or 0429 318 946
candgjohnston@bigpond.com
www.midcoast.com.au/~fernbrooklodge

Double $95-$125
Single $70, Children with adult supervision only, Full breakfast,
Three course home cooked meal available by arrangement,
Visa MC Eftpos accepted
3 Queen 2 Single (4 bdrm) Bathrooms: 4 Ensuite

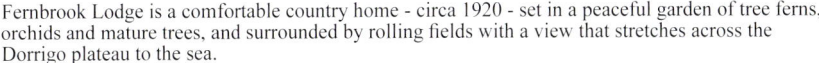

Fernbrook Lodge is a comfortable country home - circa 1920 - set in a peaceful garden of tree ferns, orchids and mature trees, and surrounded by rolling fields with a view that stretches across the Dorrigo plateau to the sea.

Enjoy old style hospitality and care, the fresh flowers, books, complimentary port and chocolates, cushions and comfy chairs, respect for your privacy, and the tranquil surrounds. Be refreshed by the charm of yesteryear in rural Australia. Afternoon tea on arrival, a very satisfying breakfast, well appointed rooms, all ensuite, 2 with verandah & garden access.

Explore Dorrigo National Park with its forest skywalk and waterfalls just minutes away.

New South Wales

Dorrigo
Lisnagarvey Cottage

Luxury Self Contained Cottage
Mark & Elaine Martin
803 Whisky Creek Road
Dorrigo
NSW 2453
8 km W of Dorrigo

Tel (02) 6657 2536 or 0428 228 160
Fax (02) 6657 2053
bookings@lisnagarvey.com.au
www.lisnagarvey.com.au

Double $145-$165
Single $120-$145, Full breakfast provisions
Accommodation only rates available
1 Queen (1 bdrm)
Bathrooms: 1 Private
Bath and shower

AAA Tourism
★★★★

Nestled amidst the lush green hills of the Dorrigo Plateau and just 8 minutes to town is a beautifully renovated, luxury, one bedroom dairy bails with loads of character, charm, privacy and spectacular views over the plateau and Dorrigo township. Relax and enjoy the views from your private deck or curl up with complimentary port and chocolates in front of the wood fire. A gourmet breakfast basket can be supplied or you can choose to self cater. Fully self-contained.

Dubbo
Pericoe Retreat B&B

Luxury B&B
Kem & Ross Irvine
12R Cassandra Drive
Dubbo
NSW 2830
12 km NE of Dubbo

Tel (02) 6887 2705 or 0407 896 828
pericoe@pericoeretreat.com.au
www.pericoeretreat.com.au

Double $225-$275
Single $155-$155
Full breakfast
Evening meals from an a-la-carte menu
Visa MC Amex Eftpos accepted
4 Queen (4 bdrm)
Bathrooms: 4 Ensuite 2 with Spas

AAA Tourism
★★★★★

Experience the wonderful seclusion and relax in 5 star luxury airconditioned suites. Featuring spa ensuites, open fires, billiard room and bar, TV room, sunroom with deck, swimming pool and tennis court. Enjoy full cooked breakfast, afternoon tea and sumptuous evening meals, served in a variety of settings. Pericoe Retreat is set on 25 acres with meandering gardens, an abundance of wildlife and birds, and magnificent views over the Talbragar Valley. Our exclusive, personalised service and attention to detail will ensure your stay is one to remember.

Dubbo - Central West
Walls Court B&B

Farmstay & Private Cottages, Country Hospitality
Neil & Nancy Lander
11L Belgravia Heights Road
Dubbo, NSW 2830
12 km S of Dubbo

Tel (02) 6887 3823 or 0407 226 606
(02) 6887 3606   Fax (02) 6887 3602
nlander@bigpond.com
www.wallscourt.com.au

Double $150
Single $125, Children $25, Extra person $30,
Full breakfast, Dinner and/or picnic basket
lunch b/a, Visa MC Amex Eftpos accepted
1 King 1 Queen 4 Single (2 bdrm)
Bathrooms: 2 Ensuite

    AAA Tourism ★★★★

Relish the tranquillity and comfort of your Walls Court suites as you laze on the veranda with a drink observing the birds in the garden. See your children's joy as they feed sheep and chooks, pat dogs and gather eggs. Gain more from your visit to the zoo; we are volunteer guides. Revel in crowd free shopping precincts or savour the tastings at nearby wineries. Explore attractions yourself or take advantage of our familiarity with the area. Your pet is welcome by arrangement. Learn a new craft - make a pair of silver earrings for a small additional cost.

When making an enquiry or booking, please tell your hosts, "We saw you in the Bed & Breakfast Book!"

New South Wales

Dunedoo – Central West

Dunedoo is a pretty country town in central west NSW, adjacent to the Talbragar River along the Golden Highway. Dunedoo is the southern gateway to Warrumbungle National Park and is well located to Dubbo and to the wine growing region of Mudgee.
Sue Graham, Redbank Gums B&B

Dunedoo - Central West
Redbank Gums B&B

Self Contained Units
Sue & Lloyd Graham
41 Wargundy Street
Dunedoo
NSW 2844
In Dunedoo

Tel (02) 6375 1218 or 0428 751 218
grahamls@bigpond.com.au
www.redbankgums.com.au

Double $75-$95
Single $55, Family $110-$125
Full breakfast provisions
Dinner by arrangement
Visa MC Eftpos accepted
1 Queen 1 Double (2 bdrm)
Bathrooms: 2 Ensuite

AAA Tourism
★★★☆

Welcome to Redbank Gums B&B which is an ideal base when touring the central west. Spacious 2 bedroom unit or 2 separate units with kitchen, laundry and lounge with television and DVD. Relax in the shady garden and enjoy a barbeque. We are in a quiet area with off street parking opposite the Golf Course and are within walking distance to most amenities. Dunedoo is a friendly, hospitable town along the Golden Highway, set alongside the Talbragar River and is well known for the annual Bush Poetry Festival. Redbank Gums accepts pets by prior arrangement.

New South Wales

Eden

Historic Eden is a popular whale watching destination with Southern Right and Humpback whales migrating between May and October. Throughout-the-year cruises to see Bottlenose dolphins, seals and penguins are popular. Eden is also centrally located for excellent bushwalking in the National Parks.
Gail and David Ward, Cocora Cottage B&B

Eden
Cocora Cottage

Traditional B&B
Gail and David Ward
2 Cocora Street
Eden
NSW 2551
0.2 km S of Centre of Eden

Tel (02) 6496 1241 or 0427 218 859
0409 961 241   info@cocoracottage.com
www.cocoracottage.com

Double $140-$160
Single $110-$120, Not suitable for children
Full breakfast, Free wireless internet,
Complimentary drink in the evening
Visa MC Eftpos accepted
2 Queen (2 bdrm)
Bathrooms: 2 Ensuite with spas

   AAA Tourism ★★★★

This Heritage listed accommodation was the original Police Station in Eden. It is located in a quiet area close to Eden's famous Killer Whale Museum, the Wharf and restaurants. Breakfast is served upstairs with spectacular views down to the Wharf and across Twofold Bay to the foothills of Mt Imlay. Both bedrooms have a Queen sized bed, an ensuite with a spa, a television and free wireless internet. The front bedroom features the original open fireplace while the back bedroom offers bay views.

New South Wales
Eden
Snug Cove B&B

B&B
Jennifer & Eric Shuwalow
25 Victoria Terrace
Eden
NSW 2551
0.4 km E of Eden

Tel (02) 6496 3123 or 0439 130 372
info@snugcove.com
www.snugcove.com.au

Double $160-$240
Single $120-$180
Full breakfast
Dinner By arrangement
Visa MC accepted
2 Queen 1 Twin (3 bdrm)
Bathrooms: 3 Ensuite

Snug Cove Bed and Breakfast is purpose built with host's area completely separate from guests. Our priority is your comfort, privacy and access to the amazing view. Each room opens onto its own balcony giving access to uninterrupted views of Twofold Bay. There is even a view from your bath. We offer complimentary welcoming drinks, and a varied breakfast served in the lounge which has expansive views of the bay. This lounge has a wood heater to keep it cosy during the colder months and opens onto a large deck.

You can find great getaways in wine regions.
Some offer wine activities.
Look for The Wine Activities Logo

New South Wales

Glen Innes

Over thirty Heritage-listed buildings dress the main street of Glen Innes in colonial charm. The Australian Standing Stones at Glen Innes are based on the first solar aligned megalithic stone circles erected thousands of years ago during the peak of Celtic civilisation. This area is rich in minerals: sapphires, topaz and quartz crystals.
Genevieve Barrett, Glen Innes Visitor Information Centre

Glen Innes - Ben Lomond
Silent Grove Farmstay B&B

B&B & Homestay & Farmstay & Self Contained Cottage
John & Dorothy Every
Silent Grove
Ben Lomond
NSW 2365
32 km N of Guyra

Tel (02) 6733 2117 or 0427 936 799
Fax (02) 6733 2117   silentgr@activ8.net.au
www.silentgrovefarmstay-bandb.com.au

Double $85
Single $45-$50, Children $15, Full breakfast
S/C Cottage - 2 Adults, 3 Children $95,
Dinner $18, Visa MC accepted
1 Queen 1 Double 2 Single (3 bdrm)
Bathrooms: 2 Guest share

AAA Tourism
★★★☆

Enjoy country hospitality in a peaceful rural setting, short detour by sealed road from the New England Highway. Working sheep and cattle property. Farm activities. 4WD tour (fee applies). Panoramic views, scenic walks, yabbying (seasonal), tennis court, fishing, occasional snow fall. Easy access to New England, Gibraltar Range, Washpool National Parks. Glen Innes Australian Stones Celtic Festival held 1st weekend May. Smoking outdoors. Winner of 2001 Big Sky Regional Tourism Hosted Accommodation. Campervans welcome. Take the time to detour you will be pleased you did.

New South Wales

Gloucester

Nestled in the foothills of the Bucketts Mountains and acclaimed for its friendliness and serene surroundings, Gloucester is your base camp to the World Heritage Barrington Tops.
Kyoko Sakamoto, Arrowee House B&B

Gloucester - Barrington Tops
Arrowee House B&B

B&B & Homestay & Separate Suite & Self Contained Apartment
Kyoko Sakamoto
152 Thunderbolts Way, Gloucester, NSW 2422
1 km N of Gloucester

Tel (02) 6558 2050
Fax (02) 6558 2050
information@gloucester.nsw.gov.au
www.arrowee.com.au

Double $130
Single $65, Child 1-11 yrs $1 per year, 12-16 years $25, Extra adult $65,
Full cooked breakfast available weekend,
Japanese dinner $35 pp, Visa MC accepted
3 Queen 4 Single (3 bdrm) Baby cot available
Bathrooms: 1 Ensuite 1 Guest share 2 Private

Commended Award 2005, 2006 and 2007. Established 1990. Northern gateway to World Heritage Barrington Tops. Walking distance to cafes, restaurants, shops, gallery and bushwalking on The Buckett and Mograni Mountains. Large undercover barbeque area with outdoor kitchen. Activities: bushwalking, fishing, canoeing, horse riding, scenic drives, golf, swimming, tennis. Events: Shakespeare on Avon Festival, Mountain Man Tri Challenge, rodeos, country music camps and community markets. During winter a 4 course Japanese dinner is available for only $35 per person, must pre book.

Grafton - Ulmarra
Rooftops B&B

B&B
Sandra & Darrel Grogan
6 Coldstream Street
Ulmarra
NSW 2462
12 km N of Grafton

Tel (02) 6644 5159
rooftopsulmarra@bigpond.com
www.rooftops.com.au

Double $130-$150
Children under six stay free
Full breakfast
2 course dinner $15 pp by prior arrangement
Honesty Bar
2 Queen 1 Double (3 bdrm)
Bathrooms: 2 Ensuite 1 Guest share, Spa bath

Rooftops is conveniently located in the centre of a Heritage listed riverport village near the beautiful Clarence River. 'You'll be Amazed' at what Rooftops has to offer; Off street parking, views of the river, quiet location, comfortably modern appointed rooms. Breakfast is served on the balcony above the rooftops. A great place to break your journey and relax, just off the Pacific Highway. Close to everything if you need it and a world away if you don't.

Hay
Bank B&B

B&B
Sally Smith
86 Lachlan Street
Hay
NSW 2711
In Hay Central

Tel (02) 6993 1730 or 0429 931 730
Fax (02) 6993 3440
ttsk@tpg.com.au
www1.tpg.com.au/users/ttsk

Double $120
Single $80
Full breakfast
1 King 1 Twin (2 bdrm) 2 luxurious rooms equipped to make your stay relaxing
Bathrooms: 1 Private

This National Trust classified mansion was built in 1891 to house the London Chartered Bank, one of the historic buildings restored to its original condition in Lachlan Street. The residence consists of a large dining room complete with period furniture and decor. The cedar staircase leads to the guest suite of two bedrooms and a fully modernised bathroom (complete with spa). The guest sitting room opens onto the balcony overlooking the main street. We look forward to you experiencing the hospitality of Hay with us.

New South Wales
Hunter Valley - Aberdeen - Scone
Craigmhor Mountain Retreat

Luxury B&B & Homestay & Separate Suite
& Self Contained Apartment
Gay Hoskings
Upper Rouchel Road
Upper Rouchel, NSW 2336
48 km E of Aberdeen

Tel (02) 6543 6393
Fax (02) 6543 6394
bnb@craigmhor.com.au
www.craigmhor.com.au

Double $135-$165
Single $70-$85, Children $35-$45, Full breakfast,
Dinner $30-$50 served with Upper Hunter Wines,
4WD tours from $100, Visa MC accepted
3 Queen 1 Twin 2 Single (4 bdrm)
Bathrooms: 2 Ensuite 1 Guest share

AAA Tourism ★★★★

Total contrast to city living - country hospitality, seclusion, splendid views, crisp mountain air in foothills of Barrington Tops. Peace and tranquillity assured - just you, your host, 1000 ha Australian bush and all its wildlife. Homestay; B&B; Self-Catered; Mix & Match to suit. Possible activities: doing absolutely nothing, picnicking by mountain streams, bush walking (50 km of forest trails), mountain biking, fishing stocked dams, Lake Glenbawn, 4-WD touring (optional extra), exploring Upper Hunter Country - magnificent horse studs, historic towns, wineries, National Parks.

Hunter Valley - Broke
Ferguson's Hunter Valley Getaway

Luxury Spacious King Suites & Spa Suites
Susie Ferguson
130 Hill Street, Broke, NSW 2330
2 km NW of Broke

Tel (02) 6579 1046
Fax (02) 6579 1054
susie@huntervalleygetaway.com.au
www.huntervalleygetaway.com.au

Double $165-$270
Children welcome - no special provisions
Full breakfast provisions
We can arrange a dinner for two in your suite
Additional person $80
Specials and group rates available
Visa MC Diners Amex Eftpos accepted
6 King (6 bdrm)   Bathrooms: 6 Ensuite

AAA Tourism ★★★★☆

Ferguson's Hunter Valley Getaway offers luxury, private suite accommodation across the Wollombi Brook from the rural village of Broke in the heart of the Hunter Valley Wine Country. Six stylish and spacious king suites with private terraces, electric BBQ and sweeping views of local vineyards and the Brokenback Range. Each suite includes a small kitchen, comfortable sofas, DVDs, reverse cycle air-conditioning and cooling ceiling fans. Gourmet breakfast hampers on weekends and generous continental breakfast midweek. Breathe fresh country air, gaze at the milky way and quite simply . . . take time out to relax.

New South Wales

Hunter Valley - East Maitland
The Old George and Dragon Guesthouse

Guest House
Nicolena & Martin Hurley
50 Melbourne Street, East Maitland, NSW 2323
5 km E of Maitland

Tel (02) 4934 6080 or 0412 995 639
Fax (02) 4933 6076
reservations@oldgeorgedragonguesthouse.com.au
www.oldgeorgedragonguesthouse.com.au

Double $140-$240
Single $130-$190, Full breakfast,
Dinner, Bed & Breakfast package $340-$380 per couple,
Visa MC Diners Amex Eftpos accepted
2 King 3 Queen (5 bdrm) All guestrooms themed individual
Bathrooms: 5 Ensuite

   AAA Tourism ★★★★

Your hosts Nicolena and Martin will greet you on arrival. Our service is discreet and professional.

Formerly a coach inn in the main route north from Sydney, the guesthouse has five guestrooms with ensuites, all individually decorated with high ceilings, flat LCD Television, DVD -CD Player & wireless broadband (fees apply).

A spacious layout convey a comforting sense of space and privacy. The guest lounge has an open fire place for the winter months. The restaurant located next to the guesthouse features an extensive menu range with a remarkable aged wine list.

The guesthouse is located close to Morpeth, famous wineries of Pokolbin , rugged glories of Barrington Tops and the sunny salty seduction of Port Stephens.

The ideal place to stay for business or pleasure, special occasions, wedding night or group getaway.

BBBook.com.au

New South Wales

Hunter Valley - Lochinvar
Lochinvar House

Luxury B&B Homestead,
Heritage Cottage & Heritage Cabin
Phillip & Heather Vickery
Kaludah Estate, 1204 New England Highway,
Lochinvar, NSW 2321
3 km NW of Lochinvar
(turn off Hwy at Kaludah Ck)

Tel (02) 4930 7873 or 0434 582 091
Fax (02) 4930 7798
enquiry@lochinvarhouse.com
www.lochinvarhouse.com

Double $121-$330
Single $99-$154, Children $66,
Special breakfast, Dinner B/A
1 King/Twin 4 Queen 2 Double (7 bdrm)
Bathrooms: 2 Guest share 1 Private

Historic Georgian-Victorian country homestead, heritage cottage and cabin circa 1841 on Kaludah Estate, an 88 acre grazing property on the Hunter River. With grand entrance and dining room, luxuriously appointed rooms featuring 13 foot ceilings and antique furnishings, Lochinvar House overlooks beautiful Loch Katrine with views over the surrounding countryside. A large swimming pool and spa with BBQ area are available. Situated 1 km north of the New England Highway, close to restaurants, Wyndham Estate, Tranquil Vale and other vineyards, equestrian centre, historic Maitland and Greta for antiques. Kennels available. Ideal for small groups and conferences.

Hunter Valley - Lovedale - Pokolbin
Hill Top Country Guest House

Luxury B&B & Homestay & Farmstay
& Self Contained Apartment & Guest House
Margaret Bancroft
288 Talga Road
Rothbury
NSW 2320
17 km N of Cessnock

Tel (02) 4930 7111
Fax (02) 4930 9048
stay@hilltopguesthouse.com.au
www.hilltopguesthouse.com.au

Double $90-$250
Special breakfast, Visa MC accepted
5 King/Twin 1 King 4 Queen 1 Double 2 Twin
(11 bdrm) Bathrooms: 9 Ensuite 2 Private

An Australian Country Experience, staying in the colonial homestead or modern Villas. Situated on the Molly Morgan Range with spectacular views of the Hunter Valley and Wine Country. Join the 4WD Night Wildlife Safari, horse riding and encounter abundant native wildlife of kangaroos, wombats, echidnas, possums roaming in their natural environment. Winery tours leave daily. The luxury guest house offers Spa Suites, wood fires, 10' billiard table, Grand Piano, delicious meals, massages, beauty treatments, sauna, pool and air-conditioning. The guest house is ideal for couples and family and friends gatherings. The Romantic Villas are ideal for couples.

Hunter Valley - Morpeth
Bronte Guesthouse

Guest House
Nicolena & Martin Hurley
147 Swan Street, Morpeth, NSW 2321
10 km E of Maitland

Tel **(02) 4934 6080** or **0412 995 639**
Fax (02) 4933 6076
reservations@bronteguesthouse.com.au
www.bronteguesthouse.com.au

Double $120-$200
Single $110-$195, Full breakfast
Visa MC Diners Amex Eftpos accepted
4 King 2 Queen 2 Single (6 bdrm)
Contemporary style accommodation
Bathrooms: 6 Ensuite, 1 room has a bath

AAA Tourism
★★★★

Historic, charming, chic and comfortable, welcoming service with attention to detail. All rooms are themed to reflect the needs of the sophisticated traveller and offer complete luxury with ensuites, individually controlled air conditioning, LCD Flat Televisions, DVD Players, CD Players and wireless broadband (fees apply).
There are two guest lounges with open fire places for the winter months. Breakfast is served on the guesthouse's balcony overlooking the township of Morpeth and the Hunter River.
Located in the heart of Morpeth, a fascinating little village, which started life in 1821 as a river port for the Hunter River.
The Hunter Wineries are a short drive away as is Port Stephens. The ideal place to stay for business or pleasure, special occasions, wedding night or group getaway.
Wireless Broadband available throughout the guesthouse and rooms - (fees apply). The guesthouse and grounds are non-smoking.

New South Wales

Hunter Valley - Morpeth
Morpeth Convent Guest House & St Bede's Cottage

Luxury B&B & Guest House & Self Contained Cottage
Scott Ranse
24 James Street
Morpeth, NSW 2321
35 km NW of Newcastle

Tel (02) 4934 4176 or 0419 622 459
info@morpethconvent.com.au
www.morpethconvent.com.au

Double $165-$330
Children only if whole house is occupied by the party, Full breakfast, Dinner by arrangement
Special tariffs available mid-week,
Visa MC Eftpos accepted
7 Queen (6 bdrm)
Bathrooms: 5 Ensuite 1 Private

Morpeth Convent Guest House is a grand two storey building once home to nuns of a teaching order, now refurbished to cater for bed-and-breakfast style accommodation with every modern comfort. The glorious house features sprawling verandas both upstairs and down, two spacious common rooms and breakfast room with bay windows. This unique accommodation experience is nestled in the heart of Morpeth NSW Australia - a town that's steeped in history and is the perfect place to get-away with family, friends or on your own.

Hunter Valley - Pokolbin
Elfin Hill

Studio Cottage & Self Contained Suites
Marie & Mark Blackmore
Marrowbone Road
Pokolbin
Hunter Valley
5 km W of Cessnock

Tel (02) 4998 7543 or 0416 209 709
0406 531 709
relax@elfinhill.com.au
www.elfinhill.com.au

Double $120-$250
Single $98-$250, Children $40,
Full breakfast, Extra person $50
Visa MC Eftpos accepted
7 Queen 2 Double 4 Twin 5 Single (7 bdrm)
Bathrooms: 7 Ensuite

AAA Tourism ★★★☆

Enjoy delightful country accommodation, serenely elevated with spectacular views of surrounding vineyards. Native wildlife. Rooms are comfy with everything you need to make your stay easy and enjoyable. BBQ beside the saltwater pool. Fabulous comfortable guest lounge. Easy bush walking. Close to Wine Tasting and Fantastic Cuisine, cheese, galleries etc. Excellent breakfast in your room or eat outside at one of many areas. Just completed a separate studio with mezzanine sleeping, ensuite, kitchen, amazing views, romantic and special.

Hunter Valley - Pokolbin
Holman Estate Pokolbin

Self Contained House
Theo and Soula Tsironis
173 (Lot 3) Gillards Road, Pokolbin, NSW 2325
120 km N of Sydney

Tel 0438 683 973
Fax (02) 6842 4513
holman@mounteyre.com
www.mounteyre.com

$800-$1000/night whole house
Accommodation only, Visa MC Eftpos accepted
3 Queen 2 Single (4 bdrm)
Two double foldout futons in Games Room
Bathrooms: 1 Ensuite 2 Family share

Holman Estate is located in the heart of Pokolbin, the Hunter Valley's premier tourist location.
Holman Estate offers spectacular views of the Hunter Valley, from the privacy of your own executive residence. Located on an operational vineyard, you will experience what it is like to live in a French chateau or Italian villa.
The house boasts 4 generously sized bedrooms, 3 bathrooms, a billiards room and kitchen. The open-plan living and dining area features cathedral ceilings and a large open fireplace.
You can simply spend a weekend drinking fine wine by the fireplace and strolling through the vineyards. Alternatively, enjoy the Hunter Valley Gardens, wine tastings, restaurants, galleries, ballooning and a myriad of other interesting pursuits.
Whether you want a romantic escape, a family and friends holiday, a corporate function or even a small wedding, Holman Estate is the ideal venue.
Holman Estate offers a unique opportunity to enjoy all the Hunter Valley has to offer, within easy reach of your own private residence.

New South Wales

Hunter Valley - Wine Country - Wollombi
Capers Guest House and Cottage

Luxury B&B & Guest House & Self Contained Cottage
Jane Young
2859 Wollombi Road, Wollombi, NSW 2325
29 km SW of Cessnock

Tel (02) 4998 3211 or 0409 305 345
Fax (02) 4998 3458   stay@capers.com.au
www.capers.com.au

Double $200-$380
Single $200-$380, Children welcome when guest house booked by single group,
Full breakfast, Dinner $55-$70,
Cottage from $75 per person per night,
Visa MC Diners Amex Eftpos accepted
1 King/Twin 2 King 3 Queen 2 Double 1 Twin
2 Single (9 bdrm)   Bathrooms: 8 Ensuite

AAA Tourism ★★★★☆

Majestic Guesthouse Retreat, set in the historic village of Wollombi. Six elegantly appointed guest rooms, reverse-cycle air-conditioning and spacious guest lounge with double sided open log fire places. Includes full country breakfast, complimentary port and chocolates. Fully licensed and dinner can be arranged. Cottage: Stay two nights in luxury three bedroom cottages which accommodate up to 7 people. Open fire or A/C in the summer, large hamper breakfast, two bathrooms one with Spa bath, gourmet kitchen, sweetest garden with BBQ, TV, CD, and DVD players.

**The difference between a hotel and a B&B.
You don't hug the hotel staff when you leave.**

Hunter Valley - Wollombi - Laguna
Arcadian Retreat

Luxury Guest House with 4 Luxury Villas
Di & Adrian Judson
3868 Great North Road
Laguna
NSW 2325
9 km S of Wollombi

Tel (02) 4998 8085
enquiries@arcadianretreat.com.au
www.arcadianretreat.com.au

Double $280-$380
Full breakfast, Dinner $35-$70
Visa MC Amex Eftpos accepted
4 Queen (4 bdrm)
Bathrooms: 4 Ensuite, Spa Baths (3double 1 single)

From the moment you thread along the private drive that winds up the valley, you're in for a special experience that combines the best of country living with style and sophistication. Each villa is stylish, bright and meticulously kept, with a lounge/dining room separate from the bedroom and includes: Open wood fire, Spa baths, Free internet connection, CD/DVD players and Complimentary DVD library, antipasto platter, beer and sherry on arrival, Kitchenette and r/c a/c. In-ground pool in bush setting. A variety of meals is available.

New South Wales

Jervis Bay

Jervis Bay is one of nature's secrets; crystal clear waters and white sandy beaches, a place where Whales rest and Dolphins live year round. Huskisson retains the character of a laid back coastal community, offering good food and a base to explore the generosity of nature.
Jervis Bay Tourism, www.jervisbaytourism.asn.au

Jervis Bay - Huskisson
Dolphin Sands Jervis Bay

B&B & Self Contained Cottages
Wayne and Beatrice Whitten
6 Tomerong Street
Jervis Bay, Huskisson
NSW 2540
25 km S of Nowra

Tel (02) 4441 5511 or 0418 476 280
Fax (02) 4441 7712
info@dolphinsands.com
www.dolphinsands.com

Double $195-$295
Children Welcome in S/C Dolphin Cottages
Full breakfast
Visa MC Amex Eftpos accepted
4 Queen 1 Twin (5 bdrm)
Bathrooms: 5 Ensuite

  AAA Tourism ★★★★☆

Dolphin Sands is what life by the ocean is all about. Dolphin Sands is a tranquil couples retreat, only minutes from the White Sands, Dolphins, and Clear Blue Waters of Jervis Bay at Huskisson. Hosts Wayne and Beatrice Whitten designed your luxury accommodations creating an intimate and relaxing atmosphere, while maintaining guest room privacy. Jervis Bay Luxury Cottage (4 bedrooms) and Dolphin Cottage (2 bedrooms) are 2 self contained cottages suitable for families, groups or a private romantic getaway.

New South Wales

Jervis Bay - Huskisson
Sandholme Guesthouse

Luxury 5 Star B&B Guesthouse
Alan & Christine Burrows
2 Jervis Street
Huskisson, NSW 2540
1 km S of Huskisson on Jervis Bay

Tel (02) 4441 8855
Fax (02) 4441 8866
guesthouse@sandholme.com.au
www.sandholme.com.au

Double $200-$310
Children under 15 not catered for
Full breakfast
Dinner by arrangement
Visa MC Eftpos accepted
5 King 2 Single (5 bdrm)
Bathrooms: 5 Ensuite 4 with Spa

     AAA Tourism ★★★★★

Sandholme Guesthouse; 5 star luxury Bed and Breakfast in Huskisson on Jervis Bay, offers a spacious couples retreat in a friendly coastal setting. Enjoy luxurious Spa guest rooms each with en-suite, guest Lounge and Games Room (separate from your Hosts), wide verandah and delicious espresso coffee, a place to relax and revive from the stress of a busy life. Just 200 meters from the water and a short walk to great restaurants, Sandholme is only 2 1/2 hours from Sydney, 3 hours from Canberra.

Jindabyne - Snowy Mountains
Troldhaugen Lodge

B&B & Guest House
John & Sandra Bradshaw
13 Cobbodah Street
Jindabyne
NSW 2627
30 km W of Berridale

Tel (02) 6456 2718 or 0409 567 718
Fax (02) 6456 2718
troldhaugen@ozemail.com.au
www.troldhaugen.com.au

Double $80-$150
Single $50-$120, Children $15-$40
Continental breakfast, cooked breakfast $8-$10
Visa MC accepted
1 Queen 8 Double 1 Single (10 bdrm)
Bathrooms: 10 Ensuite

Centrally located in Jindabyne within walking distance to shops, hotels, restaurants, club and lake. Troldhaugen is situated at the end of a quiet cul-de-sac. A friendly owner/operated lodge catering for the family or couples, holiday. Facilities include guest lounge with open fireplace, TV and videos. Game room with tennis & pool tables, drying room & ski racks. All rooms are centrally heated and have own ensuites. Features include mountain and lake views.

BBBook.com.au

New South Wales

Kiama

Kiama, a beautiful seaside town famous for its blowholes, pristine beaches and natural beauty of a magnificent hinterland with its historic dry stone walls. Visit Minnamurra Rainforest or the Illawarra Fly Tree Top Walk. Try surf schools, fishing charters, dolphin and coastal cruises, Jamberoo Action Park, vineyards and wineries.
Dianne Rendel, Seashells

Kiama
Bed and Breakfast @ Kiama

B&B or Self-Catering
Anthony & Marian van Zanen
15 Riversdale Road (off Jamberoo Road)
Kiama
NSW 2533
2 km W of Kiama

Tel (02) 4232 2844 or (02) 6084 2927
(02) 6100 7143   0428 322866
Fax (02) 4232 2844
info@bedandbreakfastatkiama.com.au
www.bedandbreakfastatkiama.com.au

Double $140-$240
Single $110-$150, Children $33, Breakfast b/a,
B&B and Self-Catering, Visa MC Eftpos accepted
2 King 2 Queen 1 Double 3 Twin 4 Single
(5 bdrm) Bathrooms: 4 Ensuite 1 Guest share

   AAA Tourism

Multi Award-winning Kiama Bed & Breakfast (now renamed Bed and Breakfast @ Kiama) has been providing luxury boutique-style B&B and Self-Catering accommodation since 1998. Enjoy a quiet nights sleep on the peaceful outskirts of the noisy bustling town of Kiama, situated overlooking the spectacular rural scenery of Jamberoo Valley and scenic rainforest escarpment. Singles, Couples, Friends, Families or Groups. 4 B&B rooms - all with ensuites. 2-bedroom Self-Catering Cottage for up to 8 people. 3-bedroom Guest House for 3 couples to share.

New South Wales

Kiama
Bed and Views Kiama

B&B
Sabine & Rudi Dux
69 Riversdale Road
Kiama
NSW 2533
3 km W of Kiama

Tel (02) 4232 3662
admin@bedandviewskiama.com.au
www.bedandviewskiama.com.au

Double $140-$160
Full breakfast
Lovebird Suite from $190
Visa MC accepted
1 King/Twin 2 King 1 Queen (4 bdrm)
Bathrooms: 4 Ensuite

   AAA Tourism ★★★★☆

Enjoy crystal clear waters at various beaches, see the world's famous Blow Hole, walk the nearby rainforest or find your favourite spot in the garden with unspoilt ocean and rural views. Only 2 minutes away from the seaside town Kiama this B&B offers modern king and queen-bed rooms, ensuites, one with spa, all air-conditioned (cool/heat). Welcoming European hospitality invites to a 'spoilt for choice' breakfast. Day-tour suggestions and booking assistance provided. "What a remarkable combination of stunning views, most comfortable bed, delicious breakfast and a warm and friendly welcome." L&D Wilson, Melbourne.

Kiama
Seashells Kiama

Luxury Self Contained House & Self Catering
Dianne Rendel
72 Bong Bong Street
Kiama
NSW 2533
0.5 km SW of Kiama PO

Tel (02) 4232 2504 or 0414 423 225
Fax (02) 4232 3419
dianne@seashellskiama.com.au
www.seashellskiama.com.au

Double $230-$440
Children's and Babies rates available
Accommodation only
2 nights min booking, Seasonal rates apply
1 Queen 1 Double 2 Single (3 bdrm)
Bathrooms: 3 Private

 AAA Tourism ★★★★☆

Unwind . . . Relax . . . and experience the delights of Kiama from this thoughtfully renovated 1960s bungalow. The spacious living area with sweeping town and ocean views is sunroom by day and cosy living room by night. Neat as a pin and full of light this retro-styled home has all the amenities you would expect and more . . . best of all, has personality. Whether looking for a weekend away or a longer stay Seashells Kiama is ideal for a summer holiday or winter retreat - the perfect getaway for couples, families and friends. Illawarra Tourism Award Winner.

BBBook.com.au

New South Wales
Lightning Ridge
Sonja's B&B

B&B & Self Contained Suites
Sonja Cairns
60 Butterfly Avenue
Lightning Ridge, NSW 2834
1.2 km S of PO

Tel (02) 6829 2010 or 0427 185 724
Fax (02) 6829 2010
info@sonjasbedandbreakfast.com
www.sonjasbedandbreakfast.com

Double $90-$120
Single $80-$95, Children $20, Special breakfast,
Dinner $35, Full cooked breakfast or
accommodation only available, Extra Adult $30,
Weekly self catering $350, Visa MC Amex accepted
2 Queen 2 Double 2 Single (4 bdrm)
Bathrooms: 4 Ensuite

AAA Tourism
★★★☆

A perfect home base to visit memorable attractions such as opal mines and fossicking. Rejuvenate in the Artesian Baths - free entry and open 24 hours a day. Art houses, indigenous art, bottle houses, cactus gardens. Wonderful wildlife, native plants and spectacular sunsets. Enjoy a scrumptious breakfast in the dining room or self cater in one of the four comfortable private self-contained units. Sleeps 10. Resident friendly cat and dog. Smoking outside. We are happy to arrange tours and complimentary pick-ups from airport or bus.

Lismore - Clunes
PJ's

B&B
Terry & Susan Hurst
152 Johnston Road
Clunes
NSW 2480
16 km N of Lismore

Tel (02) 6629 1788 or 0412 996 243
pjsbb@bigpond.com
www.pjsretreat.com

Double $160
Single $125
Full breakfast
Eftpos accepted
3 King (3 bdrm)
Bathrooms: 3 Ensuite

AAA Tourism
★★★★☆

PJ's looks over some of the most beautiful countryside in NSW. All guest rooms have panoramic views that are spectacular. The stylishly purpose built B&B which features three elegant and spacious bedrooms all with the usual comforts including complimentary port, chocolates and local coffee. A personalised country breakfast is served. PJ's is the ideal spot from which to experience the many wonders of the Northern Rivers. Or just simply relax by the saltwater pool or your own private courtyard and soak up the view. Quality accommodation at an affordable price.

New South Wales

Merimbula
Bella Vista

B&B
Judy Hori
16 Main Street
Merimbula
NSW 2548
In Town Centre

Tel (02) 6495 1373
Fax (02) 6495 1373
bellavistauno@bigpond.com
www.merimbulabellavista.com.au

Double $185-$225
Full breakfast
2 King/Twin (2 bdrm)
Bathrooms: 2 Ensuite

  AAA Tourism ★★★★☆

Bella Vista is unique - an Award winning design and a relaxing haven. The entrance opens to a large sun drenched courtyard, private entrances to large guest room - ensuite, fridge, tea, coffee. Air conditioned, underfloor heating. Your own access to the lake and large deck where you enjoy a delicious breakfast while absorbing the spectacular views - swans, pelicans and the many birds glide by. Minutes walk to shops, restaurants & clubs. Short drive to pristine beaches, golf clubs, whale watching & fishing. We are half way between Sydney & Melbourne with daily flight taking just over an hour - 2 hours to the snow fields.

Merimbula
Robyn's Nest Guest House

Luxury B&B & Self Contained Apartment
& Guest House & Self Contained Cottages
Robyn Britten
188 Merimbula Drive
Merimbula
NSW 2548
2 km N of Merimbula

Tel (02) 6495 4956
Fax (02) 6495 2426
enquiries@robynsnest.com.au
www.robynsnest.com.au

Double $175-$250
Single $140-$215, Full breakfast
Visa MC Amex Eftpos accepted
10 King/Twin 10 King 7 Queen (27 bdrm)
Bathrooms: 27 Ensuite

      AAA Tourism ★★★★★

Robyn's Nest is a 5* multi-award winning luxury BnB set amid 100acres of bushland with 25acres of Absolute Lake Frontage with water views from every room. Halfway between Sydney and Melbourne on the coastal route, 2hrs from Canberra and 2hrs from the snowfields. Facilities: heated pool, spas, sauna, tennis court, jetty/boat and mooring into prime fish breeding grounds. 3mins from the town centre that has 20 restaurants, pristine beaches, whale watching, bushwalking, deep sea & rock fishing. Romantic Indulgence packages available.

New South Wales
Milton - Mollymook - Ulladulla
Meadowlake Lodge

Luxury B&B
Diana & Peter Falloon
318 Wilfords Lane
Milton
NSW 2538
3 km S of Milton

Tel (02) 4455 7722
Fax (02) 4455 7733
enquiries@meadowlakelodge.com.au
www.meadowlakelodge.com.au

Double $230-$290
Single $190-$260, Children over 6 years old,
Full breakfast, 3 course Dinner B/A $60pp,
Visa MC Amex accepted
1 King/Twin 2 Queen (3 bdrm)
Bathrooms: 3 Ensuite

AAA Tourism
★★★★★

Meadowlake won the South Coast Tourism Award in the prestigious category of Accommodation Up to Five Stars in 2004, 2005, 2006 and 2007 This luxurious Five Star country house overlooks lakes and wetlands. Only 3 hours from Sydney and 2.5 from Canberra. Close to historic Milton. Near the beaches at Mollymook and bush walks in the Budawangs. Spacious and elegant rooms have en suites with baths. Dinners by arrangement. At Meadowlake Lodge luxury is a way of life. Listen to the sounds of nature.

Children enjoy getaways as much as adults and most properties have facilities for children. Look for The Children Welcome Logo

New South Wales

Murwillumbah

Nestled between the NSW and Queensland Border, the Tweed enchants those lucky enough to stumble upon this largely undiscovered area. Home to five World Heritage Listed National Parks, including Mt Warning, the spot where the dawn sun first touches Australia.
Tracy & Clive Parker, Hillcrest Mountain View

Murwillumbah - Crystal Creek
Hillcrest Mountain View Retreat

Luxury B&B & Separate Suite & Self Contained Cottage
Clive & Tracy Parker
Upper Crystal Creek Road
Murwillumbah
NSW 2484
12 km NW of Murwillumbah

Tel (02) 6679 1023
romance@hillcrestbb.com
www.hillcrestbb.com

Double $165-$350
Full breakfast
Dinner BBQ Packs by advance arrangement
Visa MC accepted
3 Queen (3 bdrm) in-room tv, dvd, a/c
Bathrooms: 3 Ensuite

    AAA Tourism ★★★★☆

Multi Tourism Award winning specialists in romantic getaways offering peace, privacy, spectacular views from Mt Warning to the Springbrook rainforests, solar-heated salt-water pool, luxury double spa baths, massage, wood fire, air-conditioning & jolly good food. Choose from 2 B&B suites in the main house private guest wing or 1 fully self-contained Honeymoon Spa Cottage in its own secluded garden. Centrally located to 5 World Heritage National Parks, golf, horse-riding, galleries, markets and more. Only 35 minutes from Gold Coast airport, 75 minutes from Brisbane.

New South Wales
Nambucca Heads - Macksville
Jacaranda Country Lodge

Luxury B&B, Self Contained Cottage & 3 Bedroom Farmhouse
Pamela and Donald Hallaran
292 Wilson Road
Macksville, NSW 2447
3 km N of Macksville

Tel (02) 6568 2737
Fax (02) 6568 2769
jacaranda.lodge@hotmail.com
www.jacarandacountrylodge.com.au

Double $150-$170
Single $120-$140, Children $25 for each child,
Continental breakfast, Extra Adult $35,
Visa MC Eftpos accepted
12 Queen 1 Double 18 Single (17 bdrm)
Bathrooms: 12 Ensuite 2 Family share

Country club facilities with old fashioned B&B hospitality. Boutique style accommodation surrounded by beautiful gardens set amidst 230 acres of pastoral landscape. Peacefully situated on the Nambucca River on the Mid North Coast of NSW. Outside facilities include tennis court, pool, sauna, walking track, golfing range and private jetty. Inside relax and enjoy our lounge area with its over-stuffed sofas, TV, billiard table and fireplace. An idyllic place for a quiet night's rest or a base for exploring the scenic delights of the Nambucca Valley.

Narooma - Tilba
Pub Hill Farm

B&B & Farmstay
Micki & Ian Thomlinson
566 Scenic Drive
Narooma
NSW 2546
8 km W of Narooma

Tel (02) 4476 3177
Fax (02) 4476 3177
pubhill@austarnet.com.au
www.pubhillfarm.com

Double $110-$140
Single $100-$110, Full breakfast, Karibu Cottage $160 per day
2 King/Twin 2 Queen 1 Double (5 bdrm) 5 ensuite
Bathrooms: 5 Ensuite

Pub Hill Farm is a small farm, sitting high on a hill overlooking the beautiful Wagonga Inlet and with 2 kilometres of water frontage. The birdlife is abundant and the extreme quiet makes it an ideal place to bird watch. Small mobs of kangaroos live on the property. All rooms have water views, private outdoor areas and private entrances, plus ensuites, microwaves, fridges, TV, and tea and coffee. We welcome guests' pets. The gardens are fully fenced for their safety.

If you prefer self contained accommodation, Karibu Cottage is gorgeous. Just for two, with mezzanine bedroom and fabulous views over Wagonga Inlet, Karibu sits in a secluded garden where you can enjoy water views in complete privacy. There is a cosy wood fire for winter.

We have travelled extensively and lived abroad in both UK and North and East Africa and enjoy swapping travellers' tales with our guests.

"Quite the best B&B we have ever stayed at, anywhere. Superb hospitality"
J & PJ, Woodham, Surrey, England.
"Am speechless - loved every minute - your hospitality was warm and wonderful"
Mary and Bill R, Los Osos, California USA.

BBBook.com.au

New South Wales

Narromine
Camerons Farmstay

B&B & Homestay & Farmstay & Self Contained Cottage
Ian & Kerry Cameron
Nundoone Park, 213 Ceres Road,
Narromine, NSW 2821
6 km W of Narromine

Tel (02) 6889 2978
Fax (02) 6889 5229
cameronsfarmstay@bbbook.com.au
www.bbbook.com.au/cameronsfarmstay.html

Double $110-$130
Single $90, Children welcome,
Continental breakfast, Dinner B/A,
Self Contained Cottage from $120
2 Queen 2 Double 1 Twin 4 Single (5 bdrm)
Bathrooms: 1 Ensuite 1 Guest share

AAA Tourism ★★★☆

Our home, 30 minutes west of Dubbo. We offer 4 star S/C cottage and B&B. Our house is modern and spacious with reverse cycle air-conditioning with each bedroom having a fan/heater; guest lounge has television, video, books, tea/coffee making facilities, fridge etc. It is surrounded by large gardens, all weather tennis court, and pool. Ian and Kerry run a successful Border Leicester Sheep stud - see lambs, shearing, haymaking, cotton growing and harvesting (seasonal), tour cotton gin. Visit: Rose Nursery, Iris Farm, Aviation Museum and Gliding Centre. " Excellent, comfortable accommodation and great hospitality. So good to come back." P&G, Belgium.

Newcastle

Beautiful old buildings of Newcastle are a reminder of our rich architectural heritage. Beaches to die for, a vibrant harbour and great restaurants. Nature reserves like Blackbutt, the Wetlands and the Botanic Gardens are worth a visit, as is the Art Gallery, the leading regional gallery in Australia.
Rosemary Bunker, Newcomen B&B

Tell hosts you found them in the Bed & Breakfast Book

Newcastle
Merewether Beach B&B

Self Contained Studio
Jane & Alf Scott
60 Hickson Street
Merewether
NSW 2291
5 km S of Newcastle PO

Tel (02) 4963 3526 or 0407 921 670
Fax (02) 4963 7926
janescott@bigpond.com

Double $140
Single $70-$110, Child friendly - POA
One family or friends - no stranger share
Full breakfast
Visa MC accepted
1 Queen 1 Double 3 Single (2 bdrm)
Bathrooms: 1 Ensuite

Wake up to this view! Go to sleep with only the sound of waves breaking on shore. 3 minutes to beach, 5 km from CBD, 1000 km from care. Featured on "Getaway", air-conditioned, self-contained studio with kitchenette, glassed-in verandah, private entrance and garden. Children welcome. Alf's ceramics and paintings lovingly adorn the rooms. With Jane's passion for cooking, expect a breakfast extravaganza. You are our only guests. Let us spoil you! "The view is as rare as the B&B itself..." L&DF, Bowral.

Newcastle
Newcomen B&B

B&B & Studio SC BB Accommodation
Rosemary Bunker
70 Newcomen Street
Newcastle
NSW 2300
In Newcastle Central

Tel (02) 4929 7313 or 0412 145 104
newcomen_bb@hotmail.com
www.newcomen-bb.com.au

Double $140-$150
Single $95-$105, Children $30
Full breakfast
Visa MC accepted
1 Queen 1 Double 1 Single (1 bdrm)
Bathrooms: 1 Ensuite 1 Private

Be delighted by this gem of a C19 home nestling in a vibrant garden. Explore the surrounding rich heritage area, stroll by the foreshore, enjoy the beach, savour city delights, laze by the pool, relax with every comfort, including air-conditioning, in harmonious decor featuring art works. A boutique mini holiday/work base you'll love.

New South Wales

Newcastle - Hamilton
Hamilton Heritage

B&B & Homestay
Laraine & Colin Bunt
178 Denison Street
Hamilton
NSW 2303
6 km N of Newcastle

Tel (02) 4961 1242 or 0414 717 688
Fax (02) 4969 4758   colaine@iprimus.com.au
www.accommodationinnewcastle.com.au

Double $130-$155
Single $60-$105, Children $10-$25
Budget stay shared bathroom $60 sgle $80 dble
Special breakfast
Visa MC Diners Amex Eftpos accepted
2 Queen 1 Double 3 Single (4 bdrm)
Bathrooms: 3 Ensuite 1 Family share

Children and Pets Welcome. Hamilton Heritage B&B, "Old World Charm", situated on Historic Cameron Hill. Close to Broadmeadow Station, Broadmeadow Race Course, Newcastle Entertainment Centre & All Major Sporting Venues. Beaumont Street, the Cosmopolitan Heart of Newcastle, famous for its Restaurants, Newcastle CBD, Foreshore and Beaches. Feel free to enjoy the serenity of the garden or the verandah. Breakfast of choice and time served in the Breakfast Room overlooking garden. Laundry facilities available. Fax and e-mail access.

Newcastle - Lake Macquarie
Tantarra B&B

Luxury B&B & Separate Suite
Kim & Serena Neil
119 Bayview Street
Warners Bay
NSW 2282
1 km N of Warners Bay

Tel (02) 4961 3422 or 0412 688 076
tantarra.com@gmail.com
www.tantarra.com.au

Double $110-$160
Private Suite Includes 4 Guests, Extra Guest $30,
Tariff includes a cooked or continental breakfast,
Private Suite from $220-$320 (includes first four guests), Visa MC Eftpos accepted
2 Queen 1 Double (3 bdrm)
Bathrooms: 3 Ensuite 3 Private

Tantarra, just 2 minutes drive to beautiful Lake Macquarie and 10 minutes to the shores of Newcastle, offers two well appointed Queen Bedrooms with private ensuites for couples, OR our whole guest area for small groups and families, accommodating up to 6 guests. We also offer a unique Bed & Breakfast experience where you can spend time contemplating in our tranquil Asian style gardens, sip wine by the pool or relax in our prayer garden. Included in your tariff is a cooked or continental breakfast each morning plus we are pet friendly.

New South Wales

Pacific Palms - Coomba

Set on the magnificent Wallis Lake, close to Forster-Tuncurry, a haven for fishing, boating and canoeing this small area on the mid-north coast also boasts renowned surfing and swimming beaches and walking tracks through cabbage palm and flooded gum forests . . . the perfect place in a tranquil, natural setting.
Annabelle Lewis, Whitby on Wallis

Pacific Palms - Coomba
Whitby on Wallis B&B

Luxury B&B & Homestay
Lew Dodds & Annabelle Lewis
1770 Coomba Road
Coomba Bay
NSW 2428
18 km NW of Pacific Palms

Tel (02) 6554 2448 or 0419 228 089
Fax (02) 6554 2448
info@whitbyonwallis.com.au
www.whitbyonwallis.com.au

Double $135-$160
Single $125-$135, Full breakfast
Dinner by arrangement from $35 each
Visa MC Eftpos accepted
2 King/Twin1 King (3 bdrm)
Bathrooms: 3 Ensuite

   AAA Tourism ★★★★☆

Luxurious, spacious lake-side accommodation with privacy and magnificent views. Each bedroom has its own outdoor area, TV, tea & coffee. Large guest areas - lounges, reading room, fireplaces, tea and plunger coffee makings, home-baked biscuits, fridge. Room to mix with friends or to find a quiet nook of your own. Swim in the wet-edge pool, fish from the jetty, explore the grounds, paddle on the lake or just laze the day away. Close to National Parks, recreational and tourist activities and Pacific Palms' pristine beaches.

New South Wales

Parkes

Parkes is centrally located in the Central West, easily accessible for an overnight stay. Visit our Australian icon - the world famous CSIRO Radio Telescope, "The Dish". Visitors are invited to explore the world of astronomy and discover what role The Dish plays in listening to the stars.
Helen & Mal Westcott, Kadina B&B

Parkes
Kadina B&B

Luxury B&B
Helen and Malcolm Westcott
22 Mengarvie Road, Parkes, NSW 2870
1.5 km E of Parkes CBD

Tel (02) 6862 3995 or 0412 444 452
Fax (02) 6862 6451
kadinabb@bigpond.net.au
www.kadinabnb.com

Double $130
Single $100
Children Under 12 $20, Under 16 $30
Full breakfast
Dinner 2 courses $30 pp by arrangement
Visa MC Diners accepted
2 Queen 1 Single (2 bdrm)
Bathrooms: 2 Ensuite

AAA Tourism
★★★★☆

Come and enjoy the tranquillity and ambience of this lovely modern spacious home. Watch TV, listen to music, play piano, read or just soak in the views. Dine in our traditionally furnished dining room, patio or secluded back garden. Mal is involved in cereal growing and merino sheep farming. Guests may visit when convenient. Come and see "The Dish". Relax in our luxurious therapeutic Hot Tub. Finalist in 2004 and 2006 Inland Tourism Awards. Regional Winners of Central West Region 2007 Local Business Awards.

Parkes
The Old Parkes Convent

Self Contained Apartments
Judy & Colin Wilson
33 Currajong Street
Parkes
NSW 2870
0.5 km E of Post Office

Tel (02) 6862 5385 or 0428 625 385
Fax (02) 6862 5158
parkesconvent@bigpond.com
www.parkesconvent.com.au

Double $180
Single $130, Extra Child $15, Extra Adult $30,
Full breakfast provisions, Dinner by arrangement,
1 night stay $180, minimum of 2 nights $160,
Visa MC Diners Amex accepted.
2 Double (2 bdrm) Bathrooms: 2 Ensuite

Experience spacious living in one of our exclusive apartments. You'll enjoy your own private lounge, bathroom, kitchen, and air conditioned comfort before awaking to a full and delicious breakfast. Outside you can enjoy a heated spa with barbecue area. Stay a night or a few days. Built in 1923 and set on half an acre of land in the centre of town, The Old Parkes Convent was once home to the Sisters of Mercy and girl, student boarders. The Old Parkes Convent B&B is only a short stroll to the shops, clubs, hotels, and restaurants.

Port Macquarie
Woodlands B&B

B&B & Separate Suite
Ian & Gretel McGinnigle
348 Oxley Highway
Port Macquarie
NSW 2444
3 km W of town centre

Tel (02) 6581 3913 or 0412 443 277
info@woodlandsbnb.com.au
www.woodlandsbnb.com.au

Double $130-$150
Single $110-$130
Full breakfast
Visa MC accepted
1 King/Twin 4 Queen (5 bdrm) 3 suites
Bathrooms: 1 Ensuite 2 Private

AAA Tourism ★★★★

Luxury accommodation and hospitality in a secluded setting of gardens and trees with easy access to all local attractions. Guest lounges are spacious and comfortable with air-conditioned accommodation options include the two bedroom Frangipani Suite which is partly self contained, the two bedroom Magnolia Suite with its magnificently large bathroom and the Verandah Room, an ensuited queen size bedroom which opens out to the verandah and landscaped front gardens. All rooms have the full complement of expected comforts including wireless internet connection.

New South Wales

Port Macquarie - Camden Haven
Benbellen Country Retreat

Luxury B&B & Farmstay
Sherry Stumm & Peter Wildblood
Cherry Tree Lane
Hannam Vale
NSW 2443
20 km S of Laurieton

Tel (02) 6556 7788
Fax (02) 6556 7778
info@bbfarmstay.com.au
www.bbfarmstay.com.au

Double $165-$195
Single $130-$155, Full breakfast, Dinner $40+ per person,
Visa MC Diners Amex Eftpos JCB accepted
2 Queen (2 bdrm)   Bathrooms: 2 Ensuite

AAA Tourism
★★★★☆

Revitalise yourself with fresh air, peace and quiet with country hospitality second to none. The large open-plan homestead, with its solar-passive design and its quietly stated elegance, is purpose built with your privacy and comfort in mind.

Benbellen Country Retreat is a small working alpaca farm tucked away in a lush green hidden valley at Hannam Vale, just 40 minutes from Port Macquarie, 15 minutes from Laurieton and 30 minutes from Taree. You will fall in love with the farm itself with its magical landscape of rolling hills and lotus strewn vistas in an English-style countryside.

Choose our luxury ensuite rooms and our country hospitality, not to mention locally grown produce, fresh (to die for) eggs from the farm, home-baked breads and homemade jams. Environmentally friendly. Whether on a short break escape or just "passing through", we know you will be back . . .

Port Macquarie - Camden Haven
Penlan Cottage

**Luxury B&B & Farmstay
& Self Contained House**
Sherry Stumm & Peter Wildblood
Hannam Vale Road
Hannam Vale
NSW 2443
20 km S of Laurieton

Tel (02) 6556 7788
Fax (02) 6556 7778   info@bbfarmstay.com.au
www.bbfarmstay.com.au

Double $155-$195
Single $155-$195, Children $10-$40,
Full breakfast provisions Dinner $40+ pp,
Visa MC Diners Amex Eftpos JCB accepted
1 Queen 1 Double 2 Single (2 bdrm)
Bathrooms: 1 Private

This charming holiday hideaway, with its uninterrupted valley views and set in its own garden of an acre and a half, is ideal for couples and families of up to six looking for a truly country experience. The main bedroom has a queen sized bed with French doors opening to the large veranda. The spacious combined living and dining area is tastefully furnished and the fully equipped kitchen/pantry has a good selection of "basic" supplies including home made jams and home baked bread. Environmentally friendly.

Port Macquarie - Camden Haven
Cherry Tree Cottage

**Luxury B&B & Farmstay
& Self Contained House**
Sherry Stumm & Peter Wildblood
Cherry Tree Lane
Hannam Vale
NSW 2443
20 km S of Laurieton

Tel (02) 6556 7788
Fax (02) 6556 7778   info@bbfarmstay.com.au
www.bbfarmstay.com.au

Double $155-$195
Single $155-$195, Children $10-$40,
Full breakfast provisions, Dinner $40+ pp,
Visa MC Diners Amex Eftpos JCB accepted
1 Queen 3 Single (2 bdrm)
Bathrooms: 1 Private

AAA Tourism ★★★★

High overlooking the rich green paddocks and expansive dams of Benbellen Alpaca Farm, Cherry Tree Cottage is a rural hideaway ideal for couples or families of up to five. The main bedroom has a queen bed and French doors onto the expansive balcony with breathtaking views looking down Hannam Vale to South Brother Mountain. The spacious veranda provides ample room for outdoor entertaining and relaxation while soaking up the views and watching local bird life and listening to the "sounds of nature". Environmentally friendly.

New South Wales
Port Macquarie Hinterland - Wauchope
Auntie Ann's B&B

B&B
Ann Pereira
19 Bruxner Avenue
Wauchope
NSW 2446
0.5 km W of Wauchope PO

Tel **(02) 6586 4420**
auntyannsbandb@nor.com.au
www.bbbook.com.au/auntieanns.html

Double $88
Single $66
Full breakfast
Visa MC accepted
1 Double 4 Twin (3 bdrm)
Bathrooms: 1 Guest share

   AAA Tourism ★★★☆

Wauchope is the gateway to Port Macquarie's Hinterland. Within easy driving are several national parks, nature reserves and vineyards as well as the largest single drop waterfall in the Southern Hemisphere. Overlooking the golf course, Auntie Ann's is close to clubs, restaurants and shops. Visit Timbertown Heritage Park, art, pottery and furniture galleries or just relax by the pool with some locally made fudge. Also available: Air-conditioning, TV room, BBQ, tea/coffee making facilities, heaters or air conditioner in each room.

Pets are welcome at many properties – contact hosts first to check on facilities available. Look for The Pets Welcome Logo

Port Stephens - Shoal Bay

Located on the southern headland of Port Stephens is picturesque Shoal Bay. This coastal area is rightly known as the "Blue Water Paradise". Go whale watching between June-October or dolphin cruising all year.
Philip & Christina Latham

Port Stephens - Shoal Bay
Shoal Bay B&B

Luxury B&B & Traditional
Philip & Christina Latham
15 Shoal Bay Avenue
Shoal Bay
NSW 2315
3 km E of Nelson Bay

Tel (02) 4984 9183 or 0413 995 300
0421 880 344
rest@shoalbaybedandbreakfast.com.au
www.shoalbaybedandbreakfast.com.au

Double $135-$195
Single $105-$165, Full breakfast
2 bedroom unit, S/C self catering from $120pn
Visa MC Amex Eftpos accepted
2 Queen (2 bdrm)
Bathrooms: 1 Ensuite 1 Private

Award Winning B&B - quiet, comfortable, spacious and modern. First floor accommodation, luxurious queen beds, ducted air, ceiling fans, TV/DVD. Enjoy views of Tomaree, Stephens Peak and the bay from the balcony. Guest lounge with FOXTEL. Recreation room with pool table, fridge, microwave, tea and coffee making facilities. Quiet cul-de-sac, close to cafes and restaurants. 100m walk to beach. Off street parking. Enjoy "the rest of your life", escape to Shoal Bay -share our home with us and our cat "Watson".

New South Wales

Southern Highlands - Bowral
Chorleywood B&B

B&B & Self Contained Cottage
Sue Hawick
86 Burradoo Road, Burradoo, NSW 2576
2 km S of Bowral

Tel (02) 4861 3617
Fax (02) 4861 3617
shawick@hinet.net.au
www.highlandsnsw.com.au

Double $130
Single $90, Baby in own cot only
Full breakfast provisions
Discount for 3 nights or more
Visa MC Eftpos accepted
1 Double 2 Twin (2 bdrm)
Bathrooms: 1 Ensuite 1 Private

Welcome to Chorleywood B&B set in an acre of private garden with a sunny terrace. Your self-contained cottage includes a double or twin-share bed, with ensuite bathroom, kitchenette, TV, radio, good heating and ingredients for a full breakfast. A second bedroom in the house with private bathroom is also available when families or friends are travelling together. The resident Collie is called Rose. Local attractions include bookshops, antiques shops, Bradman Museum, wineries, restaurants and excellent walks. Canberra, Sydney and the South Coast are all less than two hours away.

Southern Highlands - Bowral
Chelsea Park & Arcadia House

B&B & Country Style Home
Alex & Davidia Williams
589 Moss Vale Road, Burradoo , NSW 2576
2.5 km S of Bowral

Tel (02) 4861 7046 or 0414 468 860
Fax (02) 4862 3597   chelsea@hinet.net.au
www.chelseapark.com

Double $150-$185
Single $150, Special breakfast,
Weekend package inc. candlelight supper $330,
Arcadia House: $750-$1100/2nts. $1250/wk,
Visa MC accepted
1 King/Twin 2 Queen (3 bdrm)
Arcadia House: 5 Bedrooms
2 Private Chelsea Park
2 Bathrooms Arcadia House

Chelsea Park 'Hollywood Mansion in the Highlands' is a glamorously restored Art Deco mansion. Three delightfully restored and decorated rooms include the Mayfair with award-winning 1930s furniture, the Chelsea with lush soft furnishings and the elegant Japanese themed Shibumi. Unwind in the spa bath, relax in the woodland garden or enjoy a game of billiards in the guest lounge. Arcadia House is a two storey country-style home located close to the heart of Bowral. Delightfully renovated its spacious modern interior offers fully self-contained accommodation with 5 bedrooms, doonas, quality linen, electric blankets. Large family room with gas-log fire, TV/DVD/VCR.

Sydney
Bed & Breakfast Sydney Central

Guests, David Lucas and Pat Woodley

Luxury Homestay
Julie Stevenson
139 Commonwealth Street
Surry Hills
NSW 2010
1 km N of Sydney Central

Tel (02) 9211 9920 **or** 0419 202 779
jas@bedandbreakfastsydney.com.au
www.bedandbreakfastsydney.com.au

Double $140-$164
Continental breakfast, Christmas and New Year rates apply
3 King/Twin (3 bdrm) Air-conditioned and TV
Two bedroom suite available
Bathrooms: 1 Guest share 1 Private

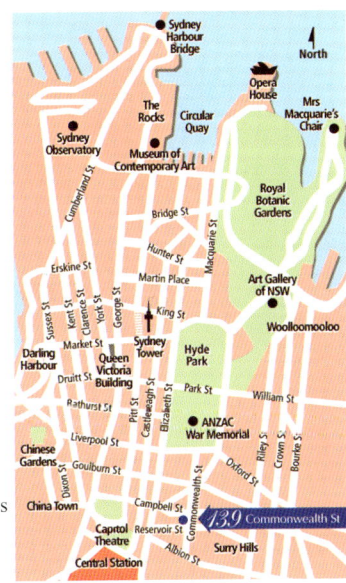

An elegant Terrace house in the heart of the best Sydney has to offer. Relax in the tranquility and comfort of a superb private inner city home. Delightful Tuscan courtyard patio garden and 2 bedrooms with balconies. 2 resident Cats to welcome you.

On your door step is a vibrant Cafe Society with an abundance of Sydney's most popular eateries. A famous area for alfresco or indoor dinning from Coffee Shops to Fine Dining. Specialty Shops, Gift, Fashion, Vintage, Contemporary Furniture, Galleries and Theatres. Walk everywhere within minutes from your B&B to all Sydney attractions ie. Capitol Theatre, Darling Harbour, Convention Centre, Opera House and Harbour Bridge. Universities, Sporting Venues, Stadium and Cricket Ground etc are close.

A fabulous central location. KST Sydney Airporter door to door. Not suitable for very young children.

New South Wales

Sydney - Balmain
An Oasis In The City

B&B
Neil Duncan
20 Colgate Avenue
Balmain
NSW 2041
2 km W of Sydney

Tel (02) 9810 3487 or 0408 476 321
Fax (02) 9810 3487
anoasis@optusnet.com.au
www.bbbook.com.au/oasis.html

Double $165-$180
Single $160, Continental breakfast,
Cooked breakfast Double $185, Single $180
2 night minimum
Christmas/New Year 7 night minimum
1 Queen (1 bdrm)   Bathrooms: 1 Ensuite

Located in one of Sydney's most historic and charming inner suburbs, Balmain Village, An Oasis offers a very large, sun-filled room with views over Sydney Harbour. The suite is completely private, with own bathroom and entrance. We offer a substantial Continental breakfast. Included in the room are a fridge, electric kettle, toaster and hairdryer, 82cm LCD television and DVD player and reverse cycle air-conditioner. There is a hot outdoor spa available to our guests with complimentary spa towels. An Oasis is a walk away from restaurants, cafes, pubs and bars. Public transport is also minutes away and include ferries and buses into Sydney. Dog friendly parks are also close by.

Sydney - Clovelly
Clovelly Bed & Breakfast

B&B & Homestay
Tony & Shirley Murray
2 Pacific Street
Clovelly
NSW 2031
6 km SE of Sydney

Tel (02) 9665 0009 or 0419 609 276
clovellybandb@yahoo.com
www.bbbook.com.au/hosts/clovelly01.html

Double $150-$180
Single $120-$150
Full breakfast
Visa MC accepted
1 Queen 1 Double 2 Twin (2 bdrm)
Bathrooms: 1 Ensuite 1 Private

 AAA Tourism ★★★★

Clovelly, Coogee and Bronte beaches and cafes are within walking distance. Transport to Sydney's tourist attractions is nearby. Afternoon tea will be served on arrival. Tea, coffee & refrigerator available all day. Breakfast includes fresh fruit, juices, home made bread and a hot dish. The air conditioned bedrooms are upstairs and each has a television, DVD, hairdryer and bathrobes. Rooms are serviced daily. Guests have a separate sitting room. "...so welcoming, spotlessly clean, wonderful breakfast...we can certainly recommend..." [Nuella, Ireland].

Sydney - Drummoyne
Eboracum

B&B & Homestay
Jeannette & Michael York
18A Drummoyne Avenue
Drummoyne
NSW 2047
5 km W of Sydney

Tel (02) 9181 3541 or 0414 920 975
mjyork@bigpond.com
www.bbbook.com.au/eboracum.html

Double $130
Single $100
Full breakfast
Dinner B/A
1 King/Twin 1 Double (2 bdrm)
Bathrooms: 1 Family share 1 Private

Charming water frontage home by the Parramatta River, amid beautiful trees, with glorious views. Boatshed and wharf at waters edge. Handy to transport, short stroll to the bus or Rivercat ferry wharf, off street under cover parking. Ideal central location for business or pleasure, 5km to Sydney CBD, Darling Harbour, Opera House, museums, theatres and sporting venues. Many restaurants and clubs, nearby... Enjoy the hospitality of Jeannette and Michael, with their two cats and the ambience of their comfortable home.

Sydney - Engadine
Engadine B&B

Luxury B&B & Self Contained Apartments
Pam & Phil Pearse
33 Jerrara Street
Engadine
NSW 2233
28 km S of Sydney

Tel (02) 9520 7009 or 0412 950 606
Fax (02) 9520 7009   jerrara@bigpond.net.au
www.engadinebnb.com.au

Double $135-$195
Single $135-$165, Children Infants in Porta Cot,
Continental breakfast, Dinner $40 pp,
Weekly rates by arrangement,
Visa MC Eftpos accepted
1 King/Twin1 King 1 Double 1 Single (3 bdrm)
Bathrooms: 3 Ensuite

Engadine B&B is just 30 minutes south of Sydney CBD and Sydney Airport in a leafy southern suburb next to The Royal National Park. Welcoming and spacious fully self-contained private apartments with kitchenettes are suitable for business and corporate stays, families or short breaks and weekends away. Facilities include Broadband with Wi Fi Internet, television, DVD, CD and barbeque. Undercover guest parking, relaxing gardens with leafy garden courtyard and quiet ambiance. Magnificent bush views with city lights on a distant horizon.

New South Wales
Sydney - Forestville - Manly
Jan's Forestville B&B

B&B & Homestay & Self Contained Apartment
Jan Fujak
49 Keldie Street, Forestville, NSW 2087
10 km N of Sydney CBD

Tel (02) 9975 6703 or 0414 351 399
Fax (02) 9975 6703
jan@accommodation-sydney.com
www.accommodation-sydney.com

Double $80
Single $60, Children negotiable, Ask Jan to stock fridge with your favourite continental breakfast provisions, Special rates are available for long stays, families and groups Visa MC accepted
1 Queen 2 Twin (3 bdrm)
Bathrooms: 1 Guest share

Jan's B&B provides travellers with fantastic Sydney accommodation at a budget price. Self contained three bedroom accommodation with fully equipped kitchen, bathroom and lounge/dining room Separate entrance, off-street parking and pool. Relax in the comfort and privacy of our forest getaway. There are no carpets and the furnishing is child friendly. The deck overlooks the national park and the tropical pool, which guests are welcome to use. We are just a twenty minute drive from Sydney CBD, a fifteen minute drive to the beach and a ten minute drive to Chatswood Shopping Centre.

Sydney - Glebe
Bellevue Terrace

Homestay
Rob & Heather Oliver
19 Bellevue Street
Glebe
NSW 2037
2.3 km W of Sydney Central

Tel (02) 9660 6096 or 0406 383 061
Fax (02) 9660 6096
bellevuebnb@pocketmail.com.au
www.babs.com.au/bellevue or
www.bellevueterrace.webhop.net

Double from $100
Single from $80
Continental provisions
1 Queen 1 Double 2 Single (3 bdrm)
Bathrooms: 2 Guest share

My spacious, elegant townhouse is situated on a quiet residential street in the inner city suburb of Glebe, where you will find a great variety of restaurants, boutiques, galleries, pubs, and the Sydney University campus. Walk to Darling Harbour, Chinatown, Paddy's Market and the Powerhouse Museum, or take a bus to the City centre (just 2.3 kms away) or Coogee Beach. We are happy to supply maps, brochures and ideas for things to see and do in Sydney.

New South Wales

Sydney - Glebe
Cathie Lesslie B&B

Homestay
Cathie Lesslie
18 Boyce Street
Glebe
NSW 2037
3 km SW of Sydney

Tel (02) 9692 0548
cathielesslie@gmail.com
www.cathielesslie.net

Double $110-$120
Single $80
Children $15
Full breakfast
Visa MC accepted
3 Double 2 Single (3 bdrm)
Bathrooms: 2 Guest share

Quiet leafy inner city, close to transport, cafes, cinemas, universities and Darling Harbour. Large comfortable room with cable TV, fridge and tea and coffee facilities. Hot "bacon and eggs" breakfast, your choice including fruit, juiced oranges and freshly baked croissants. We want you to feel welcome and at ease. Please phone first for bookings.

Sydney - Glebe
Harolden

Homestay
Leonie Dawes
Please Phone (02) 9660 5881
3 km W of Sydney Central

Tel (02) 9660 5881 or 0414 481 881
lidawes@gmail.com
www.bbbook.com.au/harolden.html

Double $110-$120
Single $80-$90
Full breakfast
1 Double 1 Single (2 bdrm)
Bathrooms: 1 Guest share

Harolden, a lovely Victorian Terrace built in 1895 in Glebe, the inner Sydney suburb with distinct village character nestled between the city, Sydney University and Blackwattle Bay. Metres from public transport to the city, Balmain and Coogee Beach. Five minutes walk to the many restaurants of Glebe Point Road. Enjoy a cooked breakfast in the lush cottage garden while watching the antics of native birds. Your host, a descendant from the First Fleet offers friendly hospitality and has travelled extensively.

BBBook.com.au

New South Wales
Sydney - Glebe
Pompei B&B

Luxury B&B
Penelope Chapple & Paull Mayne
1 Forest Street
Glebe
NSW 2037
3 km W of Sydney

Tel (02) 9660 0969 or 0416 266 179
email@pompeibedandbreakfast.com.au
www.pompeibedandbreakfast.com.au

Double $185-$200
Single $165
Full breakfast
Visa MC Eftpos accepted
2 Queen (2 bdrm)
Bathrooms: 1 Ensuite 1 Private

Pompei Bed and Breakfast offers luxury accommodation in Sydney for tourist and corporate business travellers alike. It offers an elegant, peaceful retreat and warm hospitality. Individually styled guest rooms possess period features and contemporary amenities. Luxurious touches include fine linen, antiques and original art works. Ideally located in the vibrant inner city suburb of Glebe, it is close to restaurants, cafes and shops. Most importantly it is located only minutes from the centre of Sydney.

Sydney - Greenwich
Greenwich B&B

**B&B & Homestay
& Self Contained Apartment**
Jeanette & David Lloyd
15 Hinkler Street
Greenwich
NSW 2065
5 km N of Sydney

Tel (02) 9438 1204 or 0411 409 716
info@greenwichbandb.com.au
www.greenwichbandb.com.au

Double $90-$165
Single $90-$140
Continental provisions
Visa MC Amex accepted
1 King/Twin 1 Queen (2 bdrm)
Bathrooms: 1 Ensuite 1 Private

Relaxed and friendly hosted accommodation in leafy Greenwich just 5km from the Sydney CBD. Enjoy spacious and private guests air-conditioned lounge/dining areas in a classic Australian Federation home. Kitchenette & laundry facility is available. Internet and E-mail access is available. Ample off street parking. Greenwich B&B is ideal for business or leisure stays and is conveniently located to public transport (Bus, Train, Ferry) shopping, entertainment and restaurants. Transport to St Leonard's station can be arranged. Airport shuttle is available.

Sydney - Hunters Hill
Magnolia House B&B

B&B & Homestay
Fofie Lau
20 John Street
Hunters Hill
NSW 2110
7 km NW of Sydney

Tel (02) 9879 7078 or 0418 999 553
Fax (02) 9817 3705
fofie@magnoliahouse.com.au
www.magnoliahouse.com.au

Double $150-$220
Full breakfast, Dinner B/A, Visa MC Diners accepted
1 King/Twin 1 Queen (2 bdrm)
Bathrooms: 2 Ensuite

Magnolia House is conveniently located only 7 km from the heart of Sydney and is placed within easy reach of transport that takes you directly to the city centre. Bus or ferry transport is close by.

Sydney Airport, The Sydney Opera House, Sydney Harbour and The Harbour Bridge, the CBD, galleries, museums, are all within easy reach.

Taking the ferry to Sydney Harbour and The Opera House is a memorable trip. Hunters Hill is one of Australia's oldest residential areas. Located on a peninsula between the Lane Cove and Parramatta Rivers, much of the suburb enjoys spectacular views over Sydney Harbour. Transfers from the airport can be easily arranged.

New South Wales
Sydney - Kirribilli
Terra Nova House

B&B
Vince & Jacki Johnson
46 Jeffreys Street
Kirribilli
NSW 2061
1 km N of Sydney CBD

Tel (02) 9954 9588
Fax (02) 9954 9588
vango@bigpond.com
www.kirribilliaccommodation.com.au

Double $138
Single $69
Continental breakfast
Visa MC accepted
2 King/Twin 1 Queen 1 Double 2 Twin (5 bdrm)

View from House

Terra Nova Houses is a beautifully restored 1890 National Trust listed property in the hub of Kirribilli. It has all modern conveniences and is close to the cafe life, restaurants and landmarks that make Sydney famous. The comfortable lounge has an open fire and DVD player. The rooftop garden is accessible to all guests and provides a fantastic view of the Harbour Bridge and Opera House. Close to Luna Park, North Sydney, The Ensemble Theatre and harbour foreshore walking tracks. Walk over the Harbour Bridge to the Rocks and the city. Two minutes walk to the Train and ferry

Many properties offer activities onsite such as horse riding.
Look for The Onsite Activities Logo

New South Wales

Sydney - Manly

Feel the sand between your toes after a long day at work. Get active with surfing, sailing, scuba diving. Taste an amazing array of flavours in over 100 cafes, restaurants, bars. Shop in the sunshine with over 200 stores to explore.
Sally & Lee Burnes, Manly Harbour Loft B&B and Manly Tourism

Sydney - Manly
Manly Harbour Loft

Separate Suite
Sally & Lee Burnes
1/12 George Street
Manly
NSW 2095
0.5 km W of Manly

Tel (02) 9949 8487 or 0411 898 550
Fax (02) 9949 8487
info@manlyloft.com.au
www.manlyloft.com.au

Double $120-$250
Single $100-$230
Children 1-2 extra $20pp
Special breakfast
1 King (1 bdrm)   Bathrooms: 1 Ensuite

Manly Harbour Loft is one of Sydney's finest B&B's. This luxury accommodation offers the best of both worlds. "Visit Sydney and Stay in Manly". Designed for a comfortable and memorable stay your accommodation is spacious, bright and airy with private entrance, high ceilings and your own balcony with views of Sydney Harbour and Manly. Enjoy your breakfast on the balcony. Features include King size bed, lounge, TV, CD, DVD, fridge, reverse air-conditioning, computer with broadband, wireless access, reading lamps, hair-dryer, iron with ironing board, tea and coffee facilities, crockery and cutlery, books and games.

BBBook.com.au

New South Wales

Sydney - Manly - North Balgowlah
Pepper Tree B&B

Self Contained Apartment
Conal & Louise Gain
9 Worrobil Street
North Balgowlah
NSW 2093
14 km NE of Sydney

Tel (02) 9400 3900 or 0403 138 903
Fax (02) 9400 3900
lougain@optusnet.com.au
www.peppertreebb.com.au

Double $130-$150
Breakfast provisions first night
1 King/Twin (1 bdrm)
Bathrooms: 1 Ensuite

Self-contained separate, spacious one-bedroomed garden flat with separate dining/kitchen/living area. French doors lead to large patio with views across leafy garden. Conveniently situated for easy access to city and beaches. Within walking distance of shops, between two golf courses and on cycle track to Manly.

Sydney - Marrickville
Michaela's Place

B&B
Michaela Simoni
1 Greenbank Street
Marrickville
NSW 2204
5 km SW of Sydney

Tel (02) 9591 1780 or 0401 950 605
Fax (02) 9969 6219
marcel.weyland@bigpond.com
www.bbbook.com.au/MichaelasPlace.html

Double $120-$130
Children $30, Child minding by arrangement,
Continental breakfast, High season rates apply,
Visa MC accepted
1 Queen 1 Twin (2 bdrm)
Bathrooms: 1 Ensuite 1 Private

Just renovated Federation charmer with original country kitchen but with mod cons. Secluded courtyard with barbecue. In quiet street 10 minutes from airport. One minute to station and city bus, delivery to airport available. Exotic ethnic eateries around the corner. Disabled access, children welcome, child minding available. Plenty of street parking.

Sydney - Northern Beaches Peninsula
The Pittwater Bed & Breakfast

B&B
Colette & James Campbell
15 Farview Road
Bilgola Plateau
NSW 2106
1 km N of Newport Beach

Tel (02) 9918 6932 or 0418 407 228
Fax (02) 9918 6485
colette@thepittwater.com.au
www.thepittwater.com.au

Double $175-$200
Single $175-$200, Special breakfast
Dinner $55 per person
Visa MC Amex JCB accepted
2 King/Twin 2 Queen (2 bdrm)
Bathrooms: 2 Ensuite

Comfortable beds, ensuite bathrooms, full gourmet breakfast, peace, quiet and privacy. Close to Sydney's famous Palm Beach and great local restaurants, Colette and James would be delighted to welcome you to The Pittwater. Our family home is situated on the high plateau above Newport Beach. The guest areas have spectacular panoramic views of the ocean and coastline, including an attractive garden and large solar heated swimming pool. The Pittwater offers a range of complimentary services and may include airport pickup after a long-haul flight.

Sydney - Paddington
Harts

Homestay
Katherine Hart
91 Stewart Street,
nearest cross street - Gordon
Paddington 2021
NSW 2021
2.8 km E of Sydney Central

Tel (02) 9380 5516
paddington91@bigpond.com
www.bbbook.com.au/harts.html

Double $140-$170
Single $95-$130
Special breakfast
High season rates apply
1 Queen 1 Twin 1 Single (3 bdrm)
Bathrooms: 1 Ensuite 1 Guest share 1 Private

Conveniently located 19th Century Cottage in Sydney's Historic Paddington, courtyard garden, two minutes from Oxford Street and the bus service to the CBD, Sydney Harbour, Circular Quay, The Rocks, The Opera House, Botanical Gardens, Sydney Casino, Chinatown, and Bondi Beach. Nearby Centennial Park, Fox Studios, Aussie Stadium, Sydney Cricket Ground, Art Galleries, Antique Shops, Pubs, Restaurants, Fashion Boutiques, Cinemas, Paddington Markets. All rooms with T.V, clock radios, electric blankets and feather quilts. Ironing facilities, varied breakfasts, fruit platters. One Abyssinian cat.

BBBook.com.au

New South Wales

Sydney - Paddington
Paddington B&B

B&B & Homestay
Mary J de Merindol
7 Stewart Place
Paddington
NSW 2021
2.8 km E of Sydney Central

Tel (02) 9331 5777
stay@paddingtonbandb.com.au
www.paddingtonbandb.com.au

Double $95-$110
Single $60-$70
Continental breakfast
Dinner Evening meal on request
Visa MC accepted
1 Double 1 Twin 2 Single (4 bdrm)
Bathrooms: 2 Guest share

Your hosts, originally from England, have operated the B&B for 10 years since their 4 children left home. The comfortable 5 bedroom family home dating from 1880 is furnished in traditional style and located in a tranquil cul-de-sac. It is 20 minutes from the Airport, a few minutes to Football Stadium, SCG and Fox/Hordern Pavilion, and 20 minutes by frequent bus to downtown, Opera House, ferries and Bondi Beach. Paddington is a residential area of heritage architecture enlivened by many galleries, boutiques, restaurants and cafes.

Sydney - Parramatta
Harborne Bed & Breakfast

B&B
Josephine Assaf
21 Boundary Street
Parramatta, NSW 2150
2 km S of Parramatta

Tel (02) 9687 8988
Fax (02) 9687 8998
www.bbbook.com.au/harborne.html

Double $105-$140
Single $95-$130
Continental provisions
Dinner from $20
Family suite for up to 7 adults, $10 extra person
Visa MC Diners Amex Eftpos accepted
7 Queen 1 Single (8 bdrm)
Bathrooms: 3 Ensuite 1 Guest share 1 Private

   AAA Tourism ★★★★

Harborne is a magnificent 1858 Georgian sandstone mansion. Harborne has recently been restored as a charming 8 room B&B. The beautiful home and the lush gardens have been classified by the National Trust. A glazed breakfast atrium with Tea & Coffee facilities is available. Harborne is ideal for a relaxed stay or business or team stay. Harborne, Your Home Away From Home.

Sydney - Potts Point
Victoria Court Sydney

B&B
Manager
122 Victoria Street
Sydney, Potts Point
NSW 2011
1 km E of CBD

Tel (02) 9357 3200 or 1800 63 05 05
Fax (02) 9357 7606   info@VictoriaCourt.com.au
www.VictoriaCourt.com.au

Double $99-$330
Single $88-$330, Special breakfast
Visa MC Diners Amex Eftpos JCB accepted
22 King/Twin 3 Single (25 bdrm)
Rathrooms: 25 Ensuite

    AAA Tourism ★★★★

Victoria Court, whose charming terrace house dates from 1881, is centrally located on quiet, leafy Victoria Street in Sydney's elegant Potts Point; the ideal base from which to explore Sydney.

It is within minutes of the Opera House, the Central Business District and Beaches. Friendly and personalised service is offered in an informal atmosphere and amidst Victorian charm. No two rooms are alike; most have marble fireplaces, some have four-poster beds and others feature balconies with views over National Trust classified Victoria Street.

All rooms have en-suite bathrooms, hairdryers, air-conditioning, colour television, a safe, radio-clock, coffee/tea making facilities and direct dial telephones. In the immediate vicinity are some of Sydney's most renowned restaurants and countless cafés with menus priced to suit all budgets. Public transport, car rental, travel agencies and banks are nearby. An airport shuttle bus operates to and from Victoria Court and security parking is available.

New South Wales
Sydney - Potts Point
Simpsons of Potts Point Boutique Hotel

B&B & Guest House
Keith Wherry
8 Challis Avenue
Potts Point Sydney
NSW 2011
2 km E of Sydney City

Tel (02) 9356 2199 or 0408 282 802
0414 455 562   0408 292 802
Fax (02) 9356 4476
info@simpsonshotel.com
www.simpsonshotel.com

Double $235-$325
Single $215-$315, Continental breakfast
Visa MC Diners Amex accepted
5 King 5 Queen 2 Twin (12 bdrm)
Bathrooms: 12 Ensuite

An intimate 12-room hotel, in a restored 1892 Victorian mansion. Simpsons is located in leafy tree-lined Potts Point, a vibrant and cosmopolitan neighbourhood, with many interesting restaurants, bars, galleries and cafes nearby. Just a 20 minute stroll into the City, via the beautiful Botanic Gardens and then on to the Opera House and historic Rocks area. All rooms are decorated in traditional-style, and have private en-suite bathrooms, air-conditioning, fans, tea & coffee making facilities, direct dial phones, Wi-Fi, as well as windows that actually open.

When making an enquiry or booking, please tell your hosts, "We saw you in the Bed & Breakfast Book!"

Sydney - Rose Bay
Syl's Sydney Homestay

Homestay & Self Contained Apartment
Sylvia & Paul Ure
75 Beresford Road, Rose Bay, NSW 2029
6 km E of Sydney

Tel (02) 9327 7079 or 0411 350 010
Fax (02) 9362 9192
homestay@infolearn.com.au
www.sylssydneyhomestay.com.au

Double $140-$160
Single $95-$110, Continental breakfast
Self Contained Apartment Double $190,
Extra person $40, Visa MC accepted
1 Queen 1 Double 4 Single (2 bdrm)
Bathrooms: 1 Guest share 1 Private

Rose Bay is one of Sydney's most beautiful harbourside suburbs and hospitality and friendliness are the essence of our modern, spacious family B&B with bush and harbour views, pet dog and that real home away from home atmosphere.
We are just a short stroll from cafes, restaurants, tennis, golf, sailing and the most beautiful harbour in the world and on excellent bus and ferry routes to the City and Opera House, Bondi Beach, train stations and shopping centres.
Our B&B was featured on British TV in 1991 and we were one of Sydney's first B & Bs operating since 1980. Syl and Paul are well travelled and always ready to share their local knowledge and hospitality in a relaxed informal setting to help travellers enjoy our wonderful city. So if formality is what you seek, then Syl's is not for you!
All rooms have TV and the self contained garden apartment is ideal for families. Resident gentle Pet dog. Guests are requested not to smoke inside the house.

New South Wales

Sydney - Scotland Island

From the moment you set sail for Scotland Island, you begin to experience the wonderful relaxing world of Pittwater, less than an hour's drive from the city amidst the stunning natural beauty of the magnificent Ku-ring-gai National Park and stunning surf beaches on the Northern Peninsular.
Rosemary & Colin Haskell, Scotland Island Lodge

Sydney - Scotland Island
Scotland Island Lodge

B&B
Rosemary & Colin Haskell
2 Kevin Avenue
Scotland Island
NSW 2105
5 km N of mona vale

Tel (02) 9979 3301
Fax (02) 9979 3301
rhaskell@bigpond.net.au
www.scotlandislandlodge.com.au

Double $150-$190
Single $100-$120, Full breakfast
Dinner $50 per person
Visa MC accepted
1 King 2 Queen 1 Twin (3 bdrm)
Bathrooms: 2 Ensuite 1 Private

AAA Tourism
★★★★

Unique exclusive Bed & Breakfast on beautiful Scotland Island. Ideal for couples and small groups. Kayak to Salvation Creek and experience the wonder of Pittwater. 'Too often, the breakfast part of B&B's falls by the wayside, but Rosemary is passionate about cooking and her big English breakfasts are out of this world.' 'The Beds. Perfect for a deep sleep before being woken by the birds.' Extracts from an article in the Sun Herald Travel Section by Kate Cox leading travel writer.

Tamworth - Manilla District
Oakhampton Homestead & Country Holidays

B&B & Farmstay & Self Contained Apartment & Homestead Cottage & Cabins
Belinda & James Nixon
1254 Oakhampton Road, Manilla, NSW 2346
21 km N of Manilla

Tel (02) 6785 6517 or 0429 496 936
0427 281 749   belinda@oakhampton.biz
Fax (02) 6785 6573   www.oakhampton.biz

Double $185-$240
Single $110-$210, Children under 12 half price,
Full breakfast, Cabins from $35pp,
Cottage from $135pn, Apartment from $220,
Dinner from $35 (2 course), $55 (3 course),
Visa MC JCB accepted
6 Queen 10 Twin 12 Single (17 bdrm)
Bathrooms: 5 Ensuite 1 Guest share 2 Private

AAA Tourism ★★★★

Oakhampton is a working farm of 4000 acres, offering a variety of activities including horse riding, tennis, swimming and canoeing. The 4 star rated Homestead overlooks the large garden has 3 rooms each with ensuite bathrooms. The 4 star rated unit has 2 bedrooms, private bathroom, kitchen, dining room, sitting room, air/con, a large verandah and private entrance. The Top Spot cottage was built about 1900 and has 3 bedrooms, private bathroom, kitchen, dining room, sitting room, fireplace, wonderful views. The cabins are set in a large area for games and group activities.

You can find great getaways in wine regions.
Some offer wine activities.
Look for The Wine Activities Logo

New South Wales

Taree - Wingham

Wingham, first settled in 1853, is a heritage town with many National Trust listed Federation and Victorian buildings that surround the town square. Giant Moreton Bay figs dominate the Wingham Brush Nature Reserve along with one of the largest populations of grey headed flying foxes in NSW.
Bev & Rod Petterson, The Bank Guest House & Tellers Restaurant

Taree - Wingham
Tallowood Ridge

B&B & Farmstay & Self Contained Cabin
Shirley Smith
79 Mooral Creek Road
Cedar Party via Wingham
NSW 2429
8 km NW of Wingham

Tel (02) 6557 0438 or 0411 035 945
Fax (02) 6557 0438
twr@harboursat.com.au
www.bbbook.com.au/tallowoodridge.html

Double $90-$110
Single $70-$80
Children $20
Continental breakfast
2 Double 4 Single (3 bdrm)
Bathrooms: 1 Ensuite 1 Private

Come and share the country lifestyle. Enjoy the comforts of a modern air conditioned home set on 33 hectares of undulating hills, magnificent views, colourful birds, friendly cows and Jessie the dog. There is also a fully equipped air conditioned, self contained cabin accommodation up to four persons. No smoking inside please. Relax by the pool or visit the many attractions in the area, historic buildings, a museum of past history, picturesque rainforest area alongside the Manning River or visit Ellenborough Falls. Clubs, pubs and restaurants in town. "Very hospitable - scenery fantastic - so peaceful - could stay longer."M&N C, Nthn Ireland.

Taree - Wingham
The Bank Guesthouse

B&B & Self Contained Cottage
Bev & Rod Petterson
48 Bent Street
Wingham
NSW 2429
10 km W of Taree

Tel (02) 6553 5068 or 0400 334 912
Fax (02) 6553 5863
info@thebankandtellers.com.au
www.thebankandtellers.com.au

Double $155-$175
Single $145-$165, Children 3-11 years $30,
Full breakfast, Dinner on request $40,
Visa MC Amex Eftpos JCB accepted
5 Queen 1 Double 2 Single (7 bdrm)
Bathrooms: 6 Ensuite

AAA Tourism ★★★★

The Bank Guest House & Tellers Restaurant is an oasis of stylish accommodation and dining in the beautiful Manning Valley. 5 spacious guest rooms plus a family room and Maitland Cottage (for self contained holiday accommodation). A country style breakfast is included in your tariff and is served in Tellers Restaurant. Evening meals available on request. Off street secure parking. Guest lounge and library with televsion, CD, DVD, board games, books and mazazines for guests to enjoy. Dogs welcome by arrangement. Wheelchair accessible room available. Only 10 minutes off the Pacific Highway at Taree.

New South Wales

The Entrance - Blue Bay

Blue Bay is a beautiful secluded bay close to The Entrance.
Aniello Iannuzzi, Talinga

The Entrance - Blue Bay
Talinga

Self Contained House
Eve & Soula Tsironis
54 Werrina Parade
Blue Bay
NSW 2261
90 km N of Sydney

Tel (02) 4333 6333
Fax (02) 6842 4513
iannuzzi@tpg.com.au
www.bbbook.com.au/Talinga.html

Seasonal: $1800-$4500/wk whole house
 Accommodation only
Visa MC Eftpos accepted
2 Queen 4 Single (4 bdrm)
Bathrooms: 2 Family share
One bathroom has a spa

Absolute beachfront with best views on the Central Coast. Blue Bay is one of the cleanest and safest beaches in NSW. Enjoy swimming, kayaking or fishing from the beach. Ideal for family escapes or even for a secluded romantic escape for a couple. Short drive to Sydney and Newcastle, meaning you can commute to work whilst the family relaxes on the beach. Terrigal, the Entrance, Erina and Tuggerah are short drives away, with all the restaurants and shopping you can hope for. This is a very popular destination, so advance bookings are essential. Guests are to provide their own linen and towels.

Thredbo - Jindabyne - Snowy Mountains
Bimblegumbie

B&B & Farmstay & Self Contained House
Prudence Parker
942 Alpine Way, Crackenback,
Thredbo Valley, NSW 2627
9 km SW of Jindabyne

Tel (02) 6456 2185 or 0412 484 966
Fax (02) 6456 2060
holiday@bimblegumbie.com.au
www.bimblegumbie.com.au

Double $152-$245
Single $80-$160, Children $5 to half price depending on age, Special breakfast $18.50,
Dinner $42.50 for 3-course,
Visa MC Amex Eftpos accepted
2 King/Twin 2 King 6 Queen (10 bdrm)
Bathrooms: 2 Ensuite 2 Guest share 3 Private

AAA Tourism ★★★☆

BB, Room only and Self Contained Cottages. Pets welcome. Peaceful, private and relaxing, award winning wonderful gardens, colourful birdlife and wildlife. Delicious homemade yummy breakfasts and dinners, jams, sauces and specialities. Interesting eclectic artistic decor. A collector's delight. Resident very friendly dogs. Return guests pay 10% less. 150 acres mountain virgin bush walks, close to ski fields, horse riding, trout fishing, Lake Jindabyne. Relax, recuperate, rejuvenate, reflect, respond, remember, return.

Children enjoy getaways as much as adults and most properties have facilities for children. Look for The Children Welcome Logo

New South Wales

Tilba

The National Trust villages of Central Tilba and Tilba Tilba are well known for its cheese, gold mining past, gardens and more recently art, craft, heritage and indigenous culture. Close to Narooma and Bermagui, the area has access to a pristine coastline with many secluded beaches.
Stuart Absalom, Green Gables

Tilba Tilba - Narooma
Green Gables

B&B
Stuart Absalom & Philip Mawer
269 Corkhill Drive
Tilba Tilba
NSW 2546
16 km S of Narooma

Tel (02) 4473 7435 or 0419 589 343
Fax (02) 4473 7835
relax@greengables.com.au
www.greengables.com.au

Double $150-$180
Single $90-$110, Children $20-$40
Full breakfast, Dinner $30 -$40 B/A
Visa MC Amex accepted
3 Queen 1 Twin (3 bdrm)
Bathrooms: 2 Ensuite 1 Private

AAA Tourism ★★★★

Mesmerising views, stylish accommodation, generous hospitality, fine food, endless relaxation at any time of the year, close to all the Tilba area has to offer. Set in lush gardens there are three large bedrooms with ensuite/private bathrooms and an inviting guest sitting room. Dinner is available by arrangement either served on the verandah or in the private dining room. What better way to experience the natural beauty of the unique Tilba area with its irresistible combination of mountains and unspoilt ocean beaches.

Tocumwal - Murray River
Elizas on the Murray

Luxury B&B & Farmstay & Self Contained Apartment & 9 Luxury Villas
Kevin & Sue
16 Barooga Street
Tocumwal
NSW 2714
1 km S of Tocumwal

Tel (03) 5874 2699 or 0428 975 641
info@elizasonthemurray.com
www.elizasonthemurray.com.au

Double $130-$270
Breakfast by arrangement
Visa MC Eftpos accepted
18 Queen (16 bdrm)
Bathrooms: 9 Ensuite

Many of us dream of a country retreat or country hideaway. Well you may have just discovered it. Elizas is a place of rest and tranquility, Nine gorgeous and luxuriously appointed Villas nestled into beautiful garden surrounds. All Villas are fully self contained and offer the very best accommodation available along the Murray. Whether it is rest and relaxation, or golf, tennis and water activities or maybe just enjoying all the wonderful local attractions. Tocumwal is a year round holiday destination for all ages. Elizas on the Murray provides the perfect location for your next getaway, whatever the occasion.

Some properties have restaurants attached or offer meals on request.

BBBook.com.au

New South Wales

Urunga

Urunga is one of those rare and peaceful NSW North Coast seaside towns that people dream about but never seem to be able to find. At the Eastern end of the fabulous Waterfall Way (one of the five best drives in Australia), there is a wealth of natural beauty in and around the town.
Helen & John, Aquarelle B&B

Urunga
Aquarelle Bed & Breakfast

Luxury B&B
Helen & John
152 Osprey Drive
Urunga
NSW 2455
6.5 km S of Urunga

Tel (02) 6655 3174 or 0427 553 174
info@aquarelle.net.au
www.aquarelle.net.au

Double $145-$175
Single $120-$145, Full breakfast
Dinner Winter months by prior arrangement
Visa MC Eftpos accepted
1 King suite 1 Queen suite (2 bdrm)
King bed can be configured as twin beds
Bathrooms: 2 Ensuite

AAA Tourism
★★★★☆

Aquarelle's two peaceful, elegant A/C suites suit the discerning traveller. Tall forests and a waterlily-covered lake surround the contemporary property, ensuring total privacy. Folding glass doors let you bring the outdoors into your private sitting room - gourmet breakfast accompanied by the call of the whip bird is an inspirational way to start your day. Fresh seasonal produce features on your daily breakfast menu, and we cater for special dietary requirements. "A wonderful break in this gorgeous part of the world" David & Gill UK

Wagga Wagga
Dunn's B&B

B&B
Les and Kate Dunn
63 Mitchelmore Street
Wagga Wagga
NSW 2650
2 km S of Wagga Wagga PO

Tel (02) 6925 7771 or 0435 043 079
choc1001@gmail.com
www.dunnsbedandbreakfast.com.au

Double $120
Full breakfast
Visa MC Eftpos accepted
3 Double (3 bdrm)
Bathrooms: 3 Ensuite

AAA Tourism
★★★☆

Dunn's B&B is an elegant Federation home where we combine country hospitality with elegance and comfort. The three spacious bedrooms feature brass beds and modern ensuites. They are equipped with television, refrigerator, tea/coffee making facilities and independent heating/cooling. Breakfast is served in the dining room at a magnificent mahogany table. There are facilities for wireless internet, undercover parking and a private entrance. Other facilities include guest sitting room, balcony, maps, complimentary homemade afternoon tea and vintage car ride. Be Our Guest!

Wellington
Carinya B&B and Mackays' Rest

B&B & Cottage
Miceal & Helen O'Brien
111 Arthur Street (Mitchell Highway)
Wellington, NSW 2820
0.5 km S of Wellington

Tel (02) 6845 4320 or 0427 459 794
Fax (02) 6845 3089
carinya@well-com.net.au
www.bbbook.com.au/carinyabb.html

Double $105-$112
Single $95-$99, Children under 15 $12, baby $5 plus $5 for cot if needed, Extra person $20, Full breakfast, Dinner $25 by arrangement, Whole cottage for 6 guests from $297 pn
Visa MC accepted. 1 King 2 Queen 1 Twin 2 Single (6 bdrm). Bathrooms: 4 Guest share

AAA Tourism
★★★☆

Carinya is an old homestead in a lovely garden setting situated south side of Wellington on the Mitchell Highway. We are family friendly with billiard table, pool and Tennis court. Near Burrendong Arboretum and Dam, Golf Club, Dubbo Zoo, Mudgee and Parkes. Opposite and new, Mackays Rest self-contained cottage has 3 large bedrooms, dining room, family area, 2 bathrooms, kitchen and laundry. Ideal for the executive or groups who want more independence and privacy. Minimum two rooms or two nights for cottage. Wireless internet available.

New South Wales

Wollongong - Mount Pleasant - South Coast
Above Wollongong at Pleasant Heights B&B

Luxury B&B & spa suites with kitchenette
John & Tracey Groeneveld
77 New Mt Pleasant Road, Wollongong, NSW 2519
5 km NW of Wollongong

Tel (02) 4283 3355 or 0415 328 950
Fax (02) 4283 1655   info@pleasantheights.com.au
www.pleasantheights.com.au

Double $185-$450
Children by arrangement, Full breakfast provisions,
Dinner by arrangement, Midweek specials available
Visa MC Diners Amex accepted
1 King/Twin 2 Queen (3 bdrm)
Bathrooms: 1 Ensuite 2 spa suites

Award winning boutique B&B, 'Above Wollongong at Pleasant Heights' provides exquisite accommodation which opens into a lush, tropical garden complete with stunning coastal views.
Guests choose between an eclectic trio of suites: two stylish spa suites in exotic, modern themes, and the chic, adorable studio with The View! serenity - harmony - solitude.
This is high quality accommodation offering privacy and relaxation . . . each suite has its own entrance with either a courtyard, terrace or balcony. And of course, a lavish breakfast hamper and fruit platter is provided for each morning.
Above Wollongong is a popular wedding destination and also great for pampering weekends. We are within minutes of local restaurants, beaches and just 5 kilometres from the Wollongong CBD, University and The Nan Tien Temple.
Only one hour from Sydney Airport, Southern Highlands, Jervis Bay, Kangaroo Valley and The Blue Mountains - all this makes Pleasant Heights the perfect base for day tripping!

New South Wales

Wollongong and Grand Pacific Drive

The Grand Pacific Drive encompasses 140km of some of spectacular scenery and coastline. From Royal National Park (world's second oldest) the route takes you through coastal rainforests, coastal villages, the bustling coastal city of Wollongong and the beautiful coastal towns of Shellharbour and Kiama.
Tracey Groeneveld, Above Wollongong At Pleasant Heights B&B

Yass
Kerrowgair

B&B
Judy & John Heggart
24 Grampian Street
Yass
NSW 2582
1.5 km N of Yass

Tel (02) 6226 4932 or 0417 259 982
info@kerrowgair.com.au
www.kerrowgair.com.au

$130 -$150
Full breakfast
Visa MC Diners Eftpos accepted
3 Queen 1 Twin (4 bdrm)
Bathrooms: 4 Ensuite

AAA Tourism
★★★★☆

Kerrowgair - A beautifully restored Georgian house (C.1853), in historic Yass, one hour from the Nation's capital. This outstanding heritage house has large bedrooms, all with ensuites, and gracious sitting and dining rooms, with open fires, for the use of guests. It is complimented by the shady verandahs and covered terrace. Set in over an acre of beautiful gardens, guests can enjoy the peace and tranquillity of the ancient trees, rose gardens and pond. Kerrowgair has become renowned for it's warm hospitality and superb breakfasts.

New South Wales

Yass - Rye Park
The Old School

B&B & Self Contained House
Margaret Emery
78 Yass Street, Rye Park, NSW 2586
20 km SE of Boorowa, 40 km N of Yass

Tel (02) 4845 1230 or 0418 483 613
(02) 6227 2243   Fax (02) 4845 1260
theoldschool@bigpond.com
www.theoldschool.com.au

Double $140-$180
Single $130-$150, Children $25
Special breakfast, Dinner $70 per person:
three courses and coffee - fixed price
Country House: per week: $1,650
Visa MC Amex accepted
1 King 2 Queen 1 Double 1 Twin 2 Single (5 bdrm)
Bathrooms: 2 Ensuite 1 Family share 1 Private

Fine food, warm fires, good books and a piano make this retreat a return to life's simple pleasures. Set on four acres amidst trees, roses, gardens and ponds an atmosphere is created that encourages relaxation. Margaret has built a reputation for her food and offers a seasonal menu, with influences from Belgium, the Mediterranean and Asia. The Old School won an Award of Distinction in the 2000 Capital Country Awards for Excellence in Tourism. Rye Park is half an hour north of Yass.

Young - Cootamundra
Old Nubba Schoolhouse

**Self Contained House
& Self-Contained Farm Cottages**
Fred & Genine Clark
Old Nubba
Wallendbeen
NSW 2588
3 km N of Wallendbeen

Tel (02) 6943 2513 or 0438 432 513
Fax (02) 6943 2590
oldnubba@bigpond.com
www.bbbook.com.au/oldnubbaschoolhouse.html

Double $100-$120
Single $75-$95, Children $10-$20
Full breakfast provisions
2 Queen 2 Double 8 Single (7 bdrm)
Bathrooms: 3 Private

Old Nubba is a sheep/grain farm between Cootamumdra and Young, 3 1/2 hours Sydney, 1 1/2 hours Canberra. The Schoolhouse, Killarney Cottage and Peppertree Cottage are all fully self-contained and have slow-combustion heating, reverse cycle air-conditioning, electric blankets and linen/towels provided. They sleep 4-8 and are set in their own gardens thru the trees from the homestead. Farm attractions include peace and quiet, bush walks, birdlife, bike riding, fishing and olive picking. Well behaved doggies and cats welcome. Many local tourist attractions nearby.

... a warm welcome ... a special experience

Bed & Breakfast and Farmstay NSW & ACT

Look for this logo as a sign for the highest quality of Bed and Breakfast, Farmstay and other hosted accommodation properties in:

- **Sydney & Rural New South Wales**
- **Canberra & Australian Capital Territory**

You will find friendly hosts that are committed to ensuring your stay is an experience to remember.

Bed & Breakfast and Farmstay NSW & ACT is a non profit member association of B&B and Farmstay owners abiding by a Code of Practice.

Membership enquires: www.bedandbreakfast.org.au

To find member properties - look for the logo in this book or search for accommodation online at:

www.bedandbreakfastnsw.com.au

New South Wales
Recommended Accommodation - New South Wales

Properties included below with a page reference are included in this chapter and with further details. We have also included recommended accommodation with information supplied by BFNSWACT. Contact the hosts by telephone number for further details and tell them, *"We found you in The B&B Book."*

Adaminaby - Snowy Mnts	Reynella Homestead	669 Kingston Rd	Reynella	02 6454 2386	*Page 21*
Albury	Elizabeth's Manor	531 Lyne St	Lavington	02 6040 4412	*Page 22*
Albury	Briardale B&B	396 Poplar Dv	Lavington	02 6025 5131	
Alstonville	Tallaringa Views	1344 Eltham Rd	Alstonville	02 6628 5005	
Alstonville - Ballina	Hume's Hovell	333 Dalwood Rd	Alstonville	02 6629 5371	*Page 24*
Armidale	Armidale Boutique Accom	134 Brown St	Armidale	02 6772 5276	*Page 25*
Armidale	Wattleton Farmstay	845 Sandon Rd	Metz	02 6775 3731	
Armidale - Uralla	Cruickshanks Farmstay	313 Mihi Rd	Uralla	02 6778 2148	*Page 26*
Austinmer	Austinmer Gardens B&B	4 Boyce Ave	Austinmer	02 4267 4314	
Ballina	Landfall	109 Links Ave	East Ballina	02 6686 7555	*Page 27*
Barham - Moulamein	Riverview on Edward	Balpool Rd	Moulamein	03 5887 5241	
Batemans Bay	Chalet Swisse Spa	676 The Ridge Rd	Surf Beach	02 4471 3671	*Page 27*
Batemans Bay - Malua Bay	Longridge Farm	462 Dunns Creek Rd	Malua Bay	02 4471 5943	
Bathurst	A Winter-Rose Cottage B&B	79 Morrisset St	Bathurst	02 6332 2661	
Bathurst	Barcoo's Barn	1080 Trunkey Rd	Perthville	02 6337 2383	
Bathurst	Hosies B&B	Clarke St	Hill End	02 6337 8290	
Bawley Point	Interludes at Bawley	103 Forster Dv	Bawley Point	02 4457 1494	*Page 28*
Bawley Point	The Bawley B&B	31 Murramarang Rd	Bawley Point	02 4457 1312	
Bega Vly - Bemboka	Giba Gunyah Country Cottages	224 Polacks Flat Rd	Bemboka	02 6492 8404	*Page 28*
Bega Vly - Wolumla	Jen & Tonyx B&B	264 Old Mill Rd	Wolumla	02 6494 9301	
Bellingen	Bellingen Heritage Cottages	7-9 William St	Bellingen	02 6655 1311	*Page 29*
Bellingen	CasaBelle	Gleniffer Rd	Bellingen	02 6655 9311	
Bellingen	Rivendell	10-12 Hyde St	Bellingen	02 6655 0060	*Page 29*
Bellingen	Stone Stream B&B	3072 Eastern Dorrigo Way	Brooklana	02 6654 5381	
Berry	Bellawongarah at Berry	869 Kangaroo Valley Rd	Bellawongarah	02 4464 1999	
Berry - Kangaroo Vly	Barefoot Springs	155 Carrington Rd	Beaumont	02 4446 0509	*Page 30*
Berry - Kangaroo Vly	Wombat Hill B&B	1010 Kangaroo Valley Rd	Bellawongarah	02 4464 1924	*Page 30*
Blue Mnts - Bilpin	Bilpin Springs Lodge	46 Bilpin Springs Rd	Bilpin	02 4567 0300	
Blue Mnts - Blackheath	Amani B&B	31 Days Cres	Blackheath	02 4787 8610	*Page 31*
Blue Mnts - Blackheath	Jemby-Rinjah Eco Lodge	336 Evans Lookout Rd	Blackheath	02 4787 7622	*Page 31*
Blue Mnts - Hampton	Hampton Homestead	1991 Jenolan Caves Rd	Hampton	02 6359 3337	*Page 32*
Blue Mnts - Katoomba	Edgelinks B&B	138 Narrow Neck Rd	Katoomba	02 4782 3001	
Blue Mnts - Katoomba	Melba House	98 Waratah St	Katoomba	02 4782 4141	*Page 33*
Blue Mnts - Lawson	Araluen B&B	59 Wilson St	Lawson	02 4759 1610	
Blue Mnts - Leura	Argyll House	11A Craigend St	Leura	02 4784 1555	*Page 36*
Blue Mnts - Leura	Bethany Manor B&B	8 East View Ave	Leura	02 4782 9215	*Page 35*
Blue Mnts - Leura	Broomelea	273 Leura Mall	Leura	02 4784 2940	*Page 33*
Blue Mnts - Leura	Leura's Magical Manderley	157 Megalong St	Leura	02 4784 3252	*Page 34*
Blue Mnts - Leura	Llandrindod B&B	272 The Mall	Leura	02 4784 3234	
Blue Mnts - Leura	The Greens of Leura	24-26 Grose St	Leura	02 4784 3241	*Page 35*
Blue Mnts - Lithgow	Majic Views B&B	157 McKanes Falls Rd	Lithgow	02 6353 1094	*Page 36*
Blue Mnts - Mt Tomah	Tomah Mountain Lodge	25 Skyline Rd	Mt Tomah	02 4567 2111	*Page 37*
Blue Mnts - Mt Wilson	Chimney Cottage	Waterfall Rd	Mt Wilson	02 4756 2022	
Blue Mnts - Oberon	Duckmaloi Farm	54 Karawina Dv	Duckmaloi	02 6336 1375	

New South Wales

Blue Mnts - Springwood	Mountain Jewel B&B	51 Summer Rd	Faulconbridge	02 4751 9270	Page 146
Blue Mnts - Wentworth Falls	Blue Mist Lodge	153 Falls Rd	Wentworth Falls	02 4757 2226	
Blue Mnts - Wentworth Falls	Blue Mountains Lakeside	30 Bellevue Rd	Wentworth Falls	02 4757 3777	Page 38
Blue Mnts - Wentworth Falls	Tablelands B&B	14 Miller St	Wentworth Falls	02 4757 1006	
Blue Mnts - Woodford	Braeside	97 Bedford Rd	Woodford	02 4758 6279	Page 39
Bourke	Trilby Station	Louth	via Bourke	02 6874 7420	
Braidwood	Bedervale Historic H'std & B&B	1A Monkittee St	Braidwood	02 4842 2421	
Braidwood	Mona	140 Little River Rd	Braidwood	02 4842 1288	
Byron Bay	Bay Haven Lodge	16 Shirley St	Byron Bay	02 6680 7785	
Byron Bay	Planula B&B Retreat	Lot 1 Melaleuca Dv	Byron Bay	02 6680 9134	
Byron Bay	Victoria's Byron Bay	Top of McGettigans Ln	Byron Bay	02 6684 7047	Page 39
Byron Bay Hntlnd	Green Mango Hideaway	37 Lofts Rd	Coorabell	02 6684 7171	Page 40
Byron Bay Hntlnd	The Tin Dog	Macadamia Ln	Federal	02 6688 4465	
Camden	Botanica Lodge	70 Wattle Creek Dv	Theresa Park	02 4648 1320	Page 41
Candelo - Bega Vly	Bumblebrook Farm Motel	Kemps Ln	Candelo	02 6493 2238	Page 41
Carrathool	Corynnia Station		Carrathool	02 6993 5807	
Central Coast - Avoca Bch	Avoca Ocean Breeze	55 Avoca Dv	Avoca Beach	02 4381 1566	
Central Coast - Bateau Bay	Bateau Bay Beachfront	22 Reserve Dv	Bateau Bay	02 4332 6887	
Central Coast - Brisbane Waters	Windows on the Water	25 Empire Bay Dv	Daleys Point	02 4342 2285	
Central Coast - Gosford	Wombats B&B	144 Brisbane Water Dv	Gosford West	02 4325 5633	
Central Coast - Green Point	Central Coast Waterfront	319A Avoca Dv Green Point	Gosford	02 4369 0981	
Central Coast - Lisarow	Bellbird Rest B&B	9 The Rise	Lisarow	02 4329 6661	
Central Coast - Terrigal	AnDaCer Boutique B&B	28 Serpentine Rd	Terrigal	02 4367 8368	Page 42
Central Coast - Terrigal	Cocke Bay House	1 Calool St	Kincumber South	02 4368 3394	
Central Coast - Terrigal	Forresters Beach B&B	9 Yumbool Cl	Forresters Beach	02 4385 3282	
Central Coast - Terrigal	Terrigal Hinterland B&B	26 Lea Ave	Wamberal	02 4385 5354	
Central Coast - Terrigal	Terrigal Lagoon B&B	58A Willoughby Rd	Terrigal	02 4384 7393	
Central Coast - Terrigal	Villa by the Sea	27 Table Top Rd	Terrigal	02 4385 1170	
Central Coast - Tuggerah	All Comfort B&B	34 Highland Cres	Tuggerah	0417 244 265	
Central Coast - Tuggerah	Greenacres B&B	8 Carpenters Ln	Mardi	02 4353 0643	Page 43
Central Coast - Wyong	Lake House B&B	51 Macquarie Rd	Mannering Park	02 4359 2351	
Central Tilba	The Two Story B&B	Bate St	Central Tilba	02 4473 7290	Page 43
Coffs Harbour	Boambee Palms B&B	5 Kasch Rd	Boambee	02 6658 4545	Page 44
Coffs Harbour - Bonville	Wagtail Cottage	PO Box 441	Sawtell	02 6653 4636	
Coffs Harbour - Nthn Bches	Headlands Beach GH	17 Headland Rd	Arrawarra Headland	02 6654 0364	Page 46
Coffs Harbour - Sawtell	Creekside Inn	59 Boronia St	Sawtell	02 6658 9099	
Coffs Harbour - Woolgoolga	Solitary Islands Lodge	3 Arthur St	Woolgoolga	02 6654 1335	Page 45
Cooma	Paddington Hills Rural Rtrt	26 Bransby St	Bredbo	02 6454 4207	
Cowra	Dairy Park	30 Hilton Ln	Mandurama	02 6367 5264	
Cowra	Old Milburn S'house B&B	Reg Hailstone Way	Woodstock	02 6345 1276	
Cowra - Mandurama	Millamolong	Millamolong Station	Mandurama	02 6367 5241	Page 47
Crookwell	Markdale Homestead	3 Tara St	Woollhara	02 4835 3146	Page 48
Dorrigo	Fernbrook Lodge	4705 Waterfall Way	Dorrigo	02 6657 2573	Page 49
Dorrigo	Lisnagarvey Cottage	803 Whiskey Creek Rd	Dorrigo	02 6657 2536	Page 50
Dorrigo	Tallowwood Retreat B&B	113 Old Coramba Rd	Dorrigo	02 6657 2315	
Dubbo	Boora Cottage	21R Warrie Rd	Dubbo	02 6884 2600	
Dubbo	Gortaderra B&B	43 L Peak Hill Rd	Dubbo	02 6882 9892	
Dubbo	Walls Court B&B	11L Belgravia Hts Rd	Dubbo	02 6887 3823	Page 51
Dubbo	Pericoe Retreat B&B	12R Cassandra Dv	Dubbo	02 6887 2705	Page 50

New South Wales

Dunedoo - Central West	Redbank Gums B&B	41 Wargundy St	Dunedoo	02 6375 1218	Page 52
Dungog - Patterson	CBC B&B & Café	19 King St	Paterson	02 4938 5767	
Eden	Cocora Cottage	2 Cocora St	Eden	02 6496 1241	Page 53
Eden	Crown & Anchor Inn B&B	239 Imlay St	Eden	02 6496 1017	
Eden	Snug Cove B&B	25 Victoria Terr	Eden	02 6496 3123	Page 54
Forster - Green Point	Lakeside Escape B&B	85 Green Point Dv	Green Point	02 6557 6400	
Gerroa - Seven Mile Bch	Seven Mile Beach B&B	70 Crooked River Rd	Gerroa	02 4234 2030	
Glen Innes - Ben Lomond	Silent Grove Farmstay B&B	Silent Grove	Ben Lomond	02 6733 2117	Page 55
Gloucester	Arrowee House B&B	152 Thunderbolts Way	Gloucester	02 6558 2050	Page 56
Goulburn	Pelican Sheep Station	Braidwood Rd	Goulburn	02 4821 4668	
Goulburn - Marulan	Kandoo Equine	751 Tiyces Ln	Marulan	02 4829 8338	
Grafton - Ulmarra	Rooftops	6 Coldstream St	Ulmarra	02 6644 5159	Page 57
Gundagai - Tumblong	Hillview Farmstay	3241 Hume Hwy	Tumblong	0408 863 209	
Gunning	Mallee Gum Cottage B&B	Cnr Rosamel & Cork Sts	Gundaroo	02 6236 8366	
Hawkesbury - Colo	Ossian Hall	1928 Putty Rd	Colo	02 4575 5250	
Hawkesbury - Ebenezer	Tizzana Winery B&B	518 Tizzana Rd	Ebenezer	02 4579 1150	
Hawkesbury - Kenthurst	Views at Kenthurst	182 Pitt Town Rd	Kenthurst	02 9654 9170	
Hawkesbury - Nth Richmond	Suz River Views	330 Terr Rd	North Richmond	0416 298 977	
Hay	Bank B&B	86 Lachlan St	Hay	02 6993 1730	Page 57
Hunter Vly - Aberdeen	Craigmhor Mnt Retreat	Upper Rouchel Rd	Upper Rouchel	02 6543 6393	Page 58
Hunter Vly - Bellbird	Hunter Haven B&B	351A Wollonbi Rd	Bellbird	02 4990 9291	
Hunter Vly - Broke	Ferguson's Hunter Valley	130 Hill St	Broke	02 6579 1046	Page 58
Hunter Vly - Cessnock	Abelia House	745 Lovedale Rd	Lovedale	02 4930 7118	
Hunter Vly - Denman	The Old Dairy	59 William St	East Maitland	02 6547 5033	
Hunter Vly - East Maitland	The Old George and Dragon	50 Melbourne St	East Maitland	02 4934 6080	Page 59
Hunter Vly - Greta	Camp Road Estate	165 Camp Rd	Greta	02 4938 6272	
Hunter Vly - Laguna	Arcadian Retreat	3868 Great North Rd	Laguna	02 4998 8085	Page 65
Hunter Vly - Lochinvar	Lochinvar House	28 Bridge St	Morisset	02 4930 7873	Page 60
Hunter Vly - Lovedale	Adina Vineyard	492 Lovedale Rd	Lovedale	02 4930 7473	
Hunter Vly - Lovedale	Cottages on Lovedale	636 Lovedale Rd	Lovedale	02 4930 7938	
Hunter Vly - Lovedale	Hill Top Country GH	288 Talga Rd	Rothbury	02 4930 7111	Page 60
Hunter Vly - Lovedale	Lynkeys of Lovedale	332 Lovedale Rd	Lovedale	02 4990 7605	
Hunter Vly - Lovedale	Manzanilla Ridge	442 Talga Rd	Rothbury	02 4930 9082	
Hunter Vly - Lovedale	Rose-Dale B&B	377 Lovedale Rd	Lovedale	02 4990 9537	
Hunter Vly - Lovedale	Tonic Hotel	251 Talga Rd	Lovedale	02 4930 9999	
Hunter Vly - Maitland	Peacock Grove	84 Valley St	Gosforth	02 4932 8596	
Hunter Vly - Millfield	The Vicars House	38 Wollombi Rd	Millfield	02 4998 1336	
Hunter Vly - Morpeth	Bronte Guesthouse	147 Swan St	Morpeth	02 4934 6080	Page 61
Hunter Vly - Morpeth	Convent GH and St Bede's	24 James St	Morpeth	02 4934 4176	Page 62
Hunter Vly - Pokolbin	Elfin Hill	Marrowbone Rd	Pokolbin	02 4998 7543	Page 62
Hunter Vly - Pokolbin	Holman Estate Pokolbin	173 (Lot 2) Gillards Rd	Pokolbin	0438 683 973	Page 63
Hunter Vly - Pokolbin	Hunter Valley Cooperage	41 Kelman Vineyard	Pokolbin	02 4990 1232	
Hunter Vly - Pokolbin	Misty Glen Cottage	293 Deasy Rd	Pokolbin	02 4998 7781	
Hunter Vly - Rothbury	I Villini	497 Talga Rd	Rothbury	02 4930 7384	
Hunter Vly - Wollombi	Capers GH and Cottage	2859 Wollombi Rd	Wollombi	02 4998 3211	Page 64
Hunter Vly - Wollombi	Undercliff Winery & Studio	152 Yango Creek Rd	Wollombi	02 4998 3322	
Jervis Bay - Huskisson	Dolphin Sands Jervis Bay	6 Tomerong St	Huskisson	02 4441 5511	Page 66
Jervis Bay - Huskisson	Sandholme Guesthouse	2 Jervis St	Huskisson	02 4441 8855	Page 67

Tell hosts you found them in the Bed & Breakfast Book

New South Wales

Jervis Bay - Sanctuary Point	By the Beach B&B	260 Greville Ave	Sanctuary Point	02 4443 3208
Jindabyne	Peppers over the Lake	12 Candlebark Circ	Jindabyne	02 6456 2575
Jindabyne - Snowy Mnts	**Troldhaugen Lodge**	**13 Cobbodah St**	**Jindabyne**	**02 6456 2718** *Page 67*
Kangaroo Vly	Crystal Creek Meadows	1655 Kangaroo Valley Rd	Kangaroo Valley	02 4465 1406
Kiama	**Bed & Breakfast @ Kiama**	**15 Riversdale Rd**	**Kiama**	**02 4232 2844** *Page 68*
Kiama	**Bed and Views Kiama**	**69 Riversdale Rd**	**Kiama**	**02 4232 3662** *Page 69*
Kiama	Bush Bank B&B	59 Princes Hwy	Kiama Heights	02 4232 4676
Kiama	Elli's B&B	126 Manning St	Kiama	02 4232 2879
Kiama	**Seashells Kiama**	**72 Bong Bong St**	**Kiama**	**02 4232 2504** *Page 69*
Kulnura	Forest Park Country Retreat	326 Forest Rd	Kulnura	02 4376 1340
Kyogle	Cougal Park B&B	145 Lions Rd	Kyogle	02 6636 6213
Lake Macquarie	Travellers Home B&B	51 Maud St	Cardiff South	02 4956 6513
Lightning Ridge	**Sonja's B&B**	**60 Butterfly Ave**	**Lightning Ridge**	**02 6829 2010** *Page 70*
Lismore - Clunes	**PJ's**	**152 Johnston Rd**	**Clunes**	**02 6629 1788** *Page 70*
Merimbula	**Bella Vista**	**16 Main St**	**Merimbula**	**02 6495 1373** *Page 71*
Merimbula	**Robyn's Nest Guest House**	**188 Merimbula Dv**	**Merimbula**	**02 6495 4956** *Page 71*
Milton	Acacia House B&B	203 Evans Ln	Milton	02 4454 5652
Milton	**Meadowlake Lodge**	**318 Wilfords Ln**	**Milton**	**02 4455 7722** *Page 72*
Milton	Milton B&B	124 Princes Hwy	Milton	02 4455 4449
Milton	Milton Country Cottages	83 Egans Farm Ln	Milton	02 4456 5299
Milton	Narrawilly Farm Cottages	Narrawilly	Milton	02 4456 4900
Milton	Times Past B&B	51 Princes Hwy	Milton	02 4455 5194
Moss Vale	The Pines Pastoral	Meryla Rd	Moss Vale	02 4868 3523
Mudgee	Forgandenny B&B	15-19 Short St	Mudgee	02 6372 2437
Mudgee	Protea Farm Cottages	60 Carara Rd	Mudgee	02 6373 3300
Mudgee	The Mudgee Homestead G'hse	3 Coorumbene Court	Mudgee	02 6373 3786
Murwillumbah	Wych-Wood Forest Escape	1110 Urliup Rd	Murwillumbah	02 6672 5826
Murwillumbah - Crystal Creek	**Hillcrest Mnt View Retreat**	**Upper Crystal Creek Rd**	**Murwillumbah**	**02 6679 1023** *Page 73*
Nambucca Heads - Macksville	**Jacaranda Country Lodge**	**292 Wilson Rd**	**Macksville**	**02 6568 2737** *Page 74*
Narooma - Tilba	**Pub Hill Farm**	**566 Scenic Dv**	**Narooma**	**02 4476 3177** *Page 75*
Narromine	**Camerons Farmstay**	**213 Ceres Rd**	**Narromine**	**02 6889 2978** *Page 76*
Narromine	The Abbey B&B	24 Dandaloo St	Narromine	02 6889 2213
Newcastle	Newcomen B&B	70 Newcomen St	Newcastle	02 4929 7313 *Page 77*
Newcastle - Hamilton	Chaucer Palms B&B	59 James St	Hamilton	02 4961 0111
Newcastle - Hamilton	**Hamilton Heritage**	**178 Denison St**	**Hamilton**	**02 4961 1242** *Page 78*
Newcastle - Lake Macquarie	Tantarra B&B	119 Bayview St	Warners Bay	02 4961 3422 *Page 78*
Newcastle - Merewether	Brezza Bella B&B	1 Rowan Cres	Merewether	02 4963 3812
Newcastle - Merewether	**Merewether Beach B&B**	**60 Hickson St**	**Merewether**	**02 4963 3526** *Page 77*
Newcastle - Stockton	Riverview Gardens B&B	98 Fullerton St	Stockton	02 4928 3048
Nundle	Jenkins Street Guest House	85 Jenkins St	Nundle	02 6769 3239
Oberon	Mutton Falls Colonial Accom	Mutton Falls Rd	Tarana	02 6337 5886
Oberon	RoosterHill Guesthouse	930 Lowes Mount Rd	Oberon	02 6336 3136
Orange	Cleveland B&B	9 Crinoline St	Orange	02 6362 5729
Orange	Cloudgap	224 Strathnook Ln	Orange	02 6365 1231
Orange - Manildra	The Guesthouse Manildra	97-99 Kiewa St	Manildra	02 6364 5347
Pacific Palms - Coomba	**Whitby on Wallis B&B**	**1770 Coomba Rd**	**Coomba Bay**	**02 6554 2448** *Page 79*
Parkes	**Kadina B&B**	**22 Mengarvie Rd**	**Parkes**	**02 6862 3995** *Page 80*
Parkes	**The Old Parkes Convent**	**33 Currajong St**	**Parkes**	**02 6862 5385** *Page 81*

New South Wales

Parkes	Welcome Cottage B&B	The Welcome Rd	Parkes	02 6862 3768	
Picton	Mowbray Park Farm Holiday	Barkers Lodge Rd	Picton	02 4680 9243	
Pt Macquarie	Anchors B&B	52 Anderson St	Port Macquarie	02 6582 6750	
Pt Macquarie	Azura Beach House	109 Pacific Dv	Port Macquarie	02 6582 2700	
Pt Macquarie	Woodlands B&B	348 Oxley Hwy	Port Macquarie	02 6581 3913	Page 81
Pt Macquarie - Camden Haven	Benbellen Country Retreat	Cherry Tree Ln	Hannam Vale	02 6556 7788	Page 82
Pt Macquarie - Camden Haven	Cherry Tree Cottage	Cherry Tree Ln	Hannam Vale	02 6556 7788	Page 83
Pt Macquarie - Camden Haven	Penlan Cottage	Cherry Tree Ln	Hannam Vale	02 6556 7788	Page 83
Pt Macquarie - Rollands Plains	Cedar Grove Farmstay	891 U Rollands Pl Rd	Rollands Plains	02 6585 8257	
Pt Macquarie - Wauchope	Auntie Ann's B&B	19 Bruxner Ave	Wauchope	02 6586 4420	Page 84
Pt Stephens	Kookaburra Cottage & B&B	71 Nelson Bay Rd	Bobs Farm	02 4982 6379	
Pt Stephens - Nelson Bay	Nelson Bay Getaway	31 Thurlow Ave	Nelson Bay	02 4984 4949	
Pt Stephens - Seaham	Cool Change B&B	1064 Seaham Rd	Seaham	02 4988 6132	
Pt Stephens - Shoal Bay	Shoal Bay B&B	15 Shoal Bay Ave	Shoal Bay	02 4984 9183	Page 85
Sanctuary Point	Paradise Beach Apts	119 Walmer Ave	Sanctuary Point	02 4443 2500	
Scone	Segenhoe View B&B	429 Glenbawn Rd	Scone	02 6545 2081	
Sth West Rocks - Yarrahapinni	Yarrahapinni Homestead	340 Stuarts Point Rd	Yarrahapinni	02 6569 0240	
Sthn Highlands - Bowral	Chelsea Park B&B	589 Moss Vale Rd	Burradoo	02 4861 7046	Page 86
Sthn Highlands - Bowral	Chorleywood B&B	86 Burradoo Rd	Burradoo	02 4861 3617	Page 86
Sthn Highlands - Bowral	Picket Lane	60 Bendooley St	Bowral	02 4861 1168	
Sthn Highlands - Bundanoon	Yallambee B&B	43 Garland Rd	Bundanoon	02 4883 7787	
Sthn Highlands - Burradoo	Hartnoll Park	8 Ranelagh Rd	Burradoo	02 4861 7282	
Sthn Highlands - Moss Vale	Heronswood House	165 Argyle St	Moss Vale	02 4869 1477	
Sydney - Annandale	Bet's B&B	176 Johnston St	Annandale	02 9660 8265	
Sydney - Balmain	An Oasis In The City	20 Colgate Ave	Balmain	02 9810 3487	Page 88
Sydney - Bondi	Bondi Beach Gdn Sweet	12 Forest Knoll Ave	Bondi Beach	02 9300 9111	
Sydney - Bondi Junction	Number 71	71 Denison St	Bondi Junction	02 9387 5338	
Sydney - Clovelly	Clovelly B&B	2 Pacific St	Clovelly	02 9665 0009	Page 88
Sydney - Coogee	Coogee Pet Friendly B&B	152 Carrington Rd	Coogee	02 9398 6112	
Sydney - Cronulla	Bass & Flinders B&B	23 Glaisher Pde	Cronulla	02 9527 2558	
Sydney - Cronulla	Cronulla Retreat	54 Glaisher Pde	Cronulla	02 9527 1327	
Sydney - Cronulla	Cronulla Seabreeze B&B	6 Boronia St	Cronulla	02 9523 4908	
Sydney - Drummoyne	Eboracum	18A Drummoyne Ave	Drummoyne	02 9181 3541	Page 89
Sydney - Engadine	Engadine B&B	33 Jerrara St	Engadine	02 9520 7009	Page 89
Sydney - Forestville	Jan's Forestville B&B	49 Keldie St	Forestville	02 9975 6703	Page 90
Sydney - Galston	Berrilee B&B	Jack Russell Rd	Berowra Waters	02 9655 1333	
Sydney - Glebe	Bellevue Terrace	19 Bellevue St	Glebe	02 9660 6096	Page 90
Sydney - Glebe	Cathie Lesslie B&B	18 Boyce St	Glebe	02 9692 0548	Page 91
Sydney - Glebe	Haroleden	44 Wigram Rd	Glebe	02 9660 5881	Page 91
Sydney - Glebe	Pompei B&B	1 Forest St	Glebe	02 9660 0969	Page 92
Sydney - Greenwich	Greenwich B&B	15 Hinkler St	Greenwich	02 9438 1204	Page 92
Sydney - Hunters Hill	Magnolia House B&B	20 John St	Hunters Hill	02 9879 7078	Page 81
Sydney - Kirrawee	Sekitei Boutique B&B	376 Forest Rd	Kirrawee	02 9542 5661	
Sydney - Kirribilli	Terra Nova House	46 Jeffreys St	Kirribilli	02 9954 9588	Page 94
Sydney - Lindfield	Linridge Rest	94A Bent St	Lindfield	02 9416 1684	
Sydney - Manly	Manly Harbour Loft	1/12 George St	Manly	02 9949 8487	Page 95
Sydney - Manly	Pepper Tree B&B	9 Worrobil St	North Balgowlah	02 9400 3900	Page 96
Sydney - Marrickville	Michaela's Place	1 Greenbank St	Marrickville	02 9591 1780	Page 96

New South Wales

Sydney - Nthn Bches	The Pittwater B&B	15 Farview Rd	Bilgola Plateau	02 9918 6932	Page 97
Sydney - Nthn Bches	Careel Bay Stay	101 George St	Avalon	0402 460 675	
Sydney - Oyster Bay	Oyster Bay B&B	44-46 Connell Rd	Oyster Bay	02 9528 8017	
Sydney - Paddington	Harts	91 Stewart St	Paddington	02 9380 5516	Page 97
Sydney - Paddington	Paddington B&B	7 Stewart Place	Paddington	02 9331 5777	Page 98
Sydney - Parramatta	Harborne B&B	24 Boundary St	Parramatta	02 9687 8988	Page 98
Sydney - Penrith	Penrith Lakes B&B	6 Kenilworth Crecent	Cranebrook	02 4729 4888	
Sydney - Potts Point	Simpsons of Potts Point Boutique Hotel	8 Challis Ave	Potts Point	02 9356 2199	Page 100
Sydney - Potts Point	Victoria Court Sydney	122 Victoria St	Potts Point	02 9357 3200	Page 99
Sydney - Rose Bay	Syl's Sydney Homestay	75 Beresford Rd	Rose Bay	02 9327 7079	Page 101
Sydney - Scotland Is	Scotland Island Lodge	2 Kevin Ave	Scotland Island	02 9979 3301	Page 102
Sydney - Surry Hills	B&B Sydney Central	139 Commonwealth St	Surry Hills	02 9211 9920	Page 87
Sydney - The Rocks	B&B Sydney Harbour	140-142 Cumberland St	The Rocks	02 9247 1130	
Tamworth	Jacaranda Cottage B&B	105 Carthage St	Tamworth	02 6766 4281	
Tamworth	Lavanda B&B	104 Calala Ln	Tamworth	02 6762 6026	
Tamworth	The Retreat at Froog Moore	78 Bligh St	Tamworth	02 6766 3353	
Tamworth - Manilla	Oakhampton Homestead	1254 Oakhampton Rd	Manilla	02 6785 6517	Page 103
Taralga	Sinclairs Cottage	Hollymount, Mt Rae Rd	Taralga	02 4840 2029	
Taree - Wingham	Tallowood Ridge	79 Mooral Creek Rd	Cedar Party	02 6557 0438	Page 104
Taree - Wingham	The Bank Guesthouse	48 Bent St	Wingham	02 6553 5068	Page 105
Tea Gardens - Hawks Nest	Lavender Grove Farm	55 Viney Creek Rd	Tea Gardens	02 4997 1411	
Tenterfield	Deloraine Tenterfield B&B	14 Clarence St	Tenterfield	02 6736 2777	
Tenterfield	Sylvan Park	81 Logan St	Tenterfield	02 6736 1136	
The Entrance - Blue Bay	Talinga	54 Werrina Pde	Blue Bay	02 4333 6333	Page 106
Thredbo - Jindabyne	Bimblegumbie	942 Alpine Way	Thredbo Valley	02 6456 2185	Page 107
Tilba Tilba	Green Gables	269 Corkhill Dv	Tilba Tilba	02 4473 7435	Page 108
Tocumwal	Elizas on the Murray	16 Barooga St	Tocumwal	03 5874 2699	Page 109
Tumbarumba	Mannus Lake B&B	Pineview Mannus	Tumbarumba	02 6948 5219	
Tumut	Elm Cottage	Little River Rd	Tumut	02 6947 5818	
Tumut	Goobragandra Homestead	Goobregandra Rd	Tumut	02 6947 5751	
Tweed Vly - Limpinwood	Limpinwood Lodge	531 Zara Rd	Limpinwood	02 6679 3805	
Tweed Vly - Uki	A View of Mt Warning B&B	28 Glenock Rd	Uki	02 6679 5068	
Tweed Vly - Uki	Mount Warning Forest Hdwy	460 Byrrill Creek	Uki	02 6679 7277	
Urunga	Aquarelle B&B	152 Osprey Dv	Urunga	02 6655 3174	Page 110
Wagga Wagga	Dunn's B&B	63 Mitchelmore St	Wagga Wagga	02 6925 7771	Page 111
Wagga Wagga	Little Bundah Cottages	221 Coolamon Rd	Wagga Wagga	02 6931 7016	
Wagga Wagga	Oberne Meadows B&B	Oberne Meadows	Ladysmith	02 6922 1556	
Walcha	Anglea House	Cnr Thunderbolt Way & Hill St	Walcha	02 6777 2187	
Walcha	Cheyenne Wilderness Rtrt	Cheyenne	Walcha	02 6777 9172	
Walgett	Caloola B&B	Caloola	Walgett	02 6828 1124	
Wellington	Carinya B&B	111 Arthur St	Wellington	02 6845 4320	Page 111
Wellington - Bakers Swamp	Banderra B&B	Gowan Green Rd	Bakers Swamp	02 6846 7201	
White Cliffs	PJs Underground	72 Turleys Hill	White Cliffs	08 8091 6626	
Wollongong - Mt Pleasant	Pleasant Heights B&B	77 New Mt Pleasant Rd	Mt Pleasant	02 4283 3355	Page 112
Yamba - Ashby	Ashby Cottage	2 Tullymorgan Rd	Ashby	02 6645 4686	
Yass	Country GH Schonegg	381 Hillview Dv	Murrumbateman	02 6227 0344	
Yass	Kerrowgair	24 Grampian St	Yass	02 6226 4932	Page 113
Yass - Rye Park	The Old School	76 Yass St	Rye Park	02 4845 1230	Page 114
Young - Cootamundra	Colleen & Old Sils Farmhouse	Corang	Wallendbeen	02 6943 2546	

BBBook.com.au

Northern Territory

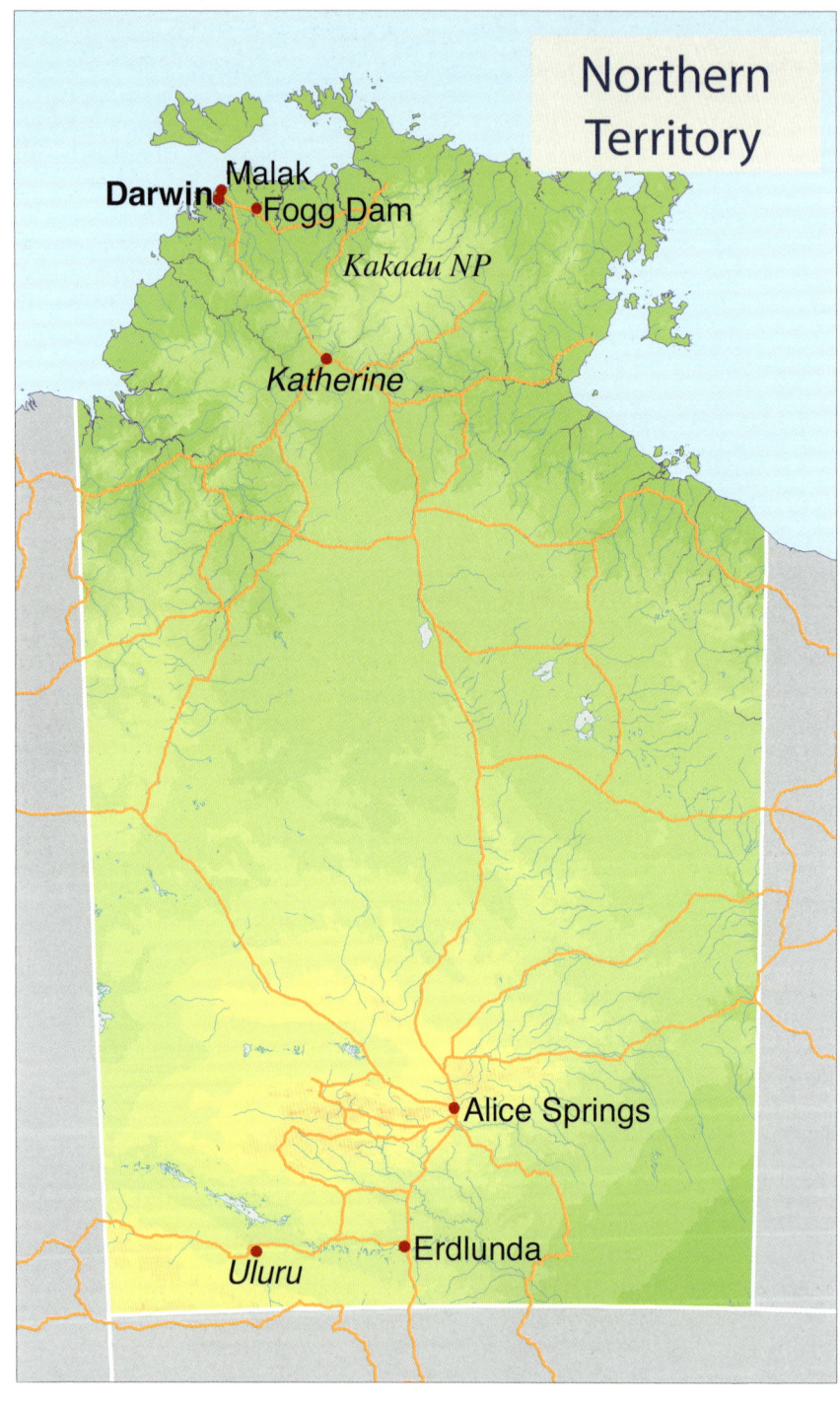

Northern Territory

Alice Springs

Beautiful scenery, with clear blue skies during the day with the sun shining, whether its, 40°C or 10°C. And clear evening skies with millions of stars to gaze at. Alice Springs is a modern town with a strong link with the past, both European settlement and Aboriginal culture.
Kathy Fritz, Kathy's Place B&B

Alice Springs
Nthaba Cottage B&B

B&B Cottage
Anne & Will Cormack & Pets
83 Cromwell Drive
Alice Springs
NT 0870
2.5 km N of Town Centre

Tel (08) 8952 9003 or 0407 721 048
Fax (08) 8953 3295
nthaba@nthabacottage.com.au
www.nthabacottage.com.au

Double $185-$210
Single $145
Full breakfast
Visa MC accepted
1 King/Twin (1 bdrm)
Bathrooms: 1 Ensuite

AAA Tourism
★★★★

Surrounded by the spectacular MacDonnell Ranges, Nthaba features a quality cottage separate from the main house. The cottage has wireless broadband, one kingsize or two single beds and the cosy sitting-room with television, has Edwardian chairs and other favourite pieces. The cottage opens onto a lovely garden with many visiting birds. Close to convention centre and many great walks. Your host, Will, is keen to share his local bird knowledge with you. Two resident friendly dogs, Toffee and Molly, and Lucy, an elegant Tonkinese cat.

BBBook.com.au   123

Northern Territory

Alice Springs
Kathy's Place B&B

B&B & Homestay & Friendly & personalised
Kathy & Karl Fritz
4 Cassia Court
Alice Springs
NT 0870
3 km E of Alice Springs

Tel (08) 8952 9791 or 0407 529 791
Fax (08) 8952 0052
kathy@kathysplace.com.au
www.kathysplace.com.au

Double $140
Single $80, Children $10 per child,
Full breakfast, Extra person in same room $30,
Visa MC Eftpos accepted. 3 Queen 4 Single
(3 bdrm). Bathrooms: 1 Ensuite 1 Family share
1 Guest share 1 Private Separate toilets

   AAA Tourism ★★★☆

Friendly Australian home, courtesy arrival transfers, tours arranged and help provided so you can enjoy the treasures the "Alice" has to offer, taking at least two days to enjoy. Air conditioning, swimming pool and garden outdoor area with native birds that come in. Combustion heating in the cooler months providing a cosy atmosphere to chat, read, watch T.V. Wireless broadband available.

Alice Springs
The Hideaway

B&B & Self Contained Apartment
John & Pauline Haden
18 Lewis Street
Alice Springs
NT 0871
500 km NE of Ayers Rock

Tel (08) 8953 1204 or 0428 531 204
Fax (08) 8953 1204
info@hideawayinalice.com
www.hideawayinalice.com

Double $120
Full breakfast provisions
Family $180
1 Queen 2 Single (2 bdrm)
Bathrooms: 1 Private

Bassa and Cocoa the resident cats will be there to add to the welcome. All rooms have fans, electric blankets and the apartment has ducted air-conditioning, a gas heater is available in winter in the separate lounge/dining area. Your hosts John and Pauline have a combined 80 years of personal local experience, we look forward to sharing this knowledge with you. We are within 5 minutes walk from the famous Cultural Precinct and a 5 minute drive from the World acclaimed Desert Park.

Northern Territory

Erldunda

Beautiful sunsets, abundant birdlife, peaceful and quite surreal with amazing colours, remarkable nights with brilliant starlight.
Paula Kilgariff, Erldunda Station

Alice Springs - Erldunda
Erldunda Station B&B

B&B & Farmstay & Self Contained Cottage
John & Paula Kilgariff
Erldunda Station
Stuart Highway, Alice Springs
NT 0872
200 km S of Alice Springs

Tel (08) 8956 0997
Fax (08) 8956 0916
jpkilgariff@bigpond.com
www.erldundastation.com

Double $130-$150
Single $110-$120, Special breakfast
Dinner $50 each -
Two course meals all you can eat
2 Queen 2 Single (3 bdrm)
Bathrooms: 1 Family share

Travelling to Uluru (Ayers Rock), Erldunda Station is half-way from Alice Springs, about 200kms south of Alice Springs and only 700m off the main highway. Erldunda Station offers a traditional bed and breakfast in fully self-contained three bedroom cottage amongst 1200 square miles of working cattle station. Relax in the comfortable lounge room with colour television and a lovely pot belly wood fire in winter. Have an evening meal with the family (by arrangement) or alternatively, cook your own in the well-equipped kitchen.

Northern Territory

Darwin

Fogg Dam is a habitat for numerous animals and Australian and migratory birds. The reserve is in the Adelaide River wetlands and known internationally to biologists, birdwatchers and photographers for its rich biodiversity. It's the only Top End wetland accessible throughout the year.
Heather Boulden & Jeremy Hemphill. Eden at Fogg Dam

Darwin - Fogg Dam - Humpty Doo
Eden at Fogg Dam

B&B & Self Contained Apartment
Heather Boulden & Jeremy Hemphill
530 Anzac Parade
Middle Point
NT 0836
25 km E of Humpty Doo

Tel (08) 8988 5599
Fax (08) 8988 5582
eden@foggdam.com.au
www.foggdam.com.au

Double $130-$190
Single $110-$170
Full breakfast, Dinner $38pp -bookings required
Special diets accommodated, Visa MC accepted
2 Queen 1 Double 2 Single (3 bdrm)
Bathrooms: 2 Private

Enjoy the bush and stay in comfort on an organic tropical fruit farm registered with Land for Wildlife, on the doorstep of internationally renowned Fogg Dam: a wildlife sanctuary reputed as paradise for birdwatchers, photographers and biologists. It's also known for spectacular sunrises and sunsets. Sunrise has the added magic of a dawn chorus of birds. Why not take a picnic breakfast! We're close to other tourist attractions and en route to Kakadu National Park. A unique location just 65km (40 miles) from Darwin.

Northern Territory

Darwin - Malak
Beale's Bedfish & Breakfast

B&B & Lodge
Heather & Allan Beale
2 Todd Crescent, Malak, Darwin , NT 0812
5 km N of Airport

Tel (08) 8945 0376
Fax (08) 8945 0379 bealesbedfish@aapt.net.au
www.bealesbedfish.com

Double $100-$200
Children Play areas and cubby house established
Continental breakfast - provisions supplied in Lodge
Full day Barra Fishing Trips, 2-6 day Fishing Safaris
Visa MC Eftpos accepted
4 Queen 12 Single (4 bdrm)   Bathrooms: 4 Ensuite

Beale's Bedfish & Breakfast is a dual purpose built establishment. Designed to cater for the B&B traveller and also to the Individuals, Families and Groups that also wish to partake in the adrenalin packed adventure of Barra or Bluewater Fishing in the Northern Territory.

It is the home of Darwin's Barra Base Fishing Safaris, which can cater for all types of fishing, from Barramundi & Bluewater fishing in coastal reefs, rivers and sheltered waters to being able to fish 15 nautical miles to sea to complete adrenalin packed pelagic, sailfish and deep sea game fishing.

For more information contain Darwin's Barra Base Fishing Safaris on www.darwinsbarrabase.com.au.

Bed & Breakfast, Farmstay and Accommodation Australia

Renowned for its colourful outback characters, casual lifestyle and unique Aboriginal culture, the Northern Territory stretches from the tropical north of Australia to its Red Centre. The capital, Darwin, at the 'Top End', has a richly diverse culture which is reflected in its food and festivals. Good roads throughout the Territory lead to frontier towns, world heritage national parks with spectacular rock formations and ancient Aboriginal art; and to the desert town of Alice Springs at the heart of Australia.

BBFAA accommodation is ideal for short breaks, romantic getaways and special occasions, travelling with pets, family stays and group reunions.

Enjoy a warm welcome and true hospitality when you stay with a BBFAA member. BBFAA brings you high quality places to stay throughout Australia that are as individual as you.

www.australianbedandbreakfast.com.au
1300 664 707

Northern Territory

Recommended Accommodation - Northern Territory

Properties included below with a page reference are included in this chapter and with further details. We have also included recommended accommodation with information supplied by BBFAA. Contact the hosts by telephone number for further details and tell them, *"We found you in The B&B Book."*

Adelaide River	Pell Mell Farmstay	Pell Airstrip Stuart Hwy	nr Adelaide River Township	08 8976 7006	
Alice Springs	A Good Rest B&B	51 Dixon Rd	Alice Springs	08 8952 5272	
Alice Springs	Cavenagh Lodge	Cavenagh Lodge	Alice Springs	08 8952 2257	
Alice Springs	**Kathy's Place B&B**	**4 Cassia Court**	**Alice Springs**	**08 8952 9791**	*Page 124*
Alice Springs	**Nthaba Cottage B&B**	**83 Cromwell Dv**	**Alice Springs**	**08 8952 9003**	*Page 123*
Alice Springs	The Gallery B&B	16 Range Cres	Alice Springs	08 8953 3514	
Alice Springs	**The Hideaway**	**18 Lewis St**	**Alice Springs**	**08 8953 1204**	*Page 124*
Alice Springs - Bond Springs Stn	Bond Springs Outback Rtrt	Bond Springs Station	Alice Springs	08 8952 9888	
Alice Springs - Erldunda Stn	**Erldunda Station B&B**	**Erldunda Station**	**PMB 122 via Alice Springs**	**08 8956 0997**	*Page 125*
Darwin - Malak	**Beale's Bedfish & Breakfast**	**2 Todd Cres**	**Malak**	**08 8945 0376**	*Page 127*
Darwin - Middle Point	**Eden at Fogg Dam**	**530 Anzac Pde**	**Middle Point**	**08 8988 5599**	*Page 126*
Humpty Doo	At Watties B&B	200 Doxas Rd	Humpty Doo	08 8988 2878	
Humpty Doo	Mango Meadows H'sty	2759 Bridgemary Cres	Humpty Doo	08 8988 4417	
Jingili	Feathers Sanctuary	49A Freshwater Rd	Jingili	08 8985 2144	
Knuckey Lagoon	Grungle Downs Trop B&B	Grungle Downs	Knuckey Lagoon	08 8947 4440	
Larrakeyah	Steeles At Larrakeyah	4 Zealandia Cres	Larrakeyah	08 8941 3636	
Palmerston	Palmerston Sunset Retreat	9 Renwick Court	Gray	0408 241 950	
Rapid Creek	Frangipanni B&B		Rapid Creek	08 8985 2797	
Rapid Creek	Lily Pad B&B		Rapid Creek	08 8985 4293	
Wagait Bch	B&B Lure Inn	PO Box 3322	Wagait Beach	08 8978 5484	

Queensland

Bed & Breakfast, Farmstay and Accommodation Australia Ltd

BBFAA is Australia's national peak industry organisation representing small to medium accommodation businesses including bed and breakfasts, farmstays, guesthouses and cottages. Our members offer a wide range of quality places to stay and all abide by a code of conduct and national standards.

Some member properties are hosted in the traditional style and others offer fully self contained accommodation.

BBFAA accommodation can be found in contemporary homes, suites and apartments, luxury country retreats, farmhouses and farm cottages, guesthouses, heritage and colonial properties and beach houses.

Look for the BBFAA logo as a symbol of quality and a commitment to your comfort and satisfaction.

Enjoy a warm welcome and true hospitality when you stay with a BBFAA member. BBFAA brings you high quality places to stay throughout Australia that are as individual as you.

www.australianbedandbreakfast.com.au
1300 664 707

Queensland

Queensland

Queensland

Airlie Beach - Whitsunday

The crystal clear aqua waters and pristine silica sand of Whitehaven - the most photographed beach in Australia - stretch over seven kilometres along Whitsunday Island, the largest of the 74 islands in the Whitsundays.

Airlie Beach - Whitsunday
Whitsunday Moorings B&B

B&B
Peter Brooks
37 Airlie Crescent
Airlie Beach
Qld 4802
0.3 km SW of Airlie Beach

Tel (07) 4946 4692
Fax (07) 4946 4692
info@whitsundaymooringsbb.com.au
www.whitsundaymooringsbb.com.au

Double $195
Single $165, Children $25, Full breakfast
$35 extra person above two
Visa MC Diners Amex Eftpos accepted
2 Queen (2 bdrm)
Bathrooms: 2 Ensuite

AAA Tourism
★★★★☆

Studio apartments, private terrace, swimming pool, overhanging Abel Point Marina and Coral Sea. Spectacular views. Traditional English breakfast, includes, squeezed juice, tropical fruit, cereals, choice cooked mains, homemade jams, teas, coffee. Apartments feature crisp starched linen, daily servicing, air-conditioning, ceiling fans, satellite TV, ensuite with shower, hairdryer, 'Gilchrist & Soames' toiletries, kitchen, refrigerator, microwave, equipped light meals, clock radio, laundry, computer and wireless facility for laptops. Relax in the pool, a cool drink, watching the sun setting on boats returning to Abel Marina below.

Queensland

Airlie Beach - Whitsunday - Jubilee Pocket
Whitsunday Lodge B&B

B&B
Cathy Zappala
12 Wildlife Road
Jubilee Pocket
Qld 4802
2 km E of Airlie Beach

Tel (07) 4948 2441
Fax (07) 4948 2447
whitsundaylodgebb@bigpond.com
www.whitsundaylodgebb.com

Double $155
$25 per extra child or adult, Continental breakfast, Dinner $50 per couple, High tea $60 per couple, Devonshire tea $15 per couple, Visa MC accepted. 2 King/Twin 3 Queen (4 bdrm). Bathrooms: 4 Ensuite

Nestled in the rainforest lined hills of Jubilee Pocket Whitsunday Lodge Bed and Breakfast is just three minutes drive from the Airlie Beach main street. Whitsunday Lodge is your quiet comfortable home away from home where your hosts Peter and Cathy provide a friendly personal holiday experience in the Whitsundays. Whitsunday Lodge is a traditional Queenslander design, including feature fret work indoors and wide verandahs outdoors. The grounds are spacious and tree lined with the rainforest creek bed behind a perfect backdrop for the pool and BBQ area. Perfect for couples or wedding groups.

Airlie Beach - Whitsundays
Whitsunday Heritage Cane Cutters Cottage

Self Contained House
Suzette & Adrian Pelt
PO Box 59
Airlie Beach, Qld 4802
7 km SW of Airlie Beach

Tel (07) 4946 7400 or 0419 768 195
Fax (07) 4946 1373
cottage@whitsunday.net.au
www.whitsundaycottage.com

Double top $150
RExtra person $20
Rollaway or double sofabed available
Breakfast by arrangement
$35 breakfast basket 2 people option
Air conditioned, secluded, Visa MC accepted
1 Double (1 bdrm) Bathrooms: 1 Ensuite

This Award Winning 100 year old beautifully restored Cane Cutters cottage is the Whitsunday's little hidden gem, perfectly located close to Airlie Beach but far away enough to experience the feeling of peace and relaxation of your private country cottage and tropical gardens. Watch wallabies and wildlife from the shady verandah, take a quiet early morning stroll around the tropical gardens and just soak up the ambience. You may never want to leave!

Queensland
Brisbane - Birkdale
Birkdale Bed & Breakfast

B&B & Traditional and private
Geoff & Margaret Finegan
3 Whitehall Avenue
Birkdale, Brisbane
Qld 4159
17 km E of Brisbane CBD

Tel (07) 3207 4442
glentrace@bigpond.com
www.bbbook.com.au/birkdalebb.html

Double $105-$115
Single $80-$90
Children $20
Full breakfast
2 Queen 1 Double 2 Single (3 bdrm)
Spacious & private with separate guest entrance
Bathrooms: 2 Ensuite 1 Private

Only 20 minutes from Brisbane CBD and airport, but with a lovely country atmosphere. Set in half an acre of beautifully landscaped gardens, Birkdale B&B is a modern English style country home, with a new luxurious guest wing with separate entrance. All bedrooms have private facilities and reverse cycle air conditioning for your comfort. Off street parking. Enjoy feeding the birds, go whale watching in nearby Moreton Bay or meet the local koalas. Qualified Aussie Hosts. Dual Tourism Award Winner. Corporate and weekly rates.

Brisbane - Shorncliffe
Naracoopa B&B

B&B & Self Contained Pavilion
Grace & David Cross
99 Yundah Street
Shorncliffe
Qld 4017
21 km NE of Brisbane

Tel (07) 3269 2334 or 0412 147 456
narabnb@bigpond.net.au
www.naracoopabnb.com.au

Double $165-$185
Single $135-$155, Children $45,
Extra person $45, Special breakfast,
S/C $180 double, 4 night minimum,
Weekly double from $780
Visa MC Eftpos accepted. 3 Queen 1 Double
(3 bdrm). Bathrooms: 3 Ensuite

AAA Tourism
★★★★

Naracoopa is all about location, luxury and tranquillity; your seaside destination on Moreton Bay; close to water, cafes, city train, airport and coasts. Two designer decorated B&B rooms, with private ensuites, verandahs, refrigerator, tea & coffee facilities, wireless broadband, air conditioning, outdoor hot spa. The Self-contained Pavilion provides more space and comfort for extended stay, all the above guest amenities and a fully equipped kitchenette, superbly appointed lounge and bedroom, outdoor deck, Foxtel digital, etc. Breakfast baskets available for $20. Indulge yourself!

Queensland

Brisbane - West End
Eskdale Bed & Breakfast

B&B & Homestay
Paul Kennedy
141 Vulture Street
West End
Qld 4101
2 km SW of Brisbane

Tel (07) 3255 2519
eskdale_brisbane@yahoo.com.au
eskdale.homestead.com

Double $120
Single $75, Children ²/₃ price
Continental breakfast, Every 5th night free,
See web site for special offers
Visa MC accepted
1 King 1 Queen 1 Double 1 Twin (4 bdrm)
Bathrooms: 1 Family share 1 Guest share

AAA Tourism
★★★

Eskdale Bed & Breakfast is a typical turn-of-the century Queensland house close to the restaurant district of West End. It's 2 km to the city centre across the Victoria Bridge, and just 1 km from the Southbank Parklands and the Brisbane Convention and Exhibition Centre, the Queensland Performing Arts Centre, Museum and Art Gallery. You'll be close to all the action and still be able to relax on the back deck and watch the birds feeding on the Australian native plants in the garden.

Bundaberg
Inglebrae

Luxury B&B
Christina & John McDonald
17 Branyan Street
Bundaberg
Qld 4670
1 km W of Bundaberg

Tel (07) 4154 4003 or 0418 889 971
Fax (07) 4154 2503
inglebrae@people.net.au
www.inglebrae.com

Double $140-$150
Single $110-$120, Full breakfast
Visa MC Eftpos accepted
2 King/Twin 2 Queen 2 Single (3 bdrm)
Bathrooms: 2 Ensuite 1 Private

Inglebrae is a restored Queenslander circa 1910 with beautifully appointed air-conditioned rooms and ensuites. Take a leisurely stroll to the city centre where you will find great shopping and many fine restaurants in which to dine. Bundaberg is situated at the Southern tip of the Great Barrier Reef and is the departure point for Lady Elliott Island. Enjoy a sumptuously cooked breakfast on the verandah overlooking beautiful gardens.

BBBook.com.au

Queensland

Cairns

Warm, sunny, tropical days tempered by cooling onshore breezes. The days are warm, the nights balmy. Cairns is the ideal base to explore and experience the many attractions of Tropical North Queensland.
Vicky Riddle, Billabong B&B

Cairns - Bayview Heights
Bayview House B&B

Luxury B&B
Bill & Margaret Morgan
3 Vine Close
Bayview Heights
Cairns
Qld 4868
8 km S of Cairns

Tel (07) 4033 6747 or 0411 898 318
margaret@cairnsluxurybandb.com.au
www.cairnsluxurybandb.com.au

Double $130-$145
Single $75-$85
Full breakfast
Visa MC accepted
1 King/Twin 2 Queen (3 bdrm)
Bathrooms: 3 Ensuite

Nestled below world heritage rainforest overlooking Cairns City, Bayview House welcomes you. We are proud to offer a modern home with spacious air conditioned en-suite bedrooms with ceiling fans, colour television and hairdryers. Guest lounge with tea/coffee making facilities, full fridge and microwave. Breakfast Menu. Laundry/Ironing facilities. Tour booking service. Secure Parking. Relax on your patio with a complimentary glass of wine and snacks whilst overlooking our 9 meter swimming pool with ocean and city views. Cairns Golf Club, restaurants, public transport nearby.

Queensland

Cairns - Brinsmead
Jenny's B&B

B&B & Self-Contained Flat
Jenny & Lex Macfarlane
12 Leon Close
Brinsmead
Qld 4870
10 km W of Cairns

Tel (07) 4055 1639 or 0428 551 639
jennysbb@jennysbandb.com
www.jennysbandb.com

Double $80-$100
Single $65-$85
Special breakfast
1 Self contained Flat $90 to $120
Visa MC accepted
1 King 1 Twin (3 bdrm)
Bathrooms: 2 Ensuite 1 Private

Jenny and Lex invite you to our home in Cairns. Wake to the sound of birds and our beautiful rainforest garden. A continental breakfast is served in the sunroom or around the pool. My husband and I are Photographers and enjoy outdoor activities. Only a short distance to tropical beaches, great restaurants, golf courses and the famous Kuranda Train and Skyrail. We are booking agents for all tours and rental cars. A complimentary pick up on arrival. "This was our 4th stay and we enjoy it more each stay" Gary & Helen Young, Seattle Washington, USA."

Cairns - Edge Hill
Galvin's Edge Hill B&B

Luxury B&B Suite
Julie and Jesse Low
61 Walsh Street
Cairns
Qld 4870
0.2 km N of Edge Hill Post Office

Tel (07) 4032 1308 or 0409 345 726
Fax (07) 4032 5968
info@galvinsonedge.com.au
www.galvinsonedge.com.au

Double $125-$150
Single $100
Family rates available
Special breakfast
1 Queen 2 Single (2 bdrm)
Bathrooms: 1 Family share

AAA Tourism ★★★★

One of Cairns' oldest & finest Queenslanders, located in quiet, leafy Edge Hill, we are one of the most conveniently located B&Bs in Cairns - five minutes drive from downtown and 5 minutes from the airport. Relax in your own private two-bedroom apartment (we only take one booking at a time so there's no need to share). Enjoy our magnificent swimming pool and gardens. Three minutes walk and you're in the village of Edge Hill with restaurants, shops, the Cairns Botanic Gardens walks, and more.

BBBook.com.au

Queensland
Cairns - Holloways Beach
Billabong B&B

B&B
Vicky & Ted Riddle
30 Caribbean Street
Holloways Beach, Cairns
Qld 4878
10 km N of downtown Cairns

Tel (07) 4037 0162 or 0427 370 044
Fax (07) 4037 0162
info@billabongbnb.com.au
www.billabongbnb.com.au

Double $155-$168
Single $120-$125
Full breakfast
Visa MC accepted
2 Queen 1 Single (2 bdrm)
Bathrooms: 2 Ensuite

Billabong is your perfect accommodation in Cairns located on an island in the heart of a large lily-covered Billabong, close to downtown Cairns and the airport. Two queen guest suites with contemporary decor include ensuite bathrooms, air conditioning and ceiling fans. Your facilities include television, CD, wireless internet, fridge, tea/coffee making, BBQ and separate entrance. Large French doors open onto a private deck overlooking the Billabong featuring spectacular bird life. A short walk to the beach and restaurants. The delicious gourmet breakfast is Billabong's speciality.

Cairns - Lake Tinaroo
Tinaroo Haven Holiday Lodge

Luxury Self Contained Pole House & Cottage
Michael & Tania Taylor
Lot 42 Wavell Drive
Tinaroo Waters (via Kairi)
Qld 4872
5 km S of Kairi

Tel (07) 4095 8686 or 0437 344 973
Fax (07) 3319 7232
tinlodge@fire-break.com
www.fire-break.com

Double $90-$185
Children $16 each, children under 2 no charge
Continental provisions
Visa MC accepted
2 Queen 1 Double 3 Single (4 bdrm)
Bathrooms: 3 Private

    AAA Tourism ★★★★

The property consists of a pole house and a cottage both hidden in the tree tops on 2.5 acres of bushland. They are both fully self-contained with all amenities, which includes Austar with National Geographic, Discovery, News, Sports, Movies, Cartoon Network, DVD Player, large selection of DVDs, a selection of games. There is also a laundry. Both units have dining areas and log fireplaces. The balconies area equipped with a BBQ.

Queensland

Cairns - Stratford
Lilybank

B&B
Mike & Pat Woolford
75 Kamerunga Road, Stratford, Cairns, Qld 4870
8 km N of Cairns

Tel (07) 4055 1123
Fax (07) 4058 1990
lilybank@bigpond.net.au
www.lilybank.com.au

Double $110-$132
Single $95, Special breakfast, Extra person in room $33
Visa MC Amex Eftpos JCB accepted
2 King/Twin 1 King 3 Queen 4 Twin
5 Single (5 bdrm) Bathrooms: 5 Ensuite

'Lilybank' - a fine example of traditional 'Queenslander' architecture. 'Lilybank' owes its success to the happy blend of hospitality and privacy offered to our guests. Bedrooms are air-conditioned, there's a guests' lounge with TV, video, salt-water pool, laundry, BBQ and off-street parking. We'll serve a wonderful breakfast and help you choose and book tours which are right for you. Our excellent local restaurants are within walking distance. Two spoodles and a galah live in our part of house. There's a beautiful tropical garden and guests are welcome to pick their own fruit in season.

BBBook.com.au

Queensland

Cardwell

Cardwell is a laid back coastal town and the gateway to Hinchinbrook Island, Australia's largest Island National Park. The 32 km Thornsbourne walking trail attracts walkers from all over the world. View Dugongs, Turtles or the Cassowary (Australia's largest flightless bird) in the area.
Jan & Bruce Ferguson, Cardwell B&B.

Cardwell - Hinchinbrook Island
Cardwell B&B

B&B Homestay
Bruce & Jan Ferguson
18 Gregory Street
Cardwell
Qld 4839
In Cardwell. Between Cairns & Townsville

Tel (07) 4066 8330 or 0408 896 013
thefergs@austarnet.com.au
www.cardwellhomestay.com.au

Double $85
Single $70
Children age 6 and over welcome
Full tropical breakfast
1 Queen 1 Double 1 Twin (3 bdrm)
Bathrooms: 1 Guest share Large bathroom

Jan & Bruce welcome you to their Tranquil Tropical Paradise. Relax and enjoy the lush tropical surrounds and bird life over a Tropical Continental Breakfast. Choose from 3 spacious air conditioned bedrooms where you can relax in comfort. Enjoy the picturesque view of Cardwell Range overlooking the golf course or take a short walk to the beach, local shops or nearby bushland. Lodged between two world heritage areas, The Wet Tropics and The Great Barrier Reef, Cardwell is the gateway to Hinchinbrook Island and Cassowary Region, best boating, fishing and wilderness experiences along the Great Greenway North Queensland.

Daintree

The Daintree Coast combines breathtaking beauty with exceptional biodiversity. The World Heritage Listed Wet Tropics Rainforest and The Great Barrier Reef meet spectacularly along the Daintree Coast and offer an unparalleled richness of rare and primitive flora and fauna.
Alison Gotts, Cape Tribulation Exotic Fruit Farm

Daintree - Cape Tribulation
Cape Trib Exotic Fruit Farm

B&B & Cottage, no kitchen
Digby and Alison Gotts
Lot 5 Nicole Drive
Cape Tribulation
Qld 4873
80 km N of Mossman

Tel (07) 4098 0057
digby@capetrib.com.au
www.capetrib.com.au

Double $140-$160
Children age 6 and over welcome
Full breakfast, Four cafes in walking distance
2 nights min, Extra person $30
Visa MC Eftpos accepted
2 Queen 2 Double (2 bdrm)
Bathrooms: 2 Ensuite

Two private, high set timber pole-framed cottages on the edge of our privately owned World Heritage Rainforest. Breakfast is a sumptuous repast, based around farm produce. The property is in a remote wilderness area and runs on solar power. We offer an ECO Certified Ecotourism experience. Located one kilometre from the beach, and the Great Barrier Reef is 45 minutes offshore.

Queensland

Daintree - Cow Bay

Two World Heritage Icons the Daintree Rainforest and the Great Barrier Reef meet on the Daintree Coast. Stay with local hosts in unique accommodation and immerse yourself in this natural wonderland!
Marion Esser, Cow Bay Homestay B&B

Daintree - Cow Bay
Cow Bay Homestay

B&B
Marion Esser
160 Wattle Close
Cow Bay
Qld 4873
58 km N of Mossman

Tel (07) 4098 9151
marion@cowbayhomestay.com
www.cowbayhomestay.com

Double $140
Single $140
Children over 6 welcome
Full breakfast, Dinner please advise
Visa MC accepted
1 Queen 1 Double 1 Twin (2 bdrm)
Bathrooms: 2 Ensuite

Cow Bay Homestay is adjacent to two World Heritage Wilderness areas the Daintree Rainforest and the Great Barrier Reef. Wake up to nature: views into vast tropical gardens and rainforest, swim in our fresh water creek, sit under trees or on the deck spotting birds, stars, butterflies or the goanna. Get active with walks to stunning Cow Bay Beach and big range of guided tours. Great breakfast. Marion can arrange all your tour bookings. Action Packed Relaxation.

Queensland

Gold Coast Hinterland - Nerang
Riviera Bed & Breakfast

B&B & Retreat
Robert & Caroline Marchesi
53 Evanita Drive
Gilston/Nerang
Qld 4211
6 km S of Nerang

Tel (07) 5533 2499 or 0421 853 189
Fax (07) 5533 2500   rivbandb@bigpond.net.au
www.rivierabandb.com.au

Double $115-$140
Single $95-$120, Children $15-$30, Continental breakfast, Dinner B/A: $25-$45, Children's meals $10-$35, Extra person $45, High Season tariff 20th Dec-3rd Jan, Visa MC Eftpos accepted.
4 Queen 3 Single (4 bdrm) Bathrooms: 1 Ensuite 1 Family share 1 Guest share 1 Private

AAA Tourism
★★★

Unique French Experience in Exquisite 100 year old Queenslander in Gold Coast Hinterland. Close proximity to all Theme Parks and National/Wildlife Parks. Peaceful, secluded in an exotic location on 7 acres of sub-tropical bushland. Franco-Australian hosts offer French Speciality Breakfasts on weekends and wholesome breakfasts of homemade/homegrown produce on weekdays. Exotic native birds to handfeed from deck while kangaroos graze nearby. Authentic French Gourmet meals by arrangement. Aussie host offers Therapeutic Massage. Pet and child friendly.

Gold Coast Hinterland - Nerang
Rumbalara B&B

B&B & Self Contained Apartment
Denise and Alan Ramage
72 Hoop Pine Court
Advancetown
Qld 4211
10 km SE of Nerang

Tel (07) 5533 2211
Fax (07) 5533 2354
ramage.construction@bigpond.com
www.home.austarnet.com.au/ramage

Double $95-$100
Single $85-$85, Children welcome, cot available
Full breakfast, Evening meal by arrangement
Visa MC accepted
3 Queen 2 Twin (5 bdrm)
Bathrooms: 1 Ensuite 1 Guest share

AAA Tourism
★★★

Rumbalara is quiet and peacefull in a semi-rainforest envioronment but still only 30 minutes to the beaches and tourist attractions. B&B rooms are very comfortable,2 have access to veranda and have tea and coffee making facilities as well as a small fridge.

BBBook.com.au

Queensland

Hervey Bay

Hervey Bay is Australia's whale watching capital and our calm waters are a playground for thousands of humpback whales on their annual migration from late July to early November. The Fraser Coast is the gateway to two World Heritage listed areas, Fraser Island and the Great Barrier Reef.
Sharon Lagan, Alexander Lakeside B&B

Hervey Bay
The Chamomile B&B

B&B
Diane & Brian Scruton
65A Miller Street
Hervey Bay
Qld 4655
0.5 km NW of Hervey Bay Marina

Tel (07) 4125 1602 or 0408 781 886
Fax (07) 4125 6975
info@chamomile.com.au
www.chamomile.com.au

Double $125-$150
Single $105
Full breakfast
Visa MC accepted
2 Queen 1 Twin (3 bdrm)
Bathrooms: 1 Ensuite 1 Guest share

Relax on the verandah as you sip a cappuccino, listen to the calming sound of water spilling over the waterfall and enjoy the peaceful sounds of the birdcalls. Stroll down to the Hervey Bay Marina and enjoy the sights and colours of the boats and people. Recharge in the garden spa. Relish the delicious breakfast and afternoon tea. A free booking service for Fraser Island, Lady Elliot Island and Whale Watch tours. A very warm welcome awaits you.

Hervey Bay
Alexander Lakeside B&B

Luxury B&B & Separate Suite
Sharon & John Lagan
29 Lido Parade
Hervey Bay
Qld 4655
1 km N of Hervey Bay

Tel (07) 4128 9448
Fax (07) 4125 5060
alexbnb@bigpond.net.au
www.herveybaybedandbreakfast.com.au

Double $130-$140
Full breakfast
Self Contained Suites $150
Visa MC Eftpos accepted
3 Queen (3 bdrm) 2 Queen Rooms & 1 S/C Suite
Bathrooms: 3 Ensuite

  AAA Tourism

Luxury accommodation located beside a peaceful wildlife lake. Wake up and enjoy a full tropical breakfast while watching our wildlife. Guests can participate in turtle feeding. Indulge yourself in our heated Lakeside Spa. Fully equipped kitchen and laundry. BBQ facilities. We can organise your tours to view the majestic Humpback Whales Aug, Sept, Oct. World Heritage listed Fraser Island the largest sand Island in the world and Lady Elliott Island beginning of the Great Barrier Reef. A warm welcome awaits you. Your Home Style Resort.

Hervey Bay - Howard
Montrave House B&B Home & Pet Stay

B&B
Jackie & George Adams
20 Pacific Haven Drive
Howard
Qld 4659
30 km N of Maryborough

Tel (07) 4129 0183 or 0407 930 106
montrave@bigpond.com
www.montrave.com

Double $105-$110
Single $95
Full traditional Aussie or Scottish Breakfast
Refreshments on arrival included, tea/coffee, evening Port.
2 Queen 1 Double 2 Twin (4 bdrm)
Bathrooms: 2 Guest share Spa bath

Enjoy the elegance of a bygone era, traditional Scottish hospitality in the ambiance of a high set historic Queenslander on rural acreage with 3 dams. Montrave House offers modern comforts, spa bath, wide verandahs in a tranquil atmosphere. Comfortable air conditioned federation rooms are individually and tastefully decorated. Close to the Burrum District Golf Club and convenient for golf courses in Hervey Bay, Maryborough and Childers. Boat ramps for two saltwater rivers are nearby and we are within walking distance of Howard CBD. Bookings available for all tours of Fraser Ireland, Lady Elliot Ireland and Whale Watching trips as well as vehicle and boat hire. Central for Hervey Bay and the historic towns of Maryborough and Childers.

Queensland
Kingaroy
Rock-Al-Roy B&B

B&B
Max & Lyn Lehmann
15 Kearney Street
Kingaroy
Qld 4610
5 km S of Kingaroy

Tel (07) 4162 3061
rockalroybb@burnett.net.au
www.rockalroy.southburnett.com.au

Double $110-$140
Single $90-$110, Children $20
Special breakfast
Dinner available
Visa MC accepted
1 Queen 1 Double 2 Single (3 bdrm)
Bathrooms: 2 Guest share

AAA Tourism
★★★☆

Just five minutes from Kingaroy, this warm modern Queenslander style house set on 7600 m2 with extensive shrub, gardens and pot plants offers quiet, peaceful surroundings with panoramic views overlooking Kingaroy. "Very welcoming and friendly, even the pets welcomed us." "Great meals. Thank you for making us feel so welcome in your beautiful home." Hosts Lyn & Max Lehmann.

Pets are welcome at many properties – contact hosts first to check on facilities available. Look for The Pets Welcome Logo

Maryborough

Glorious colonial architecture, outstanding museums, riverside dining, a first class theatre and magnificent parklands - Maryborough is a must see on the Fraser Coast region. Also known as the Queenslander Capital, Maryborough is one of Queensland's oldest provincial cities
Cecile Espigole, Eco Queenslander

Maryborough
Eco Queenslander

Self-Contained Queenslander
Cecile Espigole
15 Treasure Street
Maryborough
Qld 4650
1.5 km N of town centre

Tel 0438 195 443
info@ecoqueenslander.com
www.ecoqueenslander.com

Double $115-$120
Single $115-$120
Children welcome
Continental provisions
1 Queen 1 Double 2 Single (2 bdrm)
Two bedrooms + fold-out sofa in living room
Bathrooms: 1 Private

Experience the charm of a Maryborough Queenslander house and stay at Eco Queenslander, an environmentally friendly, self-contained holiday house with all modern facilities in the beautiful historic town of Maryborough. Craftsman built with many original features: fretwork, polished timber floors, French doors, high moulded ceilings, claw-foot bath, etc. The house accommodates 4-6 people and is ideal for touring the Fraser Coast Region with world famous tourist attractions: Fraser Island, whale watching (August to October), nesting sea turtles at Mon Repos National Park (November to March) and much more. We speak English, French and Spanish.

Queensland

Noosa - Noosa Hinterland

Noosa is renowned for its squeaky clean, white sandy beaches, azure seas and secluded beach coves. Snuggled behind the bustling coastal strip is the Noosa Hinterland, a patchwork of tranquil lakes and rivers, lush forests and pastures, quaint, historic villages and striking volcanic formations.
Christine, Eumarella Shores and Tourism Noosa

Noosa - Lake Weyba
Eumarella Shores Lake Retreat

**B&B & Self Contained House
& Self Contained Cottages and Pavlions**
Bill & Christine Tainsh
251 Eumarella Road
Lake Weyba, Noosa, Qld 4562
7 km SW of Noosa

Tel (07) 5449 1738
Fax 07 5449 1738
stay@eumarellashores.com.au
www.eumarellashores.com.au

Double $136-$450
Children $25 p.n, Breakfast b/a, BBQ Hampers available. Extra guests $25-$40 p.n, Complimentary use of canoe, Visa MC Eftpos accepted. 11 King/Twin1 King 9 Queen 9 Double 3 Single (21 bdrm). Bathrooms: 2 Ensuite 10 Private

AAA Tourism
★★★★

A unique lake front retreat, nestled in temperate rainforest on the shores of pristine Lake Weyba. Only minutes from cosmopolitan Noosa: world class beaches, national parks, restaurants and boutiques. Enchanting traditional cottages and contemporary pavilions on the lake's edge; self contained to preserve your privacy with individual lake access and beach area. Explore the creeks and lake in a canoe; go bushwalking; bird & wildlife watching; fish virtually from your doorstep; or simply relax on your verandah, listening to the gently lapping lake. Sheer bliss!

Queensland

Noosa - Noosa Valley
Noosa Valley Manor Luxury B&B

Luxury B&B
Kathleen & Murray Maxwell
115 Wust Road
Doonan, Noosa Valley
Qld 4562
6 km SW of Noosa

Tel (07) 5471 0088 or 0400 280 215
Fax (07) 5471 0066
noosavalleymanor@bigpond.com
www.noosavalleymanor.com.au

Double $220-$250
Full breakfast
Candlelight Dinners by arrangement
Visa MC Eftpos accepted
1 King/Twin 3 Queen (4 bdrm)
Bathrooms: 4 Ensuite

AAA Tourism
★★★★☆

Noosa Valley Manor is a custom built Bed & Breakfast that truly reflects its 4.5 star AAA rating. Set in 1.5 acres of award winning tropical gardens yet you are only 10 minutes pleasant drive to the heart of Noosa. All bedrooms are air conditioned with ensuites. Gourmet fresh food is a feature of your stay with us. Here is what some guests have said: "Divine food, beautiful house, perfect hosts." "So lovely to be spoilt by wonderful people in a beautiful setting."

Noosa - Peregian
Lake Weyba Cottages

B&B & Self Contained Cottages
Philip & Samantha Bown
79 Clarendon Road
Peregian Beach, Qld 4573
14 km S of Noosa

Tel (07) 5448 2285 or 0404 863 504
Fax (07) 5448 1714
info@lakeweybacottages.com
www.lakeweybacottages.com

Double $295-$445
Not suitable for children under 14 years, Full breakfast provisions, Dinner $185 per couple for 3 course dinner, Extra person $90 per night in a 4.5 star cottage, Visa MC Amex Eftpos accepted
4 King/Twin 5 Queen 2 Single (10 bdrm)
Bathrooms: 8 Ensuite 1 Guest share

AAA Tourism
★★★★☆

Relax in your own private cottage - just the two of you. Each cottage features wood fires, air conditioning, double spas and fabulous views. Enjoy a gourmet breakfast on your veranda whilst watching passing kangaroos and the abundant bird life. Swim in the natural fresh water lagoon with its own private beach. Cycle through the national park to the beach, canoe along the creek or just rejuvenate and relax with a massage treatment. The only sounds you'll hear are the morning birdsong, evening frog chorus and the ocean waves drifting across the lake at night . . . just perfect.

Queensland

Noosa Hinterland - Cooroy
Cudgerie Homestead B&B

B&B
Veronica & Steve Hall
42 Cudgerie Drive
Cooroy
Qld 4563
7 km NW of Cooroy

Tel (07) 5442 6681 or 0408 982 461
Fax (07) 5442 6681   cudgerie@hotmail.com
www.cudgerie-noosa.com

Double $155-$167
Single $90-$95, Infants can stay free with cot in parent bedroom, Full breakfast, Delicious evening meals available by arrangement, Massage therapy available by arrangement, Visa MC accepted. 3 Queen 1 Double 2 Twin (5 bdrm). Bathrooms: 4 Ensuite 1 Private

Multi-award winning Cudgerie Homestead is one of the Sunshine Coast's most popular bed and breakfasts, offering you a unique blend of hospitality and cuisine. Unwind by the sensational swimming pool in summer or around the pot belly in winter. A quiet and secluded location with fantastic views across the Noosa Hinterland. Guest Comments: "A place to indulge, superb breakfasts on the veranda. Charming hosts with helpful touring advice." "It doesn't get any better than this, splendid location, warm and friendly hosts and top notch food."

Rockhampton - The Range
Hazel Cottage

Self Contained Cottage
Liz Patrick
13 Kennedy Street
Rockhampton
Qld 4700
4 km S of Rockhampton CBD

Tel (07) 4927 4984 or 0424 846 235
lizandcolpatrick@yahoo.com.au
www.bbbook.com.au/HazelCottage.html

Double $130
Continental breakfast
1 Double 2 Single (2 bdrm)
Bathrooms: 1 Private

Come and relax at Hazel Cottage. Self Contained 2 bedroom cottage on southern outskirts of Rockhampton, 4 km from CBD. Rural views and walking track. Adjacent to Yeppen Lagoon. Within walking distance to Tropic of Capricorn Spire and Botanical Gardens. This property is ideal for a couple or two couples travelling together. Pets welcome if well behaved.

Queensland

Stanthorpe

The Granite Belt, so called because of its spectacular granite outcrops, is situated just north of the New South Wales border, around the small town of Stanthorpe. Because of its altitude, the area has become well-known for cold climate wines, 'Christmas in July' dinners and cosy log fires.
Margaret Taylor, Jireh B&B

Stanthorpe
Jireh

B&B & Homestay
Margaret Taylor
89 Donges Road
Severnlea
Qld 4380
7 km S of Stanthorpe

Tel (07) 4683 5298
ktaylor3@vtown.com.au
www.bbbook.com.au/jireh.html

Double $100-$120
Single $75-$85, Children $40, Full breakfast
Dinner $25 2 courses traditional;
$35 Indian cuisine
Extra adult $50
3 Double 1 Single (3 bdrm)
Bathrooms: 1 Ensuite 1 Guest share

Old-fashioned country hospitality in a quiet rural setting, close to the wineries and national parks of the Granite Belt. Antiques and country decor reflect family history and include many examples of Margaret's embroidery, patchwork, dolls and bears. Hearty country breakfasts are served and dinner (Traditional or Indian) is by arrangement. The combination of country home, personal attention, household pets, farm animals, and country rambles offers both a unique experience and value for money. "Wonderful friendly atmosphere and simply great food." B&B Book Commended, 2004, 2005.

Queensland
Stanthorpe
Honeysuckle Cottages & The Rocks Restaurant

Self Contained Luxury Cottages
Rick & Maxine
15 Mayfair Lane
Stanthorpe
Qld 4380
2 km N of Stanthorpe

Tel (07) 4681 1510
Fax 07 4681 1512
stay@honeysucklecottages.com.au
www.honeysucklecottages.com.au

Double $150-$225
Single $130-$225
Full breakfast provisions
Visa MC Diners Amex Eftpos accepted
10 Queen (10 bdrm)
Bathrooms: 8 Private

Escape to the crisp, clean mountain air, country hospitality and the unique scenery of the Granite Belt. Eight charming cottages with federation era decor nestled amongst thick mountain bushland next door to Old Caves Winery. One and two bedroom self contained cottages with dual spa bath, log fires, TV and stereo. Queen size beds with continental quilts, electric blankets and quality linen will ensure your comfort. A delicious country-style breakfast basket is included. The Rocks Restaurant is open for dinner five nights. Dinner can also be served in your cottage. Shops, golf course and galleries only 3 minutes away.

Sunshine Coast - Ninderry - Yandina - Coolum
Ninderry House

B&B & Traditional
Mary Lambart
8 Karnu Drive
Ninderry
Qld 4561
5 km E of Yandina

Tel (07) 5446 8556
Fax (07) 5446 8556
enquiries@ninderryhouse.com.au
www.ninderryhouse.com.au

Double $150
Single $95, Full breakfast
Dinner $25-$35 if requested on booking, can cater for special diets, Visa MC accepted
2 King/Twin 1 Queen (3 bdrm)
Bathrooms: 3 Ensuite

Central Sunshine Coast location, views overlooking Mt Ninderry and Maroochy Valley to the Ocean. Close to beaches, native plant nurseries, ginger factory, art galleries, craft and produce markets of Eumundi and Yandina. First class restaurants nearby. Three ensuite guestrooms, comfortable sitting room with fire, deck for summer breezes or winter sun. Imaginative meals using fresh local produce. Special diets catered for. Dinner available if requested on booking. Full breakfast included in tariff. Ph/Fax: 07 5446 8556. Email: enquiries@ninderryhouse.com.au

Queensland

Sunshine Coast Hinterland - Maleny
Maleny Country Cottages

Self Contained House
Claude & Teresa Goudsouzian
347 Corks Pocket Road
Reesville Via Maleny, Qld 4552
8 km W of Maleny

Tel (07) 5494 2744
Fax (07) 5494 2744
reception@malenycottages.com.au
www.malenycottages.com.au

Double $250-$410
Single $250-$380, Children $30-$50, Breakfast hampers B/A $35 per couple per morning, Two nights from $365-$410, Extra adult $30-$50, Visa MC Diners Amex Eftpos JCB accepted. 1 Queen 2 Single (2 bdrm)
Bathrooms: 1 Ensuite 2 Guest share

   AAA Tourism ★★★★

Mountain hideaway on 60acres of forested property. Fully self-contained air conditioned cottages with all linen, spa, fireplace and verandah bbq. Abundant wildlife, alpacas and bush walking tracks.

Sunshine Coast Hinterland - Maleny - Montville
Lillypilly's Country Cottages

Luxury B&B & 5 B&B Cottages
Josef & Adele Gruber
584 Maleny-Montville Road
Maleny
Qld 4552
6 km S of Town

Tel (07) 5494 3002
Fax (07) 5494 3499 lillypillys@bigpond.com
www.lillypillys.com.au

Double $198-$330
Single $187-$308, Full breakfast
Dinner $28.60-$33 (Main Course)
½ to 1 hour massage $49.50-$88
Visa MC Diners Amex Eftpos accepted
5 Queen (5 bdrm)
Bathrooms: 5 Ensuite 5 Private

   AAA Tourism ★★★★☆

At Lillypillys you have the rare opportunity to delight in exquisite meals without having to leave your own private oasis. Experience the romantic intimacy of dining in a restaurant just for two, when your sumptuous candlelit dinner is served to your individual cottage, each course at a time. Lillypilly's Cottages overlook picturesque Lake Baroon or are situated in a rainforest garden setting. All cottages are air conditioned and feature log fires, double spas, television, video, DVD and CD player, and private verandahs with double hammocks.

BBBook.com.au

Queensland

Sunshine Coast Hinterland - Montville
Secrets on the Lake

Luxury B&B & Luxury Treehouse Cabins
George and Aldy Johnston
208 Narrows Road
Montville
Qld 4560
5 km SW of Montville

Tel (07) 5478 5888
Fax (07) 5478 5166
aldy@secretsonthelake.com.au
www.secretsonthelake.com.au

Double $330-$430
Continental provisions
Visa MC Amex Eftpos accepted
1 King/Twin 13 Queen 2 Single (14 bdrm)
Bathrooms: 1 Ensuite 11 Private

Secrets on the Lake offers the perfect opportunity for romance, relaxation and intimate accommodation. Elevated wooden walkways lead you through the rainforest to 10 individually themed treehouses offering total privacy, superb attention to detail and a completely unique world-class experience. Each retreat features carved cedar furniture, double shower, kitchen facilities, special home baked treats, toasty log fire, AC, TV, CD/DVD, sunken double spa and your own balcony with BBQ. What a way to indulge... we provide a stunning view, chocolates, roses & champagne. All you need to bring is that special someone to share it with.

Sunshine Coast Hinterland - Mooloolah Valley
Mooloolah Valley Holidays

Self Contained Holiday Cottages
Atalanta Moreau
93 King Road
Mooloolah Valley
Qld 4553
1 km SW of Mooloolah

Tel (07) 5494 7109 or 0408 224 668
info@mooloolahvalley.com
www.mooloolahvalley.com

Accommodation only
Wood-fired pizza-oven set in tropical garden
$400-$725/cottage for 2 nights
Stay 4 nights, 5th night free
Visa MC accepted
4 Double 8 Single (4 bdrm)
Bathrooms: 4 Private

Discover the glorious pleasures of a country horse riding holiday at Mooloolah Valley. For romantic couples, Jacaranda Cottage is charming and full of olde-world splendour. Funky Piccaninny Cottage featuring the rainbow serpent sleeps four. For families and celebrations, Frangipani House is dazzling! Guests are treated to a fun-filled holiday. Try the tropical Hot-tub Jacuzzi spa, fabulous heated swimming pool and wood-fire pizza oven . . . Great for parties! There are fun games like giant chess set, bikes to explore picturesque Mooloolah Valley, safe Horses and cute Ponies to trek into Rainforest and Mountain-tops. Come and enjoy!

Queensland

Yeppoon - Capricorn Coast
While Away B&B

Luxury B&B
Lois & Richard Michel
44 Todd Avenue
Yeppoon
Qld 4703
2.4 km N of Yeppoon

Tel (07) 4939 5719
Fax (07) 4939 5577
whileaway@bigpond.com
www.whileaybandb.com.au

Double $130-$150
Single $110
Special breakfast
Visa MC Eftpos accepted
1 King 3 Queen 1 Twin (4 bdrm)
Bathrooms: 4 Ensuite

AAA Tourism
★★★★☆

While Away B&B is a purpose built B&B. We offer style, comfort and privacy in a modern home less than 100 m to beach. This property is ideal for couples but unsuitable for children under 10. All rooms have ensuites, television plus air-conditioning. We offer a generous tropical/cooked breakfast - tea/coffee-making facilities with cake/biscuits are available at all times. Dining room facilities available for use of guests. We will do our best to ensure you enjoy your stay in this area.

Many properties offer activities onsite such as horse riding.
Look for The Onsite Activities Logo

Queensland

Queensland Hosted Accommodation...
everything you want it to be

Get back to your roots — stay where hospitality began

Bed & Breakfast and Farmstay Queensland

PO Box 13162, George Street
Brisbane QLD 4003
T: 1800 205 030
Overseas T: +61 7 3211 5040
F: +61 7 3236 4552
E: info@bbfq.com.au
www.bbfq.com.au

Queensland

Recommended Accommodation - Queensland

Properties included below with a page reference are included in this chapter and with further details. We have also included recommended accommodation with information supplied by BBFQ and BBFAFNQ. Contact the hosts by telephone number for further details and tell them, *"We found you in The B&B Book."*

Airlie Bch	Airlie Waterfront B&B	Cnr Broadwater Ave & Mazlin St	Airlie Beach	07 4946 7631	
Airlie Bch	Island View B&B	19 Nara Ave	Airlie Beach	07 4946 4505	
Airlie Bch	**Whitsunday Heritage Cane Cutters Cottage**	**4 Braithwaite Court**	**Airlie Beach**	**07 4946 7400**	**Page 135**
Airlie Bch	**Whitsunday Moorings B&B**	**37 Airlie Cres**	**Airlie Beach**	**07 4946 4692**	**Page 134**
Airlie Bch - Cannonvale	Parkwood B&B	35 Parkwood Terr	Cannonvale	07 4948 1356	
Airlie Bch - Jubilee Pocket	**Whitsunday Lodge B&B**	**12 Wildlife Rd**	**Jubilee Pocket**	**07 4948 2441**	**Page 135**
Atherton	Atherton Blue Gum B&B	36 Twelfth Ave	Atherton	07 4091 5149	
Atherton	Isabels on the Hill B&B	8 Centenary Dv	Atherton	07 4091 6920	
Atherton - Tolga	Allawah Retreat	Lot 21 Marnane Rd	Tolga	07 4095 4900	
Atherton Tblnds - Malanda	Grandview Country Rtrt	122L Hogan Rd	Tarzali via Malanda	07 4095 1266	
Atherton Tblnds - Yungaburra	Williams Lodge	Cedar St	Yungaburra	07 4095 3449	
Baralaba	Myella Farm Stay	Myella	Baralaba	07 4998 1290	
Barmoya	Henderson Park Farmstay	88 C H Barretts Rd	Barmoya	07 4934 2794	
Beaudesert - Darlington	Ceder Glen	3338 Kerry Rd	Darlington	07 5544 8170	
Beechmont	Old Saint Johns Church	1805 Beechmont Rd	Beechmont	07 5533 3593	
Biggenden	Biggenden B&B	260 Woowoonga Hall Rd	Biggenden	0428 758 236	
Brisbane - Birkdale	**Birkdale B&B**	**3 Whitehall Ave**	**Birkdale**	**07 3207 4442**	**Page 136**
Brisbane - Holland Park	Akebia	22 Coonara St	Holland Park	07 3324 1471	
Brisbane - New Farm	Cream Gables	70 Kent St	New Farm	07 3358 2727	
Brisbane - Paddington	Aynsley	14 Glanmire St	Paddington	07 3368 2250	
Brisbane - Paddington	Fern Cottage B&B	89 Fernberg Rd	Paddington	07 3511 6685	
Brisbane - Paddington	Lucerne on Fernberg	23 Fernberg Rd	Paddington	07 3369 6686	
Brisbane - Shorncliffe	**Naracoopa B&B**	**99 Yundah St**	**Shorncliffe**	**07 3269 2334**	**Page 136**
Brisbane - West End	**Eskdale B&B**	**141 Vulture St**	**West End**	**07 3255 2519**	**Page 137**
Brisbane City	Eton	436 Upper Roma St	Brisbane	07 3236 0115	
Buderim	Buderim White Hse B&B	54 Quorn Cl	Buderim	07 5445 1961	
Buderim - Tanawha	Main Creek Bower B&B	123-125 Main Creek Rd	Tanawha	07 5476 8327	
Bundaberg	**Inglebrae**	**17 Branyan St**	**Bundaberg**	**07 4154 4003**	**Page 137**
Cairns	Abbey's Budget B&B	396 Draper St	Cairns	07 4051 7352	
Cairns - Bayview Heights	**Bayview House B&B**	**3 Vine Cl**	**Bayview Heights**	**07 4033 6747**	**Page 138**
Cairns - Brinsmead	Golden Sunbird B&B	Brinsmead Rd	Cairns	07 4055 1954	
Cairns - Brinsmead	**Jenny's B&B**	**12 Leon Cl**	**Brinsmead**	**07 4055 1639**	**Page 139**
Cairns - Caravonica	Nigana B&B	19 Figtree Dv	Caravonica	07 4058 0765	
Cairns - Clifton Bch	Clifton Beach Retreat	35 Batt St	Clifton Beach	07 4059 0452	
Cairns - Clifton Bch	Gum Tree Retreat	Lot 2 Sudbury Cl	Clifton Beach	07 4059 2793	
Cairns - Earlville	Cairns Reef R'fst B&B	112 Mansfield St	Earlville	07 4033 5597	
Cairns - Edge Hill	Cairns Edge Hill B&B	66 Walsh St	Edge Hill	07 4053 1881	
Cairns - Edge Hill	**Galvin's Edge Hill B&B**	**61 Walsh St**	**Cairns**	**07 4032 1308**	
Cairns - Edge Hill	Kookas B&B	40 Hutchinson St	Edge Hill	07 4053 3231	
Cairns - Edge Hill	The Garden Gate B&B	519 McCormack St	Edge Hill	07 4053 3748	
Cairns - Holloways Bch	**Billabong B&B**	**30 Caribbean St**	**Holloways Beach**	**07 4037 0162**	**Page 140**
Cairns - Holloways Bch	Toby's Retreat	82 Baronia Cres	Holloways Beach	07 4055 0011	

BBBook.com.au

Queensland

Cairns - Holloways Bch	Zimzala Retreat	2 Marietta St	Holloways Beach	07 4055 9972	
Cairns - Kanimbla Heights	Capers at Kanimbla	11 Hussar Cl	Kanimbla Heights	07 4034 1994	
Cairns - Kuranda	Cadaghi Cottage	135 Stoney Creek	Kuranda	07 4093 0352	
Cairns - Lake Tinaroo	**Tinaroo Haven Holiday Lodge**	**Lot 42 Wavel Drive**	**Tinaroo Waters**	**07 4095 8686**	*Page 140*
Cairns - Redlynch	Zanzoo Retreat	Lot 4 Mary Parker Dv	Redlynch	07 4039 2842	
Cairns - Stratford	**Lilybank**	**75 Kamerunga Rd**	**Stratford Cairns**	**07 4055 1123**	*Page 141*
Cairns - Trinity Bch	Palm Whispers Lux B&B	4 Madang St	Trinity Beach	07 4057 9750	
Cairns - Trinity Bch	Trinity Hideaway B&B	56 Jamieson St	Trinity Beach	07 4057 8972	
Cairns - Trinity Park	Barking Owl Retreat	409 Hough Rd	Kairi	07 4095 8455	
Cairns - Trinity Park	Bluewater B&B	12 Bataan Cres	Trinity Park	07 4055 6137	
Cairns - Yorkeys Knob	A Villa Gail	36 Janett St	Yorkeys Knob	07 4055 8178	
Cannonvale - Riordanvale	Whitsunday Coral Cruises	55 Black Rd	Cannonvale	07 4946 1698	
Cape Tribulation	**Cape Trib Exotic Fruit Farm**	**Lot 5 Nicole Dv**	**Cape Tribulation**	**07 4098 0057**	*Page 143*
Cape Tribulation	Cape Tribulation Sanc	RMB 25	Cape Tribulation	07 4098 0092	
Cardwell	**Cardwell B&B**	**18 Gregory St**	**Cardwell**	**07 4066 8330**	*Page 142*
Cardwell	Seascape B&B	18 Landsdown St	Cardwell	07 4066 2383	
Childers	Mango Hill Cottage B&B	8 Mango Hill Dv	Childers	07 4126 1311	
Condamine	Nelgai Farm B&B	Redmarley Rd	Condamine	07 4627 7124	
Daintree	Daintree Escape	17 Stewart St	Daintree	07 4098 6021	
Daintree	Daintree Valley Haven	Stewart Creek Rd	Daintree	07 4098 6206	
Daintree	Red Mill House	11 Stewart St	Daintree	07 4098 6233	
Daintree	Riverhome Cottages	c/- Post Office	Daintree	07 4098 6225	
Daintree - Cow Bay	**Cow Bay Homestay**	**160 Wattle Cl**	**Cow Bay**	**07 4098 9151**	*Page 144*
Dayboro	Dayboro Cottages	3229 Mt Mee Rd	Dayboro	07 3425 2774	
Dayboro	Kirnicama Elegant Escps	106 Woodward Rd	Dayboro	07 3425 2526	
Doonan	Kingfishers Manor	24 Kimberley Court	Doonan	07 5449 1600	
Eerwah Vale	Musavale Lodge Lux B&B	55 Musavale Rd	Eerwah Vale	07 5442 8678	
Fordsdale	Fordsdale Farmstay	171 Wagners Rd	Fordsdale	07 5462 6844	
Fraser Coast	Sealandings B&B	7 Sanctuary Place	Big Tuan	07 4129 8583	
Gladstone	Auckland Hill B&B	15 Yaroon St	Gladstone	07 4972 4907	
Gold Coast - Mermaid Bch	Mermaid Beachside B&B	115 Seagull Ave	Mermaid Beach	07 5572 9530	
Gold Coast Hntlnd - Nerang	**Riviera B&B**	**53 Evanita Dv**	**Gilston**	**07 5533 2499**	*Page 145*
Gold Coast Hntlnd - Nerang	**Rumbalara B&B**	**72 Hoop Pine Court**	**Advancetown**	**07 5533 2211**	*Page 145*
Gordonvale	Cairns Gateway B&B Cott	8 Briggs Cl	Gordonvale	07 4056 5739	
Grasstree Bch	Grasstree Beach B&B	Lot 3 20 Wrights Rd	Grasstree Beach	07 4956 6428	
Gympie - Amamoor	Amamoor Homestead	254 Kandanga/Amamoor Rd	Amamoor	07 5484 3760	
Gympie - Amamoor	Amamoor Lodge B&B	368 Kandanga-Amamoor Rd	Amamoor	07 5484 3500	
Hazeldean	Kilcoy Farmstay	3931 Esk-Kilcoy Rd	Hazeldean	07 5497 2488	
Hervey Bay	**Alexander Lakeside B&B**	**29 Lido Pde**	**Hervey Bay**	**07 4128 9448**	*Page 147*
Hervey Bay	**The Chamomile B&B**	**65A Miller St**	**Urangan**	**07 4125 1602**	*Page 146*
Hervey Bay - Howard	**Montrave House B&B Home & Pet Stay**	**20 Pacific Haven Dv**	**Howard**	**07 4129 0183**	*Page 147*
Kalbar	Wiss House B&B	7 Ann St	Kalbar	07 5463 9030	
Kilcoy	Kilcoy Upper Sandy Ck B&B	82 Cedarvale Rd	Kilcoy	07 5498 1285	
Kilcoy	Millawa Country Retreat	1501 Mt. Kilcoy Rd	Kilcoy	07 5498 1110	
Killarney	Oaklea B&B	1966 Condamine River Rd	Killarney	07 4664 7161	
Kingaroy	Minmore Farmstay B&B	583 Minmore Rd	Kingaroy	07 4164 3196	
Kingaroy	**Rock-Al-Roy B&B**	**15 Kearney St**	**Kingaroy**	**07 4162 3061**	*Page 148*
Koreelah	Kumbee Homestead	New Koreelah Rd	Koreelah	07 4666 5159	

Tell hosts you found them in the Bed & Breakfast Book

Queensland

Lake Eacham	Crater Lakes R'frst Cotts	Lot 1 Eacham Cl	Lake Eacham	07 4095 2322	
Lamb Is	Lamb Island B&B	143 Lucas Dv	Lamb Island	07 3409 4575	
Macleay Is	The Boathouse B&B	39 Attunga St	Macleay Island	07 3409 4838	
Malanda	Misty Manor B&B	15 Millaa Millaa Rd	Malanda	07 40966017	
Malanda - Lake Eacham	Rose Gums W'ness Rtrt	Land Rd	Lake Eacham	07 4096 8360	
Mareeba	Jabiru Safari Camp	Pickford Rd	Biboohra	1800 788 755	
Maryborough	**Eco Queenslander**	**15 Treasure St**	**Maryborough**	**0438 195 443**	*Page 149*
Millaa Millaa	The Long Yard	193 Malanda Rd	Millaa Millaa	07 4097 2349	
Mirriwinni	Bartle Frere B&B	1 Josphine Falls Rd	Mirriwinni	07 4067 6778	
Mission Bch	Hibiscus Lodge	5 Kurrajong Cl	Mission Beach	07 4068 9096	
Moogerah	Zengarra Country House	2225 Lake Moogerah Rd	Moogerah	07 5463 5600	
Mossman	Julatten Birdlovers Cott	1744 Rex Hwy	Julatten	07 4094 1098	
Mossman	Mossman Fantail B&B	151 Ponzo Rd	Mossman	07 4098 4997	
Mossman	Mossman Gorge B&B	Lot 15 Gorge View Cres	Mossman	07 4098 2497	
Mossman	Papillon	36 Coral Sea Dv	Mossman	07 4098 2760	
Mossman - Lower Cassowary	Treehouse B&B	Warners Rd	Mossman	07 4098 4150	
Mossman - Newell Bch	Manta Ray B&B	23 Coulthard Cl	Newell Beach	07 4098 1261	
Mossman - Newell Bch	Sea Change B&B	130 Marine Pde	Newell Beach	07 4098 2790	
Mt Molloy	Bower Bird B&B	12 Vains Cl	Mt Molloy	07 4094 1100	
Mt Barney	Lillydale Host Farm	821 Upper Logan Rd	Mt Barney	07 5544 3131	
Noosa - Lake Weyba	**Eumarella Shores Lake Retreat**	**251 Eumarella Rd**	**Lake Weyba**	**07 5449 1738**	*Page 150*
Noosa - Noosa Vly	Noosa Country House B&B	93 Duke Rd	Doonan	07 5471 0121	
Noosa - Noosa Vly	**Noosa Valley Manor Luxury B&B**	**115 Wust Rd**	**Doonan**	**07 5471 0088**	*Page 151*
Noosa - Peregian	**Lake Weyba Cottages**	**79 Clarendon Rd**	**Peregian Beach**	**07 5448 2285**	*Page 151*
Noosa Hntlnd - Cooroy	**Cudgerie Homestead B&B**	**42 Cudgerie Dv**	**Cooroy**	**07 5442 6681**	*Page 152*
Oakey	Moorlands Farmstay	Oakey-Cooyar Rd	Oakey	07 4692 8215	
Ocean View	Brockhurst Cabins Farmstay	2250 Mt Mee Rd	Ocean View	07 3425 3314	
Pt Douglas	Paradise Villa	63 Reef St	Port Douglas	07 4099 3604	
Pt Douglas	Port Douglas B&B	59 Reef St	Port Douglas	07 4099 3324	
Pt Douglas - Oak Bch	Mountain View Lodge	Lot 9 Reynolds Rd	Oak Beach	07 4098 5449	
Pt Douglas - Shannonvale	Marae	Lot 1 Ponzo Rd	Shannonvale	07 4098 4900	
Ravenshoe	Chilverton Cottages	12028 Kennedy Hwy	Ravenshoe	07 4097 6785	
Ravenshoe	The Pond Cottage B&B	844 Tully Falls Rd	Ravenshoe	07 4097 7189	
Ravenshoe - Evelyn Central	Possum Valley R'fst Cotts	Kennedy Hwy	Evelyn Central Via Ravenshoe	07 4097 8177	
Redlynch	Jungara B&B	20-22 Robb Rd	Redlynch	07 4039 1892	
Rockhampton	Athelstane House	165 Caroline St	Rockhampton	07 4922 3873	
Rockhampton	Goldston House	230 George St	Rockhampton	07 4921 4186	
Rockhampton - The Range	**Hazel Cottage**	**13 Kennedy St**	**Rockhampton**	**07 4927 4984**	*Page 152*
Roma	Telco Farm Holidays	Telco	Roma	07 4623 3791	
Scarborough	Pearl of the Bay	80 Oyster Point Esp	Scarborough	07 3203 4000	
Scarborough	Reid's Place & Camelia Cotts	377 Scarborough Rd	Scarborough	07 3203 5686	
Springbrook	Hardy House	15A Old School Rd	Springbrook	07 5533 5402	
Springbrook	The Sanctuary at Springbrook	2311A Springbrook Rd	Springbrook	07 5533 5118	
Stanthorpe	**Honeysuckle Cottages & The Rocks Restaurant**	**15 Mayfair Ln**	**Stanthorpe**	**07 4681 1510**	*Page 154*
Stanthorpe	**Jireh**	**89 Donges Rd**	**Severnlea**	**07 4683 5298**	*Page 153*
S'shn Coast - Caloundra	Currimundi Lakeside B&B	1 Rosea Court	Caloundra	07 5493 9123	
S'shn Coast - Coolum	Mount Coolum Retreat B&B	77 Mountain View Dv	Mt Coolum	07 5471 6532	
S'shn Coast - Coolum	The Dome House	15 Regent Court	Mt Coolum	07 5471 6543	

Queensland

S'shn Coast - Eumundi	Jacaranda Creek Farmstay B&B	63-73 Eumudi Range Rd	Eumundi	07 5442 7037	
S'shn Coast - Flaxton	The Tearmon Retreat	23 Old Mill Ln	Flaxton	07 5478 6282	
S'shn Coast - Ninderry	**Ninderry House**	**8 Karnu Dv**	**Ninderry**	**07 5446 8556**	**Page 154**
S'shn Coast - Ninderry	Ninderry Manor Luxury B&B	12 Karnu Dv	Ninderry	07 5472 7255	
S'shn Coast Hntlnd - Coochin Creek	Coochin Lodge	1709 Roys Rd	Coochin Creek	07 5494 6529	
S'shn Coast Hntlnd - Eudlo	Alaya Escape	1 Upper Rambert Rd	Eudlo	07 5457 3663	
S'shn Coast Hntlnd - Glasshouse Mnts	Glass on Glasshouse	182 Glasshouse-Woodford Rd	Glasshouse Mnts	07 5496 9608	
S'shn Coast Hntlnd - Glasshouse Mnts	Glasshouse Mountains Farm	31 Orchard Dv	Glasshouse Mnts	07 5496 9474	
S'shn Coast Hntlnd - Maleny	Bendles	937 Montville Rd	Maleny	07 5494 2400	
S'shn Coast Hntlnd - Maleny	Braeside B&B	305 Maleny Stanley River Rd	Maleny	07 5494 3542	
S'shn Coast Hntlnd - Maleny	**Lillypilly's Country Cottages**	**584 Maleny-Montville Rd**	**Maleny**	**07 5494 3002**	**Page 155**
S'shn Coast Hntlnd - Maleny	**Maleny Country Cottages**	**347 Corks Pocket Rd**	**Reesville**	**07 5494 2744**	**Page 155**
S'shn Coast Hntlnd - Maleny	Maleny Hideaway	130 Maleny-Kenilworth Rd	Maleny	07 5499 9520	
S'shn Coast Hntlnd - Maleny	Maleny Lodge GH	58 Maple St	Maleny	07 5494 2370	
S'shn Coast Hntlnd - Maleny	Maleny Tropical Retreat	540 Maleny-Montville Rd	Maleny	07 5435 2113	
S'shn Coast Hntlnd - Maleny	Wattle Gully Retreat	158 Ansell Rd	Witta	07 5494 4426	
S'shn Coast Hntlnd - Maleny	Wittacork Dairy Cottages	286 Tesch Rd	Maleny	07 5494 4369	
S'shn Coast Hntlnd - Montville	Avocado Grove B&B	10 Carramar Court	Flaxton	07 5445 7585	
S'shn Coast Hntlnd - Montville	**Secrets on the Lake**	**207 Narrows Rd**	**Montville**	**07 5478 5888**	**Page 156**
S'shn Coast Hntlnd - Montville	The Falls B&B & Cottages	20 Kondilla Rd	Montville	07 5445 7000	
S'shn Coast Hntlnd - Montville	The Narrows Escape	78 Narrows Rd	Montville	07 5478 5000	
S'shn Coast Hntlnd - Montville	The Spotted Chook	176-186 Western Ave	Montville	07 5442 9242	
S'shn Coast Hntlnd - Mooloolah Vly	**Mooloolah Valley Holidays**	**93 King Rd**	**Mooloolah Valley**	**07 5494 7109**	**Page 156**
S'shn Coast Hntlnd - Mooloolah Vly	Poppies B&B	16 Nicolle Court	Mooloolah	07 5494 7877	
S'shn Coast Hntlnd - Peachester	Candle Mountain Farmstay	179 Crohamhurst Rd	Peachester	07 5494 9598	
S'shn Coast Hntlnd - Woombye	Cedar Grove Cottages	80 Old Palmwoods Rd	Woombye	07 5442 3372	
Tamborine Mtn	Cedar Creek Lodges	Tambrine Mountain Rd	Tamborine Mnt	07 5545 1468	
Thangool	On Kariboe	1 Parkers Ln	Thangool	07 4995 8269	
Thorneside	Kirribilli Manor	37/247 Mooroondu Rd	Thorneside	07 3822 9311	
Toowoomba	Beccles on Margaret B&B	25 Margaret St	Toowoomba	07 4638 5254	
Toowoomba	Jacaranda Grove B&B	92 Tourist Rd	Toowoomba	07 4635 8394	
Toowoomba	Lauriston House B&B	67 Margaret St	Toowoomba	07 4632 4053	
Toowoomba	Oakleigh Country Cott	19 Bowtell Dv	Toowoomba	07 4696 7021	
Toowoomba	Sugarloaf Mountain Rtrt	36 Mount Rascal Rd	Toowoomba	07 4630 1109	
Tully - Djarawong	Djarawong Lodge B&B	717 Old Tully Rd	Tully	07 4068 6255	
Warrill View	Scenic Rim View Cotts	357 Old Rosevale Rd	Warrill View	07 5464 6508	
Warwick	Golden Rain B&B	400 Lyndhurst Ln	Warwick	07 4661 7504	
Welcome Creek	Coopers Couples Rtrt	850 Gooburrum Rd	Welcome Creek	07 4159 8805	
Woodgate	R & R @ Woodgate Bch	7 Snapper Court	Woodgate	07 4126 8767	
Woolooga	Staple House	3541 Bauple-Woolooga Rd	Woolooga	07 5484 7146	
Wynnum	Waterfront Escape	193 Wynnum Esp	Wynnum	07 3393 6802	
Yeppoon	**While Away B&B**	**44 Todd Ave**	**Yeppoon**	**07 4939 5719**	**Page 157**
Yungaburra	Breamber by the Lake	81 Kulara Rd	Yungaburra	07 4095 2299	
Yungaburra	Mt Quincan Crater Retreat	Peeramon Rd	Yungaburra	07 4095 2255	
Yungaburra	Calm Water Landing B&B	8 Oleander Dv	Yungaburra	07 4095 2666	

South Australia

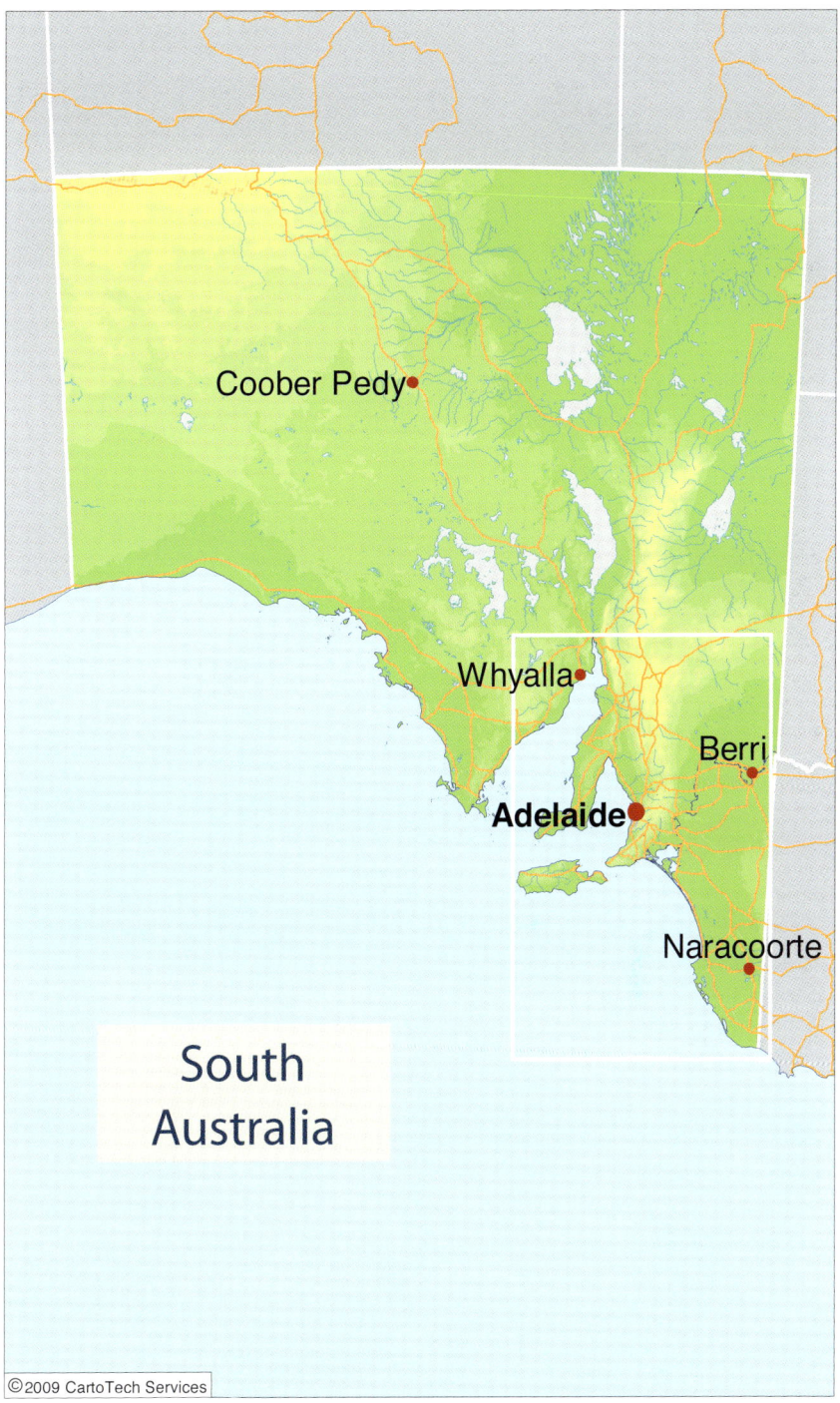

South Australia

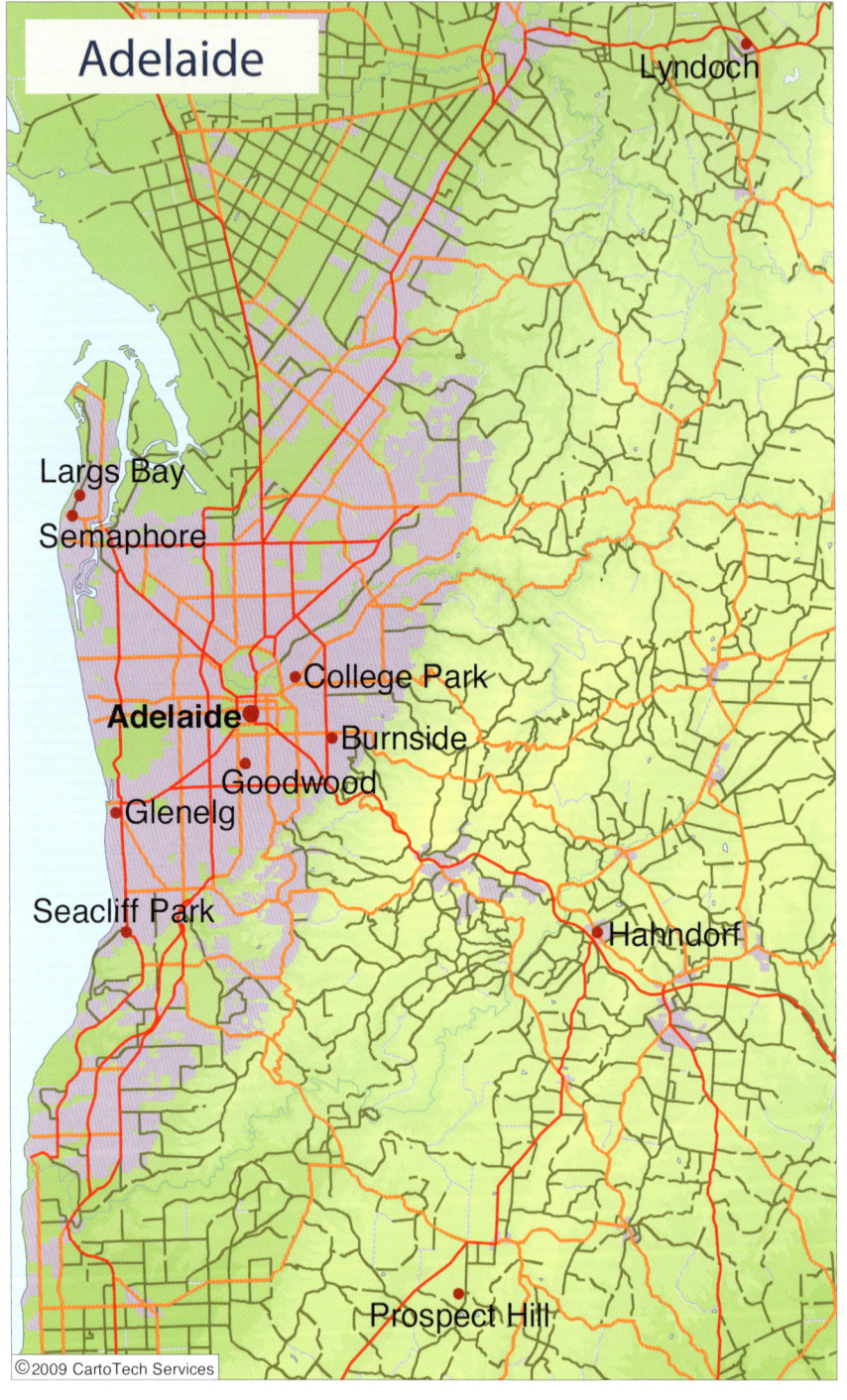

Bed & Breakfast, Farmstay and Accommodation Australia

Australia-Wide Accommodation Gift Vouchers

From the tropical north to the temperate south, in the cities, country, beaches or the bush BBFAA Accommodation Gift Vouchers are the key to a unique accommodation experience.

Great for Personal Gifts - Engagements, Weddings, Birthdays, Thank You, Christmas, Valentine's Day, Mother's Day, Father's Day, whatever the occasion BBFAA Vouchers are the perfect gift.

Versatile for Corporate Gifts - Retirements, Team Incentives, Client Gifts, Staff Bonuses. Tangible gifts, always appreciated.

Ideal for short breaks, romantic getaways and special occasions, travelling with pets, family stays and group reunions. Voucher holders choose where to stay and when to go. The vouchers are valid for twelve months.

Over 900 unique places to stay throughout Australia featured in the Australian Bed & Breakfast Book and on the BBFAA website.

Purchase your accommodation gift vouchers online
www.australianbedandbreakfast.com.au

or call the BBFAA Gift Voucher Hotline
1300 664 707 (Australia only)

South Australia

Adelaide - Burnside - St Georges
Kirkendale

B&B & Self Contained Apartment
Jenny & Steve Studer
16 Inverness Avenue
St. Georges
SA 5064
5 km SE of Adelaide

Tel 0413 414 140 or (08) 8338 2768
kirkendale@ozemail.com.au
www.kirkendale.com.au

Double $135-$155
Single $125-$135, Children $30-$40
Continental provisions
Not suitable for children under 10 years
Visa MC accepted
1 Queen 2 Twin (2 bdrm)
Bathrooms: 1 Private

Idyllic "Country-style" 3 room apartment, nestled in peaceful, leafy garden, sun-dappled patio, French doors, terracotta floors, rose garden. Hint of the Provence. Fresh flowers, fruit basket, generous breakfast provisions, books, tourist information. Separate entrance, private bathroom, living room, kitchenette, sole occupancy. Quiet location. 5km city, near restaurants, wineries, wildlife parks. Jenny and Steve are extremely well travelled, this is reflected by their gracious but unobtrusive hosting. Smoking outdoors. "We loved our accommodation - our best yet in 6 weeks of travel," SS & DC, USA.

Adelaide - College Park
Possums Rest B&B

Separate Suite
Sue & Phil Ogden
8 Catherine Street
College Park
SA 5069
2 km NE of Adelaide CBD

Tel (08) 8362 5356 or 0412 092 881
Fax (08) 8362 5356
possumsrest@gmail.com
www.possumsrestbedandbreakfast.com.au

Double $135
Single $125
Special breakfast
2 night minimum stay
1 Queen (1 bdrm)
Bathrooms: 1 Ensuite

Possums Rest Bed & Breakfast is ideally located in the leafy heritage area of Adelaide. Accommodation is quiet and luxurious, yet only 2 km from the CBD. within walking distance of Adelaide events such as WOMAD, Clipsal 500, Fringe Festival and Festival of Arts. Walk to the Adelaide Zoo, Museum, Art Galleries and numerous shopping and restaurant precincts. Guests are welcome to enjoy the pleasant garden and inground swimming pool in summer. Home cooked breakfasts cater for special dietary requirements. Comfortable fully air conditioned accommodation, has wireless internet connection, television, DVD and cooking facilities. Laundry facilities are available.

BBBook.com.au

South Australia
Adelaide - Glenelg
Water Bay Villa B&B

Luxury B&B - Self Contained Suite
Kathy & Roger Kuchel
28 Broadway
Glenelg South
SA 5045
11 km SW of Adelaide

Tel 0412 221 724
glenelg@waterbayvilla-bnb.com.au
www.waterbayvilla-bnb.com.au

Double $245-$285
Single $200
Children $20-$45
Full breakfast provisions
Visa MC Diners Amex accepted
2 Queen 2 Single (2 bdrm)
Bathrooms: 1 Ensuite

Indulge! Experience the luxury of this historic 1910 Queen Anne Villa in seaside Glenelg. 'The Attic' - your upstairs 4 room suite with private entry and off street parking. Welcoming bottle of wine, fresh flowers, fruit and chocolates. Antiques, open fire, claw foot bath and laundry. Kitchenette with cooking facilities. Living area with tourist info, TV, DVD and video player, CD/Radio. A few minutes stroll via the award winning garden to the nearby beach, Jetty Road, trams, restaurants, cinema, 7-day shopping, summer markets, The Beachouse fun park and marina. Close to airport and public transport. Come and enjoy!"A little piece of heaven." HF, Canada.

Adelaide - Goodwood
Rose Villa

Luxury B&B Homestay
Doreen Petherick
29 Albert Street
Goodwood
SA 5034
2 km S of Adelaide

Tel (08) 8271 2947
Fax (08) 8271 2947
doreen@rosevilla.com.au
www.rosevilla.com.au

Double $125-$145
Single $100-$125, Children $10
Continental breakfast
Cooked breakfast available on request
1 King 1 Queen (2 bdrm)
Bathrooms: 1 Ensuite 1 Guest share

Treat yourself to a romantic candle lit breakfast in my newly decorated Tea Rose salon. Rose Villa offers an elegant private suite (own entrance) overlooking the garden. Inside is an additional guest room with the use of the exquisite Blue-White-Russian Tea Cup bathroom. Stroll to trendy Hyde Park Road with its delightful cafes and coffee shops, boutiques and flower shops. Close by are buses and trams (to the Bay) and city and The Ghan Terminal. Free wireless internet. "Rose Villa" is roses, romance and caring hospitality. You are most welcome. "A romantic and warm place to be. Great hospitality." Erwin Zwijnenburg, The Hague, Holland.

South Australia

Adelaide - Largs Bay
Seapod B&B

B&B & Separate Suite
Bernadette McDonnell
146 Esplanade
Largs Bay
SA 5016
18 km NW of Adelaide

Tel (08) 8449 4213 or 0418 851 680
info@seapod.com.au
www.seapod.com.au

Double $180-$210
Single $150-$180, Children $50
Full breakfast
Visa MC Diners Amex Eftpos JCB accepted
1 Queen (1 bdrm)
Bathrooms: 1 Private

   AAA Tourism ★★★★

Seapod is wonderful beachfront bed & breakfast accommodation with great views and within walking distance of shops, restaurants, cafes, and public transport. Delicious breakfasts served daily in your suite or on the verandah overlooking the sea. Natural, free range and organic produce with unlimited freshly brewed coffee and tea are standard. See dolphins and magnificent sunsets from your table, go for a run on the track across the road, walk along the jetties, swim with the dolphins, or stroll along the beach for miles.

Adelaide - Seacliff Park - Brighton
Homestay Brighton

B&B & Homestay
Ruth & Tim
PO Box 319
Brighton
SA 5048
2 km S of Brighton

Tel (08) 8298 6671 or 0417 800 755
Fax (08) 8298 6671
timbb@hotmail.com
www.bbbook.com.au/brighton.html

Double $65-$80
Single $45-$60
Full breakfast
1 Double 2 Single (2 bdrm)
Bathrooms: 1 Guest share 1 Private

Spacious home and grounds in quiet suburb close to Brighton/Seacliff beach. Public transport to the city and nearby large Westfield Shopping Centre. Ideal for day trips to the Fleurieu Peninsula with its picturesque wine areas and southern vales and coast. Guest rooms are upstairs including a television lounge with heating and cooling. Laundry and off-street parking are available. Sascha, our friendly Border Collie dog, stays outside the house "Great value in a relaxing suburb of Adelaide. Outstanding host, helpful, supportive and friendly." J&GB, UK. "Home from Home." LJ, UK.

South Australia

Adelaide - Semaphore
Time and Tide Beach Apartment

Self Contained Apartment
Lindy Revill
8 Newman Street
Semaphore
SA 5019
12 km NW of Adelaide CBD

Tel (08) 8449 7102 or 0438 872 510
timeandtidebeachapartment@gmail.com
www.timeandtidebeachapartment.com.au

Double $180-$200
Breakfast by arrangement
Visa MC accepted
1 King/Twin (1 bdrm)
Bathrooms: 1 Ensuite

With panoramic views of the Semaphore coastline, this modern private self-contained one-bedroom apartment will provide you with peace and tranquillity. There is wheelchair access including to the shower. Walking trails, swimming (a picnic pack is available), shopping and restaurants are all at your doorstep. Return to Time and Tide and relax in the elegantly appointed living area, and watch the sun set with your favourite drink. The perfect place for some relationship maintenance, a quiet business trip or your own place to stay while you visit relatives. Time and Tide waits for you.

Adelaide Hills - Hahndorf
Amble at Hahndorf

B&B & Self Contained Cottage
Di & Roger
10 Hereford Avenue
Hahndorf
SA 5245
In Hahndorf

Tel (08) 8388 1467
Fax (08) 8388 1267
bookings@amble-at-hahndorf.com.au
www.amble-at-hahndorf.com.au

Double $170-$190
Single $170-$190, Full breakfast provisions
Visa MC accepted
4 Queen (4 bdrm)
Bathrooms: 3 Ensuite

AAA Tourism ★★★★

Amble at Hahndorf Bed and Breakfast is just 150m from Hahndorf's Main Street and only 25km east of Adelaide CBD. Nestled in the Adelaide Hills region of South Australia, Amble at Hahndorf Bed and Breakfast is perfectly located for an enjoyable and peaceful escape. Set in lovely gardens, it offers tranquillity, romance and seclusion. This beautiful Hahndorf accommodation is offered in either 'Amble Wren', 'Amble Fern' or 'Amble Over'. 'Amble at Hahndorf is life at your own pace'..

South Australia

Adelaide Hills - Mt Pleasant
Saunders Gorge Sanctuary

Self contained family cottage & Six buildings for couples
Brenton & Nadene Newman
Mt Pleasant
SA 5237
18 km E of Mt Pleasant

Tel (08) 8569 3032
nature@saundersgorge.com.au
www.saundersgorge.com.au

Double $120-$180
Single $100-$150, Family cottage sutable for children $10 per night, Continental provisions, Restaurant availabile on the property, Family Cottage $20 per extra adult per night sleeps 6 Visa MC accepted. 4 King 3 Queen 2 Single (7 bdrm). Bathrooms: 5 Ensuite 1 Guest share

    AAA Tourism

ECO Tourism accredited Saunders Gorge Sanctuary is a private property of 1364 ha on the rugged Eastern slopes of the Mt Lofty Ranges (Adelaide Hills). Offering visitors the opportunity to experience the rugged Australian landscape, learn about and enjoy the natural environment. The property is a combination of conservation and sheep grazing. Relax in self contained accommodation. Experiance the tranquility & beauty of the property. Explore the many scenic walks or drive the 4WD trail. Enjoy an evening meal in the licensed restaurant.

When making an enquiry or booking, please tell your hosts, "We saw you in the Bed & Breakfast Book!"

South Australia

Barossa Valley

The old hills of the Barossa Ranges look down on a colourful patchwork of vineyards and picture book villages whose historic churches, stone buildings and cottages beckon explorers. The Barossa is one of the world's great wine regions, acclaimed for food, wine and a rich European heritage.
Mandy Creed, Bellescapes

Barossa Valley - Lyndoch
Barossa Shiraz Estate

Self Contained B&B Cottages
Alex & Nellie
Lot 292, Barossa Valley Way
Lyndoch, SA 5351
60km N of Adelaide

Tel **(08) 8333 3103** or **0422 030 303**
Fax (08) 8333 3103
bookings@barossashirazestate.com.au
www.barossashirazestate.com.au

Double from $220
Children 0-4 $25 if bedding required; 5-15 $45 pn, Full breakfast provisions, Restaurant bookings, Platters, Tours, Massages can be arranged, Visa MC accepted. 4 cottages, 1-3 bedrooms, each cottage with ensuite/spa and log fire. Bathrooms: 4 Ensuite

Exclusive vineyard stay. Choice of four luxury cottages among the finest in Barossa Valley. Sensational views to vineyards and Barossa ranges, spa baths, log fire, private, historic with contemporary conveniences, modern kitchen facilities, a/c, lounges, TV, DVD and CD players, Internet access, bottle of Estate's wine, full breakfast provisions. The property is in a major tourism precinct close to the township of Lyndoch and is central to several restaurants, wineries, Helicopter Rides, Balloon Adventures, Rose Garden, Lyndoch Lavender Farm, Peter Franz Gallery and other attractions.

South Australia

Barossa Valley - Lyndoch - Tanunda - Angaston
Bellescapes

Self Contained B&B Cottages
Mandy & Mark Creed
PO Box 481
Lyndoch, SA 5351
1 km N of Barossa Valley

Tel **(08) 8524 4825** or **0412 220 553**
Fax (08) 8524 4046 escape@bellescapes.com
www.bellescapes.com

Double $150-$250
Single $140-$250, Children welcome in properties with more than one bedroom, Full breakfast provisions, Dinner Platters and BBQ packs can be arranged, Tours can be arranged, Visa MC accepted
14 properties, ranging from 1 to 3 bedrooms
Each property has its own bathroom facilities

Bellescapes properties are exclusively yours, private & self contained, properties can accommodate between 2-12 guests. Indulge in one of our stunning B&B's designed to spoil, all located within the beautiful Barossa Valley. Choose from either heritage or contemporary properties, 10 with spa and 10 with cosy log fires. Your choice between vineyard views, the townships of Angaston, Lyndoch, Tanunda or getaway from it all in the Barossa foothills of Eden Valley. We pride ourselves on providing quality service and accommodation with a very personalised touch.

You can find great getaways in wine regions. Some offer wine activities. Look for The Wine Activities Logo

South Australia
Berri

Berri is a beautiful river town on the banks of The River Murray. It is a centre for fruit growing as well as home to the huge Berri winery - the largest in Australia.
Kerin Vallelonga, Ohanez Holiday House

Berri
Ohanez Holiday House

Holiday House
Kerin Vallelonga
1 Ohanez Street
Berri
SA 5343
In Berri

Tel (08) 8584 1357 or 0428 116 577
ohanezholidayhouse@bigpond.com
www.ohanezholidayhouse.com.au

Double $135
Children Under 2 yrs free
2-12 yrs $25
Accommodation only
$30 per extra adult
2 Queen 1 Twin 2 Single (4 bdrm)
Bathrooms: 1 Private

Ohanez Holiday House is a beautifully presented self contained 4 bedroom home accommodating up to 8 people with modern conveniences: ducted air conditioning and heating, kitchen, laundry, sunroom, TV/DVD and all linen and towels. You have a fully enclosed yard for privacy with large outdoor entertainment area, lockup parking and room for boats. Conveniently located within the township of Berri in the heart of the Riverland of South Australia, it is the perfect place to discover the region. A short walk to shops and restaurants Ohanez offers accommodation for business trips, family holidays or just a weekend away.

South Australia

Kangaroo Island

Kangaroo Island is blessed with a temperate 'Mediterranean' climate with warm dry summers and cool mild winters. Renowned for its spectacular scenery and abundant and diverse variety of wildlife and flora. The spectacular South Coast has incredible rock formations, whilst the calmer north coast has rolling hills, secluded bays and beautiful beaches.

Kangaroo Island - Emu Bay
Seascape Lodge on Emu Bay

Luxury B&B & Small Luxury Lodge
Mandy and Paul Brown
Bates Road, Emu Bay
Kangaroo Island
SA 5223
1 km N of Emu Bay

Tel (08) 8559 5033
Fax 08 8559 5088   info@seascapelodge.com.au
www.seascapelodge.com.au

Double $432-$592
Single $327-$407, For child rates please contact us for a quote, Full breakfast, Dinner 3 course set menu using local produce, quality local wines, Luxury 4WD island tours available, Visa MC Eftpos accepted. 2 King/Twin 3 King (3 bdrm). Bathrooms: 3 Private

Explore Australia's premier wildlife destination on one of our exclusive 4WD tours. Our hosted dinner, bed and breakfast property provides an intimate, homely experience whilst Enjoying stunning beach, sea and rural views from every room in the house. Sit back on the open deck in summer, nestle up against the fire in winter or simply relax with a wine in the privacy of your room and soak up the quiet tranquillity. This together with Mandy's elegant home-style cooking will make for a memorable experience.

BBBook.com.au

South Australia

Mount Gambier

Crater Lakes Complex including the Unique Blue Lake. Background: The City of Mount Gambier which has formed on the slopes of the volcanic craters.
Mae Steele, City of Mount Gambier

Mt Gambier
Metro on Alexander

Self Contained Townhouse
Deborah Kirkup
Unit 1/ 33A Alexander Street
Mount Gambier
SA 5290
In Mt Gambier

Tel (08) 8723 9617 or 0407 384 087
deborah@metroonalexander.com.au
www.metroonalexander.com.au

Double $130-$150
Single $110-$130
Children Contact us for details
Full breakfast provisions, Visa MC accepted
3 Queen (3 bdrm)
Bathrooms: 1 Ensuite 1 Guest share

AAA Tourism
★★★★☆

Metro on Alexander is an award winning, self contained, contemporary style inner city townhouse with all the privacy and convenience of home. It is ideal for business or pleasure. Featuring 3 bedrooms with ensuite, walk-in robe and LCD TV in the master bedroom. Separate office with free wireless broadband. Spacious lounge room with large Sony LCD panel or in-house DVDs. The fully equipped kitchen includes a microwave and dishwasher. Outside there is a barbecue and enclosed courtyard garden. A double remote control garage provides security. At Metro on Alexander, it's the little extras we provide that sets us apart.

Tell hosts you found them in the Bed & Breakfast Book

South Australia

Naracoorte

Naracoorte is central to four renowned wine growing regions - Coonawarra, Wrattonbully, Padthaway and Mt. Benson. Naracoorte Caves National Park is South Australia's only World Heritage Site that preserves a continuous fossil record of the past 500,000 years.
Lynette & John Lauterbach, Willowbrook Cottages B&Bs

Naracoorte
Willowbrook Cottages B&B's

2 Self Contained B&B Cottages
Lynette & John Lauterbach
3 & 3A Jenkins Terrace
Naracoorte
SA 5271
1 km E of Post Office

Tel (08) 8762 0259 or 0419 802 728
stay@willowbrookcottages.com.au
www.willowbrookcottages.com.au

Double $120-$140
Single $90-$100, Children $15 per child
Full breakfast provisions
Visa MC Amex accepted
2 Queen 1 Twin (3 bdrm) per cottage
Bathrooms: 1 Private per cottage

AAA Tourism
★★★★

The allure and charm of bygone years combined with all the modern conveniences expected by today's traveller - that's the brilliant blend of Willowbrook Cottages B&Bs. Centrally located in Naracoorte, within walking distance to shops and eateries, Willowbrook Cottages are the ideal base for exploring the Limestone Coast including World Heritage Fossil site, Coonawarra & Padthaway wine regions.

South Australia
Prospect Hill
Chamel Fields Farmstay

Farmstay Cottage
Judith Hamel
Blackfellows Creek Road
Prospect Hill
SA 5121
45 km SE of Adelaide CBD

Tel (08) 8556 7442
chamel.fields@activ8.net.au
www.chamelfields.com.au

Double $170
Children Under 2yr free, 3-12yr half price
Full breakfast provisions
2 night minimum stay, Extra adult $35
Breakfast $10-$15pp
1 Queen 3 Single (2 bdrm) Plus sofa bed
Bathrooms: 1 Private

Chamel Fields Farmstay, home of 'Adopt a Horse Holiday' offers a quality farm experience in a comfortably and cosily appointed 1930's refurbished cottage. Accommodation includes a large master bedroom with a queen sized bed and a second bedroom with a bunk bed and trundle. The sofa in the lounge room also serves as a double foldaway bed, thus comfortably catering for at least 6. The spacious dining room, kitchen and lounge open out onto a shady sun porch. The cottage is easily warmed with a slow combustion stove. Electric blankets and electric heaters are also provided. Continental or farm breakfast provisions are available.

Strathalbyn - Fleurieu Peninsula
Callistemon Cottage

Stone Cottage
Raelene & Bob Gaffney
Lot 10, Stirling Hill Road
Strathalbyn
SA 5255
8 km NE of Strathalbyn

Tel 0458 294 882
bookings@callistemoncottage.com.au
www.callistemoncottage.com.au

Double $150
Breakfast provisions first night
2 night minimum stay
Rates for longer stays on application
1 Queen 1 Twin (2 bdrm)
Bathrooms: 1 Private

We offer a totally self sufficient holiday experience with superb views of the Coorong and surrounding areas. Callistemon Cottage is situated on 100 acres just 5 minutes from the township of Strathalbyn. This comfortable environmentally friendly, solar powered stone cottage has slate floors and stone walls to keep you cool in summer and warm in winter, slow combustion heating for winter warmth and country kitchen cooking - with gas! Digital TV, DVD/CD player. Fully paved entertaining area and barbecue. Native wildlife frequents the cottage environment. Centrally located for Adelaide Hills, McLaren Vale, Currency Creek and Langhorne Creek wineries.

South Australia

Victor Harbor
Encounter Hideaway Cottages

2 Self Contained Cottages
Jill Fairchild
26 Giles Street
Encounter Bay
SA 5211
4 km S of Victor Harbor

Tel (08) 8552 7270 or 0409 527 270
Fax (08) 8552 8386
jill@encounterhideaway.com
www.encounterhideaway.com

Double $160 Single $100
Children $10 per child, Full breakfast provisions
$50 per extra person per night
Visa MC accepted
1 Queen 2 Single (2 bdrm)
Bathrooms: 1 Private Bathroom includes spa

Encounter Hideaway has two self-contained cottages. Ruby and Bud Cottages are situated just one street back from the sea in the historic part of Encounter Bay, only five minutes drive from the centre of Victor Harbor. Set in a charming garden, each cottage has a queen-size bed in the main bedroom, plus twin beds (Ruby) or double bed (Bud) in the second bedroom, a sparkling bathroom with a large spa, a well equipped kitchen with generous provisions for a cooked breakfast, a comfortable living room with A/C, TV, VCR, CD player, flowers, port and fresh fruit.

Whyalla
B&B on the Beach

Self Contained Cottage
Petrah Kirby Bastians
6 Neagle Terrace
Whyalla
SA 5600
In Whyalla

Tel 0428 262 326
Fax (08) 8127 8070
Bookings@BandBontheBeach.com.au
www.bandbonthebeach.com.au

Double $130-$200
Continental breakfast, Full breakfast provisions available for small additional charge
Please request rates for additional persons
Visa MC Diners Amex Eftpos accepted
1 Queen 2 Single (2 bdrm) Bathrooms: 1 Private

AAA Tourism
★★★★

B&B on the Beach is a self contained cottage located just 200 metres from the main Whyalla beach. It has been exclusively renovated with quality fittings, is set in a spacious well maintained garden and is located in a prime but quiet and private location with off street parking. Facilities include, full kitchen with dishwasher, laundry, reverse cycle air-conditioning, television, DVD and large secure outdoor area for children or pets. It is ideal for business, couples, small families and honeymooners. Enjoy the tranquil beach walks, sea views, the Ada Ryan Gardens and restaurants.

Bed & Breakfast, Farmstay and Accommodation Australia

No matter what time of year you visit South Australia there are many diverse experiences just waiting to be discovered. Explore Adelaide, the festival capital of Australia. Enjoy the relaxed lifestyle and mild Mediterranean climate, the stunning landscapes of the Flinders Ranges, the Outback and magnificent coastlines. Delight in spectacular natural wildlife attractions, exciting international events, regional festivals, arts, music and food. Experience Australia's finest wines from the Clare Valley, Barossa, McLaren Vale, Coonawarra and beyond.

BBFAA accommodation is ideal for short breaks, romantic getaways and special occasions, travelling with your pet, family stays, and family and group reunions.

Enjoy a warm welcome and true hospitality when you stay with a BBFAA member. BBFAA brings you high quality places to stay throughout Australia that are as individual as you.

www.australianbedandbreakfast.com.au
1300 664 707

South Australia

Recommended Accommodation - South Australia

Properties included below with a page reference are included in this chapter and with further details. We have also included recommended accommodation with information supplied by BBFAA. Contact the hosts by telephone number for further details and tell them, *"We found you in The B&B Book."*

Adelaide	Adelaide Old Terraces	26 Blackburn St	Adelaide	08 8364 5437	
Adelaide - Burnside	Kirkendale	16 Inverness Ave	St Georges	0413 414 140	Page 167
Adelaide - Burnside	Petts Wood Lodge	542 Glynburn Rd	Burnside	08 8331 9924	
Adelaide - College Park	Possums Rest B&B	8 Catherine St	College Park	08 8362 5356	Page 167
Adelaide - Craigburn Ridge	Kingfisher House B&B	58 Kingfisher Circuit	Craigburn Ridge	08 8358 6397	
Adelaide - Glenelg	Water Bay Villa B&B	28 BRdway	Glenelg South	0412 221 724	Page 168
Adelaide - Goodwood	Rose Villa	29 Albert St	Goodwood	08 8271 2947	Page 168
Adelaide - Hackney	Athelney Cottage	7 Athelney Ave	Hackney	08 8132 0069	
Adelaide - Largs Bay	Seapod B&B	146 Esp	Largs Bay	08 8449 4213	Page 169
Adelaide - Nth Adelaide	North Adelaide Heritage	109 Glen Osmond Rd	Eastwood	08 8272 1355	
Adelaide - Norwood	Norwood B&B	6 Rosemount St	Norwood	08 8431 7097	
Adelaide - Seacliff Park	Homestay Brighton	PO Box 319	Brighton	08 8298 6671	Page 169
Adelaide - Semaphore	Time And Tide Beach Apartment	8 Newman St	Semaphore	08 8449 7102	Page 170
Adelaide Hills - Aldgate	Aldgate Creek Cottage	3 Rugby Rd	Aldgate	08 8339 1987	
Adelaide Hills - Aldgate	Aldgate Lodge	27 Strathalbyn Rd	Aldgate	08 8370 9957	
Adelaide Hills - Aldgate	Aldgate Ridge Vineyard B&B	23 Nation Ridge Rd	Aldgate	08 8388 5225	
Adelaide Hills - Aldgate	Chippings Cottage B&B	32 Ludgate Hill Rd	Aldgate	08 8339 1008	
Adelaide Hills - Aldgate	Cladich Pavilions	27-29 Wilpena Terr	Aldgate	08 8339 8248	
Adelaide Hills - Balhannah	Hannah's Cottage	Lot 14 Jones Rd	Balhannah	08 8388 4148	
Adelaide Hills - Basket Range	Bishops Adelaide Hills	Lobethal Rd	Basket Range	08 8390 3469	
Adelaide Hills - Basket Range	Burdetts Country Rtrts	Burdettes Rd	Basket Range	08 8390 0296	
Adelaide Hills - Basket Range	St Githas Garden	12 Rosewarne Cres	Bridgewater	08 8339 1264	
Adelaide Hills - Birdwood	Birdwood B&B	38 Olivedale St	Birdwood	08 8568 5444	
Adelaide Hills - Crafers	Corktree Cottage	34 Piccadilly Rd	Crafers	08 8339 4151	
Adelaide Hills - Gumeracha	Randell's Mill B&B	37 Victoria St	Gumeracha	08 8389 1064	
Adelaide Hills - Hahndorf	Amble At Hahndorf	10 Hereford Ave	Hahndorf	08 8388 1467	Page 170
Adelaide Hills - Hahndorf	Evelyn's B&B	15 Auricht Rd	Hahndorf	08 8188 0181	
Adelaide Hills - Littlehampton	Woodman's Cottage	Lot 202 Junction Rd	Littlehampton	08 8398 3993	
Adelaide Hills - Macclesfield	Mirrabooka	Strathalbyn Rd	Macclesfield	08 8388 9733	
Adelaide Hills - Macclesfield	Popblebonk B&B	Lot 54 Edmonds St	Macclesfield	08 8388 9481	
Adelaide Hills - Macclesfield	Riddlesdown Cottage	72 Vennables St	Macclesfield	08 8388 9213	
Adelaide Hills - Macclesfield	The Stumps B&B	Hilltop Rd	Macclesfield	08 8388 9513	
Adelaide Hills - Meadows	Colancy Gardens	Tynan Rd	Meadows	08 8388 3240	
Adelaide Hills - Meadows	The Old Oak B&B	Bald Hill Rd	Bull Creek	08 8536 6069	
Adelaide Hills - Mt Barker	Dumas House	11 Druids Ave	Mt Barker	0417 814 815	
Adelaide Hills - Mt Barker Springs	Little Undermount	Springs Rd	Mt Barker Springs	08 8391 1031	
Adelaide Hills - Mt Pleasant	Stoneybank Settlement Cotts	Lot 100 Stoneybank Ln	Mt Pleasant	08 8568 2075	
Adelaide Hills - Oakbank	Adelaide Hills Country Cotts	Oakwood Rd	Oakbank	08 8388 4193	
Adelaide Hills - Palmer	Saunders Gorge Sanctuary	Saunders Gorge	Palmer	08 8569 3032	Page 171
Adelaide Hills - Stirling	Castle Keep B&B	2 Glenside Ln	Stirling	08 8339 6748	
Adelaide Hills - Stirling	The Retreat at Stirling	9 Hoylake Ave	Stirling	08 8339 4702	
Adelaide Hills - Summertown	Summertown H'std B&B	4 Cummins Dv	Summertown	08 8390 0497	

South Australia

Adelaide Hills - Tungkillo	Sunnybrook B&B	Mannum Rd	Tungkillo	08 8568 2159
Aldinga Bch	Cockleshell Cottage	10 Boomerang Ave	Aldinga Beach	0409 702 208
Aldinga Bch	Kalabity Jane Holiday Cotts	8 Cox Rd	Aldinga Beach	08 8557 4396
Aldinga Bch	Silver Sands B&B	277 Esp	Aldinga Beach	08 8557 4002
Barossa Vly - Angaston	Angaston Views B&B	8 Collins St	Angaston	08 8564 2144
Barossa Vly - Angaston	Bluebird Cottage	15 Murray St	Angaston	08 8570 8843
Barossa Vly - Angaston	Caithness Manor	12 Hill St West	Angaston	08 8564 2761
Barossa Vly - Angaston	Collingrove Homestead	Eden Valley Rd	Angaston	08 8564 2061
Barossa Vly - Angaston	Country Pleasures B&B	54/56 Penrice Rd	Angaston	08 8564 3477
Barossa Vly - Angaston	Sorby Adams Jellicoe Hse	Saw Pit Gully Rd	Angaston	08 8564 2071
Barossa Vly - Angaston	Wroxton Grange	Flaxman Valley Rd	Angaston	08 8565 3227
Barossa Vly - Cockatoo Vly	Kooringal Homestead	Cnr Yettie Rd & Millington Rd	Cockatoo Valley	08 8524 6196
Barossa Vly - Lyndoch	Barossa Country Cotts B&B	55 Gilbert St	Lyndoch	08 8524 4426
Barossa Vly - Lyndoch	**Barossa Shiraz Estate**	**Lot 292 Barossa Valley Way**	**Lyndoch**	**08 8333 3103** *Page 172*
Barossa Vly - Lyndoch	**Bellescapes**	**PO Box 481**	**Lyndoch**	**08 8524 4825** *Page 173*
Barossa Vly - Maranaga	Treetops	Seppeltsfield Rd	Maranaga	08 8562 2522
Barossa Vly - Nuriootpa	Walnut Cottage	8 French St	Angaston	08 8562 4556
Barossa Vly - Pewsey Vale	Applecroft Cottages	Block 6, Trial Hill Rd	Pewsey Vale	08 8524 4531
Barossa Vly - Seppeltsfield	Seppeltsfield Vineyard Cott	Gerald Roberts Rd	Seppeltsfield	08 8563 4059
Barossa Vly - Seppeltsfield	The Lodge Country House	Seppeltsfield Rd	Seppeltsfield	08 8562 8277
Barossa Vly - Tanunda	Barossa House	Barossa Valley Way	Tanunda	08 8562 4022
Barossa Vly - Tanunda	Miriam's Cottage	22 College St	Tanunda	08 8562 8103
Barossa Vly - Tanunda	Stonewell Cottages	Stonewell Rd	Tanunda	0417 848 877
Barossa Vly - Williamstown	Tungali Cottage	Williamstown to Springton Rd	Williamstown	08 8524 6251
Booleroo Centre	Booleroo View B&B	Gordon Sanders Rd	Booleroo Centre	08 8667 2238
Cape Jervis	Cape Jervis Station	Main Rd	Cape Jervis	1800 805 288
Carrickalinga	Dee's Villa	Cnr Smith Hill Rd & Wattle Flat Rd	Carrickalinga	0409 124324
Carrickalinga	Panorama At Carrickalinga	7 Stacey Dv	Carrickalinga	0405 13 7272
Christies Bch	Christies Seahorse	1 The Esp	Christies Beach	0437 133 500
Clare	Brice Hill Country Lodge	56-66 Warenda Rd	Clare	08 8842 2925
Clare	Bungaree Station	12km N of Clare on Hwy B82	Clare	08 8842 2677
Clare	Clare Manor	Lot 2 Kurrang Ave	Clare	08 8842 1819
Clare	Mundawora Mews	Main North Rd	Clare	08 8842 3762
Clare	The Stationmaster's Res	4 New Rd	Clare	08 82616270
Clare	Wuthering Heights	PO Box 288	Clare	08 8842 3196
Clare Vly - Auburn	Annabelle's Cottage	15 Henry St	Auburn	08 8849 2081
Clare Vly - Auburn	Dennis Cottage	St Vincent St	Auburn	08 8843 0048
Clare Vly - Balaklava	Balaklava B&B	3 Fisher St	Balaklava	N/A
Clare Vly - Burra	Burra Heritage Cotts	8-18 Truro St	Burra	08 8892 2461
Clare Vly - Laura	Talyala Hills Farmstay	PO Box 38	Laura	08 8663 2576
Clare Vly - Leasingham	Ethel's Cottage	Main North Rd	Leasingham	08 8342 0406
Clare Vly - Mintaro	Millers House Mintaro	Young St	Mintaro	08 8271 6601
Clare Vly - Mintaro	Mintaro Country Cotts	Sandow Rd	Mintaro	N/A
Clare Vly - Mintaro	Mintaro Hideaway	41 Copper Ore Rd	Mintaro	08 83901995
Clare Vly - Snowtown	Hummocks Station	Barunga Homestead Rd	Snowtown	0417 084 377
Clare Vly - Watervale	Battunga B&B	Skilly Rd	Watervale	08 88430120
Clare Vly - Watervale	Granma	Main North Rd	Watervale	08 8843 0193
Clare Vly - Watervale	Stanley Grammar C'try Hse	Lot 25 Commercial Rd	Watervale	08 8843 0224

Coober Pedy	Underground B&B	Lot 1647 Potch Gully Rd	Coober Pedy	08 8672 5301	
Coonawarra	Koonara Cottage	Tricia Reschke Rd	Coonawarra	08 8737 3222	
Delamere	Southern Ocean Retreats	Deep Creek Conservation Park	Deep Creek	08 8598 4169	
Goolwa	Rose-Eden House	27 Cadell St	Goolwa	08 8552 2012	
Goolwa	Vue de M B&B	11 Admiral Terr	Goolwa	08 8555 1487	
Inman Vly	Rattleys At Pear Tree Hollow	9 Nosworthy Rd	Inman Valley	08 8558 8234	
Kangarilla	Aunt Amanda's Cottage	Peters Creek Rd	Kangarilla	08 8383 7122	
Kangarilla SA	Mt. Bold Estate	Cnr. Mt. Bold Rd & White Rd	Kangarilla	08 8383 7185	
Kangaroo Is	Cape Cassini W'ness Rtrt	PO Box 609	Cape Cassini	08 8559 2215	
Kangaroo Is	Eleanor River H'std	Gregors Rd	Parndana	08 8559 5234	
Kangaroo Is	Lindsays of Kang Is	Lot 14 Bates Way	Penneshaw	08 8553 1280	
Kangaroo Is	Sea Dragon at Pink Bay	Lot 398 Willoughby Rd	Cape Willoughby	0407 878 668	
Kangaroo Is	**Seascape Lodge on Emu Bay**	**Bates Rd, Emu Bay**	**Kangaroo Island**	**08 8559 5033**	*Page 175*
Maslin Bch	Bott's Beach Retreat	79 Gulf Pde	Maslin Beach	08 8332 2200	
McLaren Flat	Villa Grenache B&B	Lot 29c Kangarilla Rd	McLaren Flat	08 8383 0204	
McLaren Vale	Bellevue B&B	12 Chalk Hill Rd	McLaren Vale	08 8323 7929	
McLaren Vale	Jessica' Place	14 Vine St	McLaren Vale	08 8323 8233	
McLaren Vale	Rosebank Studio	11 Jarred St	McLaren Vale	08 8323 8890	
McLaren Vale	The Flower Fields	73 Main Rd	McLaren Vale	08 8323 8675	
McLaren Vale	The Linear Way B&B	41 Caffrey St	McLaren Vale	08 8323 7328	
Meningie	Dalton On The Lake	30 Narrung Rd	Meningie	N/A	
Meningie	The Cottage No.12 On North	12 North Terr	Meningie	08 8575 1250	
Meningie - Narrung	Poltalloch Station	PMB3	Tailem Bend	08 8574 0043	
Middleton	Middleton Cottage	29 Goolwa Rd	Middleton	08 8554 3743	
Middleton	Wenton Farm Holiday Cottages	Sect 163 Burgar Rd	Middleton	08 8555 4126	
Mt Gambier	Amble In Cottage	7 Davison St	Mt Gambier	0428 254 611	
Mt Gambier	Colhurst House	3 Colhurst Place	Mt Gambier	08 8723 1309	
Mt Gambier	Eliza Cottage	30 Wehl St South	Mt Gambier	0407 422 877	
Mt Gambier	Lemon Gum B&B	Peweena Rd	Mt Gambier	08 8725 0010	
Mt Gambier	Mackenzie's on Jardine	9 Jardine St	Mt Gambier	0409 420 864	
Mt Gambier	**Metro on Alexander**	**1/33A Alexander St**	**Mt Gambier**	**08 8723 9617**	*Page 176*
Mt Gambier	Talbot Hill Farm	RSD 6055 Bay Rd	Mt Gambier	08 87231670	
Mundulla	Mundulla Hosted Accom	Lot 146 Chark Rd	Mundulla	08 8753 4133	
Murraylands - Barmera	Barmera Rose Cott	33 Lake Ave	Barmera	0417 119 689	
Murraylands - Barmera	Berrinbo	PO Box 95	Barmera	0414 882 659	
Murraylands - Berri	**Ohanez Holiday House**	**1 Ohanez St**	**Berri**	**08 8584 1357**	*Page 171*
Murraylands - Loxton	Mill Cottage Loxton	2 Mill Rd	Loxton	0439 866 990	
Murraylands - Lyrup	Pike River Woolshed	Lot 5 Pike Creek Rd	Lyrup	08 8583 8196	
Naracoorte	**Willowbrook Cottages B&B's**	**5 Jenkins Terr**	**Naracoorte**	**08 8762 0259**	*Page 177*
Normanville	Shore Indulgence B&B	2 Marjory St	Normanville	08 85583726	
Normanville	Yankalilla Bay Homestead	39 Jetty Rd	Normanville	08 8558 3223	
Orroroo	Nuccaleena Cottage	Government Rd	Orroroo	08 8648 4861	
Padthaway	Padthaway	Riddoch Hwy	Padthaway	08 8765 5555	
Penola	Georgie's Cottage	1 Riddoch St	Penola	08 87373540	
Pt Elliot	Brooklands Heritage B&B	Heysen Rd	Port Elliot	08 8554 3808	
Pt Elliot	Tarooki B&B	13 Charteris St	Port Elliot	08 8554 2886	
Pt Elliot	Trafalgar House Accom	25 The Strand	Port Elliot	08 8554 3888	
Pt MacDonnell	The Customs House	3 Charles St	Port MacDonnell	0400 251 196	

South Australia

Pt Willunga	Saltaire	4 Marlin Rd	Port Willunga	08 8339 4151	
Prospect Hill	**Chamel Fields Farmstay**	**Blackfellows Creek Rd**	**Prospect Hill**	**08 8556 7442**	*Page 178*
Quorn	Endilloe Lodge B&B	319 Schmidt Rd	Quorn	08 8648 6536	
Robe	Cricklewood Cottage	24 Woolundry Rd	Robe	08 8768 2137	
Robe	Robe House	1A Hagen St	Robe	08 8768 2770	
Robe	Robe Retreats	9 Agnes St	Robe	08 87578224	
Strathalbyn	**Callistemon Cottage**	**Lot 10 Stirling Hill Rd**	**Strathalbyn**	**0458 294 882**	*Page 178*
Strathalbyn	Hamilton House	70 Watson St	Strathalbyn	08 8536 4990	
Tintinara	O'Deas Cottage	Dukes Hwy	Tintinara	08 8575 8023	
Victor Harbor	Close Encounters B&B	69 Whalers Rd	Victor Harbor	08 8552 4850	
Victor Harbor	**Encounter Hideaway Cottages**	**66 Rapid Dv**	**Victor Harbor**	**08 8552 7270**	*Page 179*
Victor Harbor	Encounter House	Franklin Pde	Victor Harbor	N/A	
Victor Harbor	Encounter Lakes B&B	45 Matthew Flinders Dv	Victor Harbor	08 8552 7758	
Victor Harbor	Morgan Park B&B	1 Shetland Court	Victor Harbor	08 8552 8781	
Victor Harbor	Scenic Encounter B&B	27 Bolger Way	Victor Harbor	08 8552 2043	
Victor Harbor - Encounter Bay	All Seasons Lakefront G'way	1 Ketch Place	Encounter Bay	0419 868 143	
Victor Harbor - Mt Jagged	Welcome Springs	Victor Harbor Rd	Mt Jagged	08 85549503	
Whites Vly	Linger Longer Vineyard	California Rd	Whites Valley	08 8556 2358	
Whyalla	**B&B On The Beach**	**6 Neagle Terr**	**Whyalla**	**0428 262 326**	*Page 179*
Whyalla Playford	Playford Lodge	55 Rudall Ave	Whyalla Playford	0419 840 142	
Willunga	Bindarah Valley	Off St. Johns Terr East	Willunga	08 8556 2819	
Willunga	Escape to Willunga	73 Aldinga Rd	Willunga	08 8556 4493	
Willunga	McCaffrey Cottage	21 St James St	Willunga	08 8556 2902	
Willunga	Port Willunga Cottages	Aldinga Rd	Willunga	08 8557 8516	
Willunga	Willunga House	1 St Peter's Terr	Willunga	08 8556 2467	
Wirrabara	Taralee Orchards	Forest Rd	Wirrabara	08 8668 4343	
Yankalilla	Sleepy Hollow Farm Cott	Woodvale Rd	Yankalilla	08 8558 3190	
Yorke Pen	Cletta	PO Box 61	Warooka	08 8854 5052	
Yorke Pen	Evening Waves	42 Alexander St	Wallaroo	08 8258 0347	

Tasmania
Beauty Point
Pomona Spa Cottages

Luxury Self Contained Cottages
Paula & Bruce Irvin
77 Flinders Street
Beauty Point
Tas 7270
40 km N of Launceston

Tel (03) 6383 4073
relax@pomonaspacottages.com.au
www.pomonaspacottages.com.au

Double $180-$250
Single $180-$240
Full breakfast provisions
Visa MC Eftpos accepted
2 King/Twin2 King 2 Single (4 bdrm)
Spacious bedrooms with river views
Bathrooms: 4 Ensuite Spa and separate shower

AAA Tourism
★★★★☆

Relax and enjoy a wine or a delicious breakfast in your private Rotunda, overlooking beautiful views of the Tamar River/valley, a travellers retreat. Spoil yourself in the new luxurious, spacious, sunny 1 and 2 bedroom/2 ensuite S/C Spa Cottages. Water views from your king bed or in front of your cosy wood fire. Stroll in the rambling gardens, orchard, vines and along river to Restaurants, Seahorses, Platypus House. Explore the Tamar Valley Scenic Wine Route, National Parks, Penguins. Ferry & Airport: within 1 hour. Ideally located between Freycinet and Strahan. B.B.Qs. Visit our website for rates for longer stays.

The difference between a hotel and a B&B.
You don't hug the hotel staff when you leave.

Deloraine
Bowerbank Mill B&B

Heritage B&B, S/C Cottages, 2-Bedroom Suite & Rooms
Anne & JD
4455 Meander Valley Road
Deloraine, Tas 7304
50 km W of Launceston

Tel (03) 6362 2628
info@bowerbankmill.com.au
www.bowerbankmill.com.au

Double $149-$229
Single $139-$209, Children $29-$49 depending on age,
Special breakfast, Extra adult $49-$59, Visa MC accepted
7 Queen 1 Double 5 Single (11 bdrm)
Bathrooms: 3 Ensuite 3 Guest share

Situated in picturesque farmland with the backdrop of the hauntingly beautiful Great Western Tiers Mountains is magnificent Bowerbank Mill offering world class accommodation in a colonial setting - original Georgian architecture, stone walls, huge beams, six storey chimney, plus modern comforts and genuine hospitality. Add charming decor/antique furnishings and you have a restful, timeless ambience. "Overwhelming! So wonderful to see such respect & love for beauty, both with the building & furnishing. Very, very special", praised a Queenslander.
Your Hosts will pamper you with gourmet breakfasts, port/cheese and afternoon tea served in your Cottage, Suite or Room - all creating a repose second to none.
NEW: Deloraine Holiday Retreat - spacious & modern with 180 degree views over pretty Deloraine and the spectacular Mountain Range. Accommodates 8.
Both a great base (Central North): near pristine Lakes, Wilderness, Cradle Mountain, Tamar Wineries, Galleries and Gourmet Food. 30 minutes to Launceston and Devonport (Airports & Ferry).

Tasmania

Derwent Bridge

Derwent Bridge is almost the geographical centre of Tasmania. The village is surrounded by Forestry Land, Wildlife Reserves and National Parks in particular The Cradle Mountain/Lake St Clair World Heritage National Park. Enjoy wonderful walks near Lake St Clair - Australia's deepest, fresh water lake.
John & Louise, Derwent Bridge Chalets & Studios

Derwent Bridge
Derwent Bridge Chalets & Studios

Self Contained Chalets & Studios
John & Louise
15478 Lyell Highway
Derwent Bridge
Tas 7140
0.5 km E of Lake St Clair Turnoff

Tel (03) 6289 1000 or (03) 6289 3210
Fax (03) 6289 1230
info@derwent-bridge.com
www.derwent-bridge.com

Double $155-$385
Single $155-$385, Children 11 years and younger $25, 12 years and over $35, Continental breakfast, Visa MC Diners Amex Eftpos accepted. 2 King/Twin2 King 10 Queen 4 Single (14 bdrm). Bathrooms: 10 Ensuite

   AAA Tourism
★★★☆

Edged by a snow gum forest and the Derwent River, 5km from the World Heritage listed Cradle Mountain Lake St Clair National Park - half way between Hobart and Strahan this quality 3 1/2 star property is "simply magic" in summer or winter. Featuring 6x Chalets (2x spa bath) and 4x Studios, with complimentary port wine, chocolate mints, ground coffee and a morning newspaper. All with TV, DVD, microwave etc.

Tasmania

Hobart - Battery Point
Grande Vue

Private Hotel
Annette McIntosh
8 Mona Street
Battery Point
Tas 7005
0.8 km S of Hobart Central

Tel (03) 6223 8216 or 0400 591 457
Fax (03) 6224 1724 jarem8@bigpond.com
www.grande-vue-hotel.com

Double $165-$280
Children and Extra Guests $30, Continental provisions, Winter Specials Available, Weekly rates in apartments on request
Visa MC Amex Eftpos accepted
2 King/Twin 7 Queen 2 Double (7 bdrm)
Bathrooms: 7 Ensuite 5 spa suites

   AAA Tourism ★★★★

Grande Vue Private Hotel is located in Hobart's historic Battery Point. (8 Mona Street). This gracious Edwardian mansion c1906 has spectacular views of the Derwent River, Mount Wellington, just 5 minutes walk to the city, restaurants, Salamanca Place and Hobart's waterfront. We also offer studio, water view rooms and spa suites.

Hobart - Glebe
Corinda's Cottages

Luxury Self Contained Cottages
Matthew Ryan & Wilmar Bouman
17 Glebe Street
Glebe
Tas 7000
0.5 km S of Hobart

Tel (03) 6234 1590
Fax (03) 6234 2744
info@corindascottages.com.au
www.corindascottages.com.au

Double $220-$250
Breakfast provisions first night
Visa MC Diners Amex Eftpos accepted
3 Cottages with Queen & Single Beds
1 bathroom in each cottage

    AAA Tourism ★★★★

Corinda's historic outbuildings, Gardener's Cottage, the Servant's Quarters and Coach House are delightful self-contained cottages furnished with period antiques and bric-a-brac. Corinda was originally part of the convict-run vegetable garden, with the garden wall dating from that period with cobbled courtyards, extensive formal gardens, lawns, quaint topiary animal shapes, woodland areas and a mighty horse chestnut. Each cottage includes a fully equipped kitchen, laundry, bathroom, wood fire, television and CD player. Corinda's Cottages, beautiful heritage accommodation, is located just a few minutes walk from downtown Hobart.

BBBook.com.au

Tasmania
Hobart - Lindisfarne
Orana House

B&B
Maria & Tony Grincais
20 Lowelly Road
Lindisfarne
Tas 7015
6 km E of Hobart

Tel (03) 6243 0404
Fax (03) 6243 9017
welcome@oranahouse.com
www.oranahouse.com

Double $150-$220
Single $120-$170
Children $50 (only children 5 years or older)
Full breakfast, Visa MC Eftpos accepted
7 Queen 3 Double 4 Single (10 bdrm)
Bathrooms: 10 Ensuite

A large Federation home circa 1909 offering warm hospitality. Orana House is 12 minutes from the airport and six minutes to Hobart. Situated near picturesque Lindisfarne Bay, it is a convenient base to explore southern Tasmania. Some of our many features include superb breakfasts, great views from the verandah and guest lounge, afternoon tea daily, genuine antiques and open fire. A choice of standard, deluxe or spa rooms, all with ensuites.

Hobart - Rose Bay
Roseneath B&B

B&B & Self Contained Studio
Susan & Alain Pastre
20 Kaoota Road
Rose Bay
Tas 7015
3.5 km NE of Hobart

Tel (03) 6243 6530 or 0418 121 077
Fax (03) 6243 0518   pastre@bigpond.com
www.roseneath.com

Double $115-$170
Single $100-$165, Full breakfast
Dinner $40-$50 BA
Low season/long stay available
Visa MC Diners Amex Eftpos JCB accepted
2 King/Twin 1 Queen 2 Double (5 bdrm)
Bathrooms: 5 Ensuite

For true Tasmanian hospitality and warmth with a French accent. Only 5 minutes from CBD/Salamanca and 10 from airport. Spectacular views of Mt Wellington, the Tasman Bridge and Derwent River. An ideal base for exploring southern Tasmania or for business. Choose from a SC studio (kitchenette) or in-house accommodation with ensuites (1 spa). Guest lounge with log fire; conservatory; inground heated (summer) pool; spacious, secluded gardens; BBQ; off street parking. Dinner BA with your French chef host. Pet on property.

Tasmania

Hobart - Rosetta
Undine Colonial Accommodation

B&B & Traditional, Heritage Listed
Patricia & Rocco Di Carlo
6 Dodson Street
Rosetta, Hobart
Tas 7010
10 km N of Hobart CBD

Tel (03) 6273 3600 or 0409 658 209
Fax (03) 6273 3900
undine@ozemail.com.au
www.undine.net.au

Double $170-$210
Single $130-$150
Extra persons $60, Full breakfast
Visa MC Diners Eftpos accepted
1 King/Twin 4 Queen 6 Single (5 bdrm)
Bathrooms: 5 Ensuite

AAA Tourism
★★★★☆

Undine - circa 1816, is a splendid Georgian Colonial home set in a large cottage garden with luxurious rooms, complimentary chocolates and port. Relax and enjoy your stay. Swim in the heated, indoor pool. Tea/Coffee and fresh home baked treats. Indulge in a country style, cooked breakfast as you plan the day. Undine is located only 10 minutes from Hobart CBD. Children welcome. Sorry no pets.

Hobart - Sandy Bay
Apartments on Star

Self Contained Serviced Apartments
Kate & James McIntosh
22 Star Street & 11 Jersey Street
Sandy Bay
Tas 7005
1 km S of Hobart CBD

Tel 0419 104 417 or (03) 6223 8216
info@apartmentsonstar.com.au
www.apartmentsonstar.com.au

Double $165-$280
Single $125-$165
Accommodation only
Children and extra guests $30 each
Visa MC Amex Eftpos accepted
1 King 4 Queen 3 Double (8 bdrm)
Bathrooms: 8 Ensuite

AAA Tourism
★★★★

Apartments on Star are modern contemporary designed one, two and three bedroom stylish apartments and townhouses fully equipped to suit all your requirements for short or long term stays. Each apartment has a fully equipped kitchen, including dishwasher, fridge and stove, lounge/dining rooms with TV, DVD and Stereo. Apartments on Star have water views of the Derwent River or a private courtyard, secure undercover/off street parking. Walking distance to Battery Point restaurants, Salamanca Place, the city centre and the University of Tasmania.

BBBook.com.au

Tasmania
Launceston
Edenholme Grange

Luxury B&B & Self contained apartments
& 2 bed cottage
Paul & Rosemary Harding
14 St Andrews Street
Launceston
Tas 7250
1.5 km SW of Post Office

Tel (03) 6334 6666 or 0419 894 269
Fax (03) 6334 3106   sales@edenholme.com
www.edenholme.com

Double $150-$240
Single $130-$220, Children $25 up to age 13,
Full breakfast , Dinner nearby restaurants
Visa MC Diners Amex Eftpos JCB accepted
2 King/Twin2 King 4 Queen 3 Double 2 Twin
(10 bdrm) Bathrooms: 10 Ensuite

AAA Tourism
★★★★

Edenholme Grange, Settlers Cottage and The Coachhouse Apartments. Experience past times in this private Victorian mansion. set amongst secluded and substantial grounds, on the edge of the City and near the magnificent Cataract Gorge. There are uniquely themed rooms, furnished with antiques & some with spa baths. Close to the City yet secluded in the spacious grounds of the House are a self-contained rustic cottage, with modern amenities, including double spa bath and extra ensuite and 2 luxury apartments.

Launceston
Alice's Cottages and Spa Hideaways

Cottages and Spa Hideaways
Rob & Louise Widdowson
129 Balfour Street, Launceston, Tas 7250
0.5 km W of Launceston

Tel (03) 6334 2231
Fax (03) 6334 2696
alicescottages@bigpond.com
www.alicescottages.com.au

Double $170-$206
Single $130-$170, Children can be
accommodated in fold out beds. Hearty
continental breakfast provisions are provided.
All cottages have their own cooking facilities.
Visa MC Diners Amex Eftpos accepted.
6 cottages each with a queen bed
3 with spas baths & 3 with showers and baths

AAA Tourism
★★★★

A wickedly wonderful romantic retreat awaits for lovers in one of Alice's Spa Hideaways tucked away in the historic heart of Launceston. The accommodation, which welcomes pets and children by arrangement, is fully self-contained for your privacy. Roaring log fires and bubbling spas warm the bodies and stir the passion whilst being cocooned in a different world with all the modern comforts. Launceston's finest restaurants and fabulous Cataract Gorge are a pleasant stroll away, or you may decide to prepare and enjoy dinner in the intimacy of your own fireside. Saviour the complimentary bedtime port, chocolate truffles, brewed coffee and sweet treats which all just tops a tremendous experience.

Tasmania

Port Arthur

The Tasman Peninsula has it all. The coastal rock formations, forests, bays, beaches and towering sea cliffs will have you pointing your camera in no time. The historic remains at Port Arthur, Point Puer, the Isle of the Dead, the Salt River Coal Mines and Eaglehawk Neck will have you pondering the sometimes sad saga of human history.
Lorella Matassini, Norfolk Bay Convict Staion

Port Arthur - Taranna
Norfolk Bay Convict Station

B&B & Guest House
Lynton Brown & Lorella Matassini
5862 Arthur Highway
Taranna
Tas 7180
10 km N of Port Arthur

Tel (03) 6250 3487
Fax (03) 6250 3701
norfolkbay@convictstation.com
www.convictstation.com

Double $110-$180
Single $80-$120, Children Up to 12 yo $30
Continental breakfast, Nearby restaurants
Visa MC Eftpos accepted
2 Queen 2 Double 1 Twin 4 Single (5 bdrm)
Bathrooms: 3 Ensuite 2 Private

Stay in living history and indulge yourself. Nature, adventure, history, culture, it's all here! Convict built in 1838 on this picturesque waterfront location, we are just minutes from Port Arthur, Eaglehawk Neck and all that the Tasman Peninsula has to offer. We offer warm, comfortable rooms, a guest sitting room with a log fire and a wonderful breakfast. This friendly B&B has history, charm and all the modern comforts. Enjoy a complimentary glass of Port, watch a DVD or explore our extensive library.

Tasmania
Richmond
Mulberry Cottage B&B

B&B & Homestay & Self Contained House
Miriam Cooper
23a Franklin Street
Richmond
Tas 7025
In Richmond

Tel (03) 6260 2664 or 0407 473 015
miriam23@bigpond.net.au
www.mulberrycottage.com.au

Double $110-$160
Single $85-$110, Children B/A, Special breakfast, Dinner or platters B/A with Grannie, Seasonal Specials, Show included in Grannie Rhodes Cottage, Visa MC accepted
1 King 3 Queen 1 Double 4 Twin 1 Single (4 bdrm)
Bathrooms: 2 Ensuite 1 Guest share 1 Private

Charming, hosted B&B, in 'old worlde' cottage, built from the reclaimed wall of Hobart's Old Penitentiary. Self contained cottage on site 'Dobbin's Hole.' 'Excellent' Tourism Award Winning show included (Highly Commended, Cultural Heritage section). Valley views. Rustic gardens. Glass of wine on arrival. Cosy guest sitting room (pet free). Host lounge shared with greeting retrievers, cuddly cat. For the history & theatre lover; unique entertainment, by your hostess, a performance of 'Turn the Key of Time' about a cottage, a key and a convict in Grannie Rhodes' Cottage, on site 1830.

Children enjoy getaways as much as adults and most properties have facilities for children. Look for The Children Welcome Logo

Tasmania

Swansea - Freycinet Coast

The historic township of Swansea encompasses a charming collection of heritage homes. Visit world class restaurants or shuck oysters and sip local wines on sandy, unspoiled beaches. Wineglass Bay in the beautiful Freycinet National Park with white sandy beaches and pure clear turquoise waters is perfect for sea kayaking, swimming and scuba diving.
Cameron & Jodie Finlayson, Schouten House

Swansea
Schouten House

B&B
Cameron and Jodie Finlayson
1 Waterloo Road
Swansea
Tas 7190
0.5 km E of Swansea

Tel (03) 6257 8564
Fax (03) 6257 8767
enquiries@schoutenhouse.com
www.schoutenhouse.com.au

Double $150-$180
Single $130-$150, Children Welcome, additional charge applies, Full breakfast, Dinner by arrangement, Visa MC Eftpos accepted
5 Queen 1 Twin (6 bdrm)
Bathrooms: 6 Ensuite

Schouten House is c1844 Georgian Bed and Breakfast Accommodation. A landmark Heritage Listed property in the seaside town of Swansea, overlooking Great Oyster Bay and Freycinet Peninsula on the East Coast of Tasmania. Your hosts, Cameron and Jodie, welcome you to this gracious home. The house offers six suites, all with queen sized beds and private ensuites. Guests can enjoy two lounge areas, one with open fire, and a dining room where a generous full cooked breakfast is served. Enquire about meals by arrangement.

Bed & Breakfast, Farmstay and Accommodation Australia

Australia's island State has an abundance of historic towns and villages; dramatic mountain scenery; lush rainforest wilderness; coastal hamlets with magnificent beaches along the east coast and a wild, rugged western coastline. Mount Wellington provides a stunning backdrop to Tasmania's picturesque capital, Hobart, where you can visit the Salamanca Market the old settlers cottages and historic homes at Battery Point. With its pristine environment, Tasmania is acclaimed for the quality and variety of its produce and cool climate wines.

BBFAA accommodation is ideal for short breaks, romantic getaways and special occasions, travelling with pets, family stays and group reunions.

Enjoy a warm welcome and true hospitality when you stay with a BBFAA member. BBFAA brings you high quality places to stay throughout Australia that are as individual as you.

www.australianbedandbreakfast.com.au
1300 664 707

Recommended Accommodation - Tasmania

Tasmania

Properties included below with a page reference are included in this chapter and with further details. We have also included recommended accommodation with information supplied by BBFAA. Contact the hosts by telephone number for further details and tell them, *"We found you in The B&B Book."*

Beauty Point	Pomona Spa Cottages	77 Flinders St	Beauty Point	03 6383 4073	Page 186
Bicheno	Greenlawn Cottages	16999 Tasman Hwy	Bicheno	03 6375 1114	
Burnie	The Duck House	26-28 Queen St	Burnie	03 6431 1712	
Coles Bay	Sheoaks on Freycinet	47 Oyster Bay Court	Coles Bay	03 6257 0049	
Deloraine	Bowerbank Mill B&B	4455 Meander Valley Rd	Deloraine	03 6362 2628	Page 187
Derwent Bridge	Derwent Bridge Chalets & Studios	15478 Lyell Hwy	Derwent Bridge	03 62891000	Page 188
Hobart	The Elms of Hobart	452 Elizabeth St	Hobart	03 6231 3277	
Hobart - Battery Point	Colville Cottage	32 Mona St	Battery Point	03 6223 6968	
Hobart - Battery Point	Grande Vue	8 Mona St	Battery Point	03 6223 8216	Page 189
Hobart - Bellerivre	Bellerive House	89-91 Cambridge Rd	Bellerive	03 6244 7798	
Hobart - Crabtree	Crabtree House & River Cotts	130 Crabtree Rd	Crabtree	0429 626 640	
Hobart - Gembrook	Brilynbrook at Hobart	1/18 Chadwick Court	West Hobart	03 5968 1938	
Hobart - Glebe	Corindas Cottages	17 Glebe St	Glebe	03 6234 1590	Page 189
Hobart - Lindisfarne	Orana House	20 Lowelly Rd	Lindisfarne	03 6243 0404	Page 190
Hobart - Rose Bay	Roseneath B&B	20 Kaoota Rd	Rose Bay	03 6243 6530	Page 190
Hobart - Rosetta	Undine Colonial Accom	6 Dodson St	Rosetta	03 6273 3600	Page 191
Hobart - Sandy Bay	Apts on Star	22 Star St	Sandy Bay	0419 104 417	Page 191
Hobart - Sandy Bay	Merre Be's	17 Gregory St	Sandy Bay	03 6224 2900	
Huonville	Walton House	2720 Huon Hwy	Huonville	03 6264 1640	
Launceston	Airlie on the Square	Civic Square	Launceston	03 6334 0577	
Launceston	Alice's Cottages & Spa Hideaways	129 Balfour St	Launceston	03 6334 2231	Page 192
Launceston	Edenholme Grange	14 St Andrews St	Launceston	03 6334 6666	Page 192
Launceston	The Edwardian Apts	227 Charles St	Launceston	03 6334 7771	
Launceston - Bridport	Platypus Park Country Rtrt	20 Ada St	Bridport	03 6356 1873	
Launceston - Lilydale	Plovers Ridge Country Rtrt	132 Lalla Rd	Lilydale	03 6395 1102	
Launceston - Longford	The Racecourse Inn	114 Marlborough St	Longford	03 6391 2352	
Launceston - Riverside	Riverside B&B	273 West Tamar Rd	Riverside	03 63274696	
Launceston - Ross	Ross Bakery Inn	15 Church St	Ross	03 6381 5246	
Moina	Cradle Chalet Btq Lge	1422 Cradle Mountain Rd	Moina	03 6492 1401	
Nth West - Arthur River	Arthur River Holiday Units	2 Gardiner St	Arthur River	03 6457 1268	
Pt Arthur - Taranna	Norfolk Bay Convict Station	5862 Arthur Hwy	Taranna	03 6250 3487	Page 193
Queenstown	Comstock Cottage	45 McNamara St	Queenstown	03 6471 1200	
Richmond	Laurel Cottage	9 Wellington St	Richmond	03 6260 2397	
Richmond	Mulberry Cottage B&B	23a Franklin St	Richmond	03 6260 2664	Page 194
Stanley	Cable Station	435 Greenhills Rd	Stanley	03 6458 1312	
Swansea	Schouten House	1 Waterloo Rd	Swansea	03 6257 8564	Page 195
Ulverstone	B&B at Winterbrook	28 Eastlands Dv	Ulverstone	03 6425 6324	

Victoria

Victoria

Apollo Bay
Arcady Homestead

B&B & Homestay & Farmstay
Marcia & Ross Dawson
925 Barham River Road
Apollo Bay - Great Ocean Road
Vic 3233
10 km W of Apollo Bay

Tel (03) 5237 6493 or 0408 376 493
Fax (03) 5237 6493
arcadyhomestead@fastmail.fm
www.bbbook.com.au/arcadyhomestead.html

Double $110-$120
Single $75-$85
Children 50%
Full breakfast, Dinner B/A
2 Queen 1 Double 3 Single (4 bdrm)
Bathrooms: 1 Guest share

Set on sixty scenic acres, part farmland and part natural bush. Share breakfast with our Kookaburras, explore the Otway Forest trails, tree-fern and glow worm gullies and waterfalls, see some of the tallest trees in the world or visit Port Campbell National Park, which embraces Australia's most spectacular coastline. The Otway Ranges are a bushwalkers paradise. Bird-watchers? We have identified around thirty species in the garden alone! Many visit our kitchen window! Our home has wood fires & spring water. Our beds are cosy, our meals country-style, and our atmosphere relaxed and friendly.

Apollo Bay
Paradise Gardens

B&B & Self Contained Cottages
Jo and Jock Williamson
715 Barham River Road
Apollo Bay
Vic 3233
7.5 km W of Apollo Bay

Tel (03) 5237 6939 or 0417 330 615
Fax (03) 5237 6105
paradisegardens@bigpond.com.au
www.paradisegardens.net.au

Double $120-$220
Continental provisions provided
in Cottages by request
Visa MC Eftpos accepted
1 King/Twin 2 King 1 Queen (4 bdrm)
Bathrooms: 4 Ensuite All ensuite with spas

AAA Tourism
★★★★☆

Situated on 3 acres of Award Winning landscaped gardens in a lush rainforest valley, our facility is only 10 minutes from Apollo Bay on a (sealed) scenic road. Our charming self-contained cottages (one and two bedroom) are built over a lake and feature wood fires, spas, bar-b-cues on the decking and air conditioning. Continental breakfast available by request. Laundry facilities. Our in-house B&B unit is comfortable with double spa and external entrance and includes continental breakfast. Enjoy walks, birdlife and glow-worms. Most often repeated comment by guests, "We wish we could stay longer."

Victoria
Apollo Bay
Point of View

Luxury B&B & Self Contained Apartment
Alan & Glenda Whelan
165 Tuxion Road
Apollo Bay, Vic 3233
1 km N of Apollo Bay

Tel 0427 376 377
info@pointofview.com.au
www.pointofview.com.au

Double $250-$340
Continental provisions, 2 night minimum stay ($580/620)
Visa MC Eftpos accepted
5 King (5 bdrm) modern, open plan
Bathrooms: 5 Ensuite Double shower and spa

Breathtaking views from every location in our architect designed luxury villas. Perfect retreat for couples for those special occasions.

Features wood fire, king beds, double shower, full kitchen, dishwasher, satellite tv, large therapeutic spa, DVD, electric heating, air conditioning, robes, toiletries, surround sound, spacious sundecks, BBQ, washing machine, dryer, fresh flowers, beach towels, hairdryer, continental breakfast supplies.

Ideal base to explore the 12 Apostles, Great Ocean Road or as a romantic, secluded getaway for you and your partner. Wine and chocolates on arrival. Spoil yourself.

Victoria

Apollo Bay - Great Ocean Road
Claerwen Retreat

Self Contained Apartment & Self Contained House & Guest House
Cornelia Elbrecht
480 Tuxion Road, Apollo Bay , Vic 3233
5 km N of Apollo Bay

Tel (03) 5237 7064
Fax (03) 5237 7054
cornelia_elbrecht@claerwen.com.au
www.claerwen.com.au

Double $99-$360
Single $99-$250, Pre-school children only welcome in cottages, Full breakfast, Cheese and wine upon request, Cottage sleeps up to six adults/children: $295-$350, Visa MC Diners Amex Eftpos JCB accepted. 4 King 5 Queen 3 Twin (12 bdrm) . Bathrooms: 10 Ensuite

Exclusively situated on top of the highest hill overlooking the coast with panoramic ocean views from all rooms we offer spacious suites, self contained three-bedroom cottages or one-bedroom studios. Set in the peaceful solitude of 130 acres of park, bush and rainforest, it features saltwater swimming pool, hot spa and tennis court. It is close to the famous Great Ocean Road, to the Twelve Apostles and the Otway National Park. We offer in-house massages, facials and art classes. In winter every third night is free.

Bairnsdale
Tara House

B&B
Phillip
37 Day Street
Bairnsdale
Vic 3875
1.2 km W of town centre

Tel (03) 5153 2253
Fax (03) 5153 2426
enquiries@tarahouse.com.au
www.tarahouse.com.au

Double $160-$170
Single $130-$140, Children fold out bed in parents room $60, Full breakfast, Dinner by arrangement, Visa MC accepted
2 King/Twin 1 Queen (3 bdrm)
Bathrooms: 3 Ensuite

Share a beautiful garden with a retired gardener. Be welcomed by the hostess, Tara, a seven year old Sydney Silky. A relaxing and refreshing time is assured. Sit on the verandah and watch the setting sun or have a glass of wine. Many areas to sit and forget your troubles. Come and smell the roses. Two hours to the snow, 20 minutes to lake, 30 minutes to sea. The perfect place to stay.

BBBook.com.au

Bairnsdale - Sarsfield

Stringybark Cottages B&B

Self Contained B&B Cottages
Lois & Neil Triggs
77 Howards Road
Sarsfield
Vic 3875
19 km NE of Bairnsdale

Tel (03) 5157 5245 or 0412 130 028
Fax (03) 5157 5639
neil@stringybarkcottages.com
www.stringybarkcottages.com

Double $160-$180
Single $100-$120, Children under 2 stay for free, Full breakfast provisions, Dinner avaliable by prior arrangement, Extra person $35 per night, Visa MC Eftpos accepted
4 Queen 4 Single (6 bdrm) Bathrooms: 3 Private

Finalist
2008 Victorian
Tourism Awards
Environmentally
Friendly

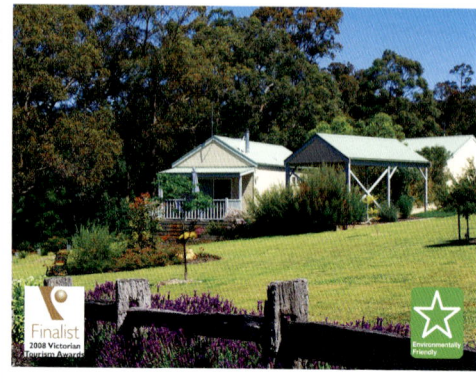

AAA Tourism ★★★★

Experience that little piece of paradise, tranquil and delightfully different. Enjoy those cool evenings snuggled up in front of the wood fire, warmer nights spent relaxing on your verandah with a ceiling of millions of stars. Multi Award winning Stringybark Cottages are situated 19kms from Bairnsdale just off The Great Alpine Road. There are four cottages, accommodating from two to five people. Each cottage is fully self contained.

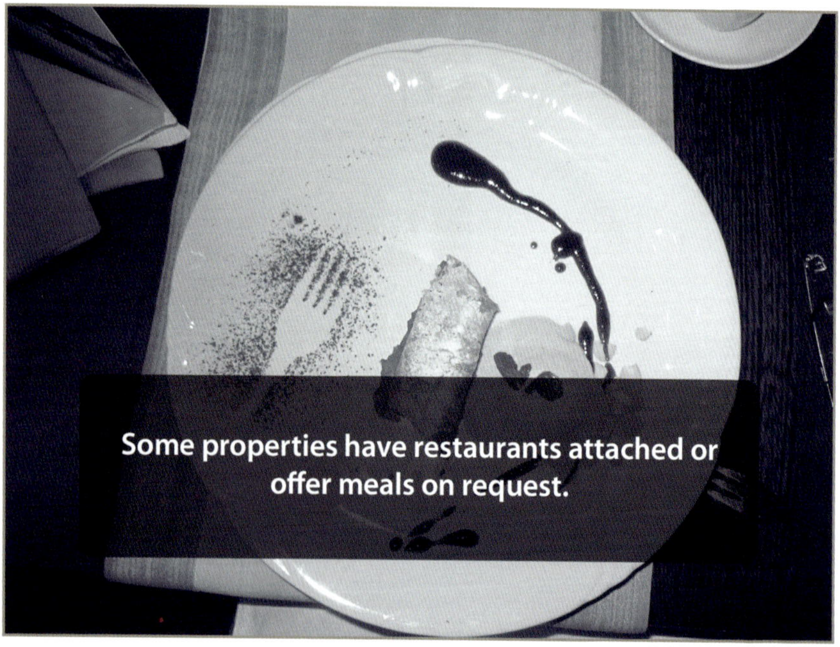
Some properties have restaurants attached or
offer meals on request.

Victoria

Beechworth

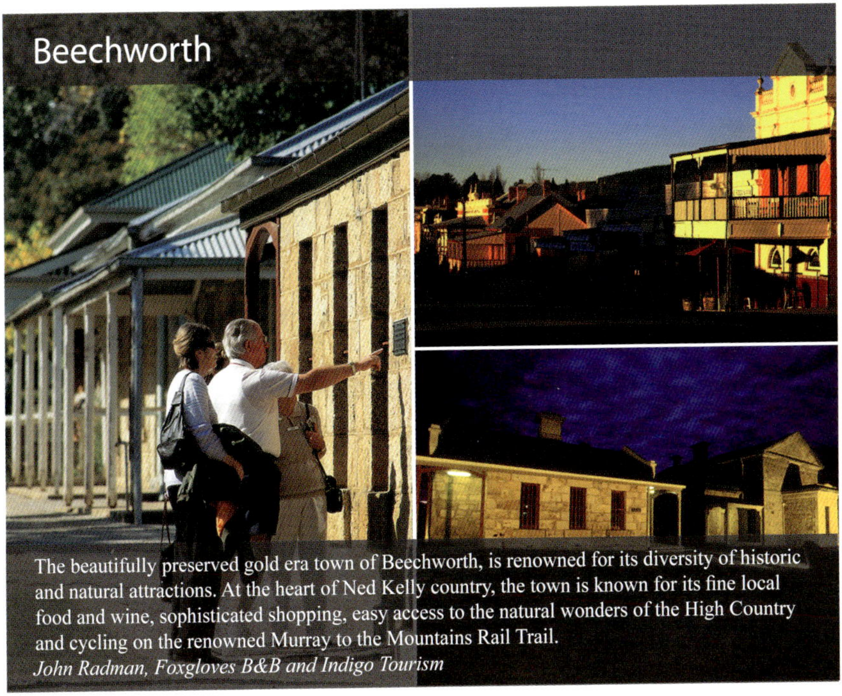

The beautifully preserved gold era town of Beechworth, is renowned for its diversity of historic and natural attractions. At the heart of Ned Kelly country, the town is known for its fine local food and wine, sophisticated shopping, easy access to the natural wonders of the High Country and cycling on the renowned Murray to the Mountains Rail Trail.
John Radman, Foxgloves B&B and Indigo Tourism

Beechworth
Country Charm Swiss Cottages

Self Contained House
Judy & Greg Lazarus
22 Malakoff Road
Beechworth
Vic 3747
1.4 km W of Beechworth

Tel **(03) 5728 2435 or 0417 376 819**
Fax (03) 5728 2436
info@swisscottages.com.au
www.swisscottages.com.au

$175-215 per cottage per day
Children No charge under 4, Full breakfast
Visa MC Amex Eftpos accepted
5 Queen 6 Single (8 bdrm)
Bathrooms: 5 Ensuite 2 Family share
2 Guest share

AAA Tourism
★★★★

Delightful, well appointed self-contained cottages set high overlooking the Beechworth Gorge. Our 1 or 2 Bedroom cottages offer tranquillity, privacy and a perfect setting for any occasion. Each cottage has open fires in winter, reverse cycle air conditioning, spa baths, along with TV, CD/DVD players. A guest laundry and outdoor BBQ area are available. Enjoy generous breakfast provisions to be prepared at your leisure. Along with the complimentary treats provided, the ambience of the property and wonderful hosts will ensure a wonderful stay.

Victoria

Beechworth
Freeman on Ford

5 Star Luxury B&B
Heidi Freeman & Jim Didolis
97 Ford Street
Beechworth
Vic 3747
35 km E of Wangaratta

Tel (03) 5728 2371 or (03) 5728 2055
0409 958 340
Fax (03) 5728 2504
freemanford@westnet.com.au
www.freemanonford.com.au

Double $195-$350
Single $185-$300, Full breakfast
Visa MC Diners Amex Eftpos accepted
1 King/Twin2 King 3 Queen (6 bdrm)
Bathrooms: 6 Ensuite

   AAA Tourism ★★★★★

Freeman on Ford is the only 5 star and Green Star Accredited B&B in Beechworth with environmentally friendly policies with luxury appointments. It stands alone in quality and furnishings. The hosts have paid much attention to detail with Victorian decor to match its historical significance. Built in 1866, a former bank it was once the second Brigidine Convent in Australia. There is onsite secure parking. Situated in the main street, near the Post Office, Historical Precinct, restaurants and quality shops. If you enjoy being pampered and appreciate antiques and quality and 'position, position, position', this venue is for you.

Beechworth
Foxgloves

Luxury B&B & Separate Suite
John & Sheila Rademan
21 Loch Street
Beechworth
Vic 3747
0.3 km N of PO

Tel (03) 5728 1224
Fax (03) 5728 1228
foxgloves1@westnet.com.au
www.foxgloves.com.au

Double $165-$205
Single $140-$205, Twin share $185
Full breakfast
Visa MC Eftpos accepted
4 Queen 1 Single (4 bdrm)
Bathrooms: 4 Ensuite

Welcome to our tastefully restored Victorian cottage (c 1897) in the heart of historic Beechworth. We offer country hospitality in quietly elegant surrounds with all the delights of contemporary comforts. Our personal attention includes traditional cooked breakfast, homemade afternoon teas & complimentary port/sherry in our cosy lounge or on the plant-filled patio. All fully serviced bedrooms have heating/cooling, electric underblankets and quality linen. The guest lounge/dining room has TV/DVD, log fire in winter and cooling in summer for your comfort.

Chiltern
The Mulberry Tree B&B & Tea Rooms

B&B
Regina Welsh
28 Conness Street
Chiltern
Vic 3683
In Chiltern

Tel (03) 5726 1277
mulberrytree@bbbook.com.au
www.mulberrytreechiltern.com.au

Double $160-$180
Single $130-$160
Special breakfast
Dinner by arrangement
Tearooms next door
2 Queen (2 bdrm)
Bathrooms: 1 Ensuite 1 Private

AAA Tourism ★★★★

Just 1 km off the highway. Indulge yourself in the heart of Country Victoria. At The Mulberry Tree you will find a haven to relax and enjoy delightful accommodation with gourmet breakfast. Choose from "The Bank Residence" with it's own lounge with open fire, private bathroom or "The Henry Handel Richardson Suite" with ensuite dining area. This delightful building was built in 1879 as "The Bank of Australasia" and is on the Historic Building Register. Be assured of a warm welcome with special attention to every detail. Situated in the centre of town. Come and see our beautiful cats, 'Paris' & 'Tina'.

Cudgewa - Corryong
Elmstead Cottages

B&B & Farmstay & Self Contained House
Marja & Tony Jarvis
61 Ashstead Park Lane
Cudgewa
Vic 3705
12 km W of Corryong

Tel (02) 6077 4324 or 0427 774 324
Fax (02) 6077 4324
elmstead@corryongcec.net.au
www.bbbook.com.au/elmstead

Double $90
Single $90, Extra person $15
Children 12 and under $10
Breakfast by arrangement, Eftpos accepted
2 Queen 4 Single (3 bdrm)
Bathrooms: 2 Private

AAA Tourism ★★★☆

Elmstead Cottage: A one room cottage set amongst magnificent elm trees on a working farm, cute cosy and affordable. Arthur's Cottage: An eco-friendly, historic two bedroom cottage (circa 1887). Secluded location on the banks of the Cudgewa Creek where platypus and trout abound. Fully equipped kitchen, BYO linen.

Victoria

Dandenong Ranges

Less than an hour from Melbourne . . . but "A World Away" is the catch phrase for this spectacular mountain area. Villages, specialty shops, restaurants, cafes, tearooms, magnificent public gardens, Puffing Billy Steam train, William Ricketts sanctuary and farm gate shops. The Yarra Valley wineries are only half an hour drive.
Peta Rolls, Candlelight Cottages Retreat Retreat and Andrew Chapman, photographer

Dandenong Ranges
Candlelight Cottages Retreat

Self Contained Cottages
Peta & Laurie Rolls
7-9 Monash Avenue, Olinda Village , Vic 3788
0.3 km N of Olinda

Tel (03) 9751 2464 or 1300 553 011
Fax (03) 9751 0552
stay@candlelightcottages.com.au
www.candlelightcottages.com.au

Double $220-$300
Single $210-$320, Extra couple $50 p/
Children 0-3 yrs $10, 4-10 yrs $20p/n
Full breakfast provisions
Mini-bar dinner available
Visa MC Amex Eftpos accepted
1 King/Twin 2 Queen 1 Double (4 bdrm)
Bathrooms: 4 Ensuite 1 Guest share

AAA Tourism ★★★★

Two exquisite cottages in Olinda Village, Candlelight Cottage & Cottage in the Village offering privacy, serenity. Spabath, luxurious beds, comfortable lounge, open-log fire, full kitchen, outdoor area - minutes stroll to restaurants, shops, cafes, galleries. A Cottage in the Forest invites you to soak in the spa, lounge on your kingsize bed, sip wine by the open fire - hidden away on 1 acre.

Victoria

Dandenong Ranges - Emerald
Fernglade on Menzies

Luxury B&B & Self Contained Suites
Helen & Stewart Spence
11 Caroline Crescent
Emerald
Vic 3782
2 km N of Emerald

Tel (03) 5968 2228 or 0411 024 021
Fax (03) 5968 2228
info@fergladeonmenzies.com.au
www.fergladeonmenzies.com.au

Double $135-$190
Full breakfast, Dinner B/A, Special occasion packages with dinner available, Special rates midweek and for longer stays, Visa MC accepted
4 Queen 1 Double (5 bdrm)
Bathrooms: 5 Ensuite

AAA Tourism
★★★★☆

Fernglade on Menzies provides great hospitality, home cooking, in-suite dining, personalised service - perfect base for exploring tourist attractions of the Dandenong Ranges and Yarra Valley. Secluded relaxing location with direct access to superb walking tracks. Luxury spa suites offer cosy gas log fires for romantic winter nights, cooling for summer comfort. The two self-contained suites have mini kitchens, a BBQ area and are perfect for a romantic escape or a getaway with family or friends. Personalised gift certificates available. Group dining room/home theatre/conference room seats 12.

Dandenong Ranges - Mount Dandenong
Observatory Cottages

Luxury B&B & 4 Self Contained Cottages
Leeanne & Daniel Gazzola
8 Observatory Road
Mt Dandenong
Vic 3767
2 km N of Mt Dandenong

Tel (03) 9751 2436
Fax (03) 9751 2904
enquiries@observatorycottages.com.au
www.observatorycottages.com.au

Double $220-$320
Children $25 per child, $50 per extra person
Full breakfast provisions
Visa MC Amex Eftpos accepted
4 Queen (4 bdrm) Open plan living
Bathrooms: 4 Ensuite

Sip wine by the twinkling night light views of the city skyline on a lazy summers evening. Slide into a deep hot bubbling spa with a good book or your true love. Curl up in an ultimately romantic four posted bed and watch the mountain mist roll in through the winter nights. Sleep late and enjoy a hearty breakfast to the serenade of the birds, the fragrance of the forest, and the tranquillity of a stunning garden paradise.

Victoria

Dandenong Ranges - Olinda
A Sunrise View

Log Homestead Suites
Nick & Lisa Sanders
34 McCarthy Road
Olinda
Vic 3788
2 km SE of Monbulk

Tel 0412 621 259
contact@sunriseview.com.au
www.sunriseview.com.au

Double $130-$220
Breakfast provisions first night
Extra person $40/night
Visa MC accepted
2 Queen (2 bdrm) Full lounge room with open fire, chaise lounge, and lots of cushions
Bathrooms: 2 Ensuite

Awake to the sound of Kookaburras and the most gorgeous sunrises on this magnificent 5 acre, private and secluded property with magnificent views over the Valley. Located next to the Silvan Dam this property offers natural forest and gardens with many secluded areas to get away from it all. A fabulous log homestead nestles on the slope with all bedrooms facing the Eastern sunrises and overlooking the valley. Rooms are spacious, warm, clean and comfortable with private entrances and parking. This is the perfect place for lovers of all ages. Close to Wineries, Restaurants, Trout and Tulip farms and market gardens.

Dandenong Ranges - Sassafras
Clarendon Cottages

B&B & Self Contained Cottages
Pam & Ian Hankey
11 Clarkmont Road
Sassafras
Vic 3787
1 km S of Sassafras

Tel (03) 9755 3288 or 0438 529 220
Fax (03) 9755 3288
pam@clarendoncottages.com
www.clarendoncottages.com

Double $140-$288
Single $140-$288, Extra bedroom $50 per person or foldout bed $30, Full breakfast provisions, Visa MC Eftpos accepted
3 Queen 1 Double (4 bdrm)
Bathrooms: 3 Private

Clarendon's boutique guest accommodation consists of three charming cottages in a secluded, peaceful and romantic setting. Two acres of English country gardens and meadow nestle amongst a huge variety of beautiful century old trees. The cottages are within easy walking distance of Sassafras Village and Sherbrooke Forest. Three cosy 1 & 2 bedroom cottages each with its own individual charm are located separately on the two acre property. Log fires, spas, fully equipped kitchens, air conditioning and private decks are just some of the many features. TV, DVD & CD in all cottages. Full breakfast provisions are provided.

Victoria

Daylesford - Hepburn Springs
Pendower House

B&B
René Ludekens
10 Bridport Street
Daylesford
Vic 3460
0.1 km NW of Daylesford PO

Tel (03) 5348 1535 or 0438 103 460
Fax (03) 5348 1545
bookings@pendowerhouse.com.au
www.pendowerhouse.com.au

Double $150-$380
Single $105-$290, Children B/A
Full breakfast
Visa MC accepted
3 Queen 1 Twin (4 bdrm)
Bathrooms: 4 Ensuite

AAA Tourism
★★★★

Pendower House, a beautifully restored Victorian House, situated in the heart of Australia's Spa Capital - Daylesford. RACV Rated 4 Pendower House offers first class amenities: fine linen, antique furnishings, big brass beds, loungeroom/library with open fire. Our luxurious Spa Suite, with corner spa, T.V/DVD & private courtyard is perfect for privacy, peace & pampering. Fantastic country breakfast, Muffins, hollandaise sauce drizzled on Eggs - more like brunch than breakfast! Easy walk to restaurants/galleries. Close to Spa resort. Massages & Spa packages or Gift Vouchers available.

Daylesford - Smeaton
Tuki Retreat

Stone Cottages
Robert & Jan Jones
60 Stoney Rises Road
Smeaton
Vic 3364
20 km NW of Daylesford

Tel (03) 5345 6233
Fax (03) 5345 6377
info@tuki.com.au
www.tuki.com.au

Double $150-$260
Full breakfast provisions
Visa MC Diners Amex Eftpos JCB accepted
2 King 6 Queen 2 Single (9 bdrm)
1 and 3 bedroom cottages
Bathrooms: 7 Ensuite 1 Private

AAA Tourism
★★★★

A unique rural retreat, offering tranquillity, 70km views. Tuki Retreat is situated on historic "Stoney Rises", a traditional sheep grazing property. The cottages offer a wonderful view of the Loddon-Campaspe Valley and are surrounded by dry stonewalls, landscaped gardens and established trees. There is a private lake in front of the stone cottages. All have open fireplaces, cathedral ceilings and a veranda to watch the sunset on. The master bedroom has a Queen size bed, with electric blankets and linen and towels are all provided. There is a double sofa bed in the lounge room for additional guests.

Victoria
Echuca
Ayr House B&B

Luxury B&B
Doug Hall
62 Hare Street
Echuca
Vic 3564
In Echuca

Tel (03) 5482 1973
Fax (03) 5482 1901
esobab@mcmedia.com.au
www.ayrhouse.com

Double $165
Single $125
Full breakfast
Visa MC accepted
2 Queen (2 bdrm)
Bathrooms: 2 Ensuite

Ayr House brings over 25 years experience and a well deserved reputation for exceptional hospitality skills. Situated within easy walking distance to restaurants and Echuca's shopping precinct, guests are offered the personal touches one would expect when visiting friends. Ayr House is furnished with wonderful period pieces collected by the owner over the years. The elegant bedrooms each with ensuites exude warmth and comfort, which is mirrored by the sumptuous library lounge and dining rooms. Here's Bed & Breakfast accommodation in the grand style, right in the heart of the historic river port of Echuca.

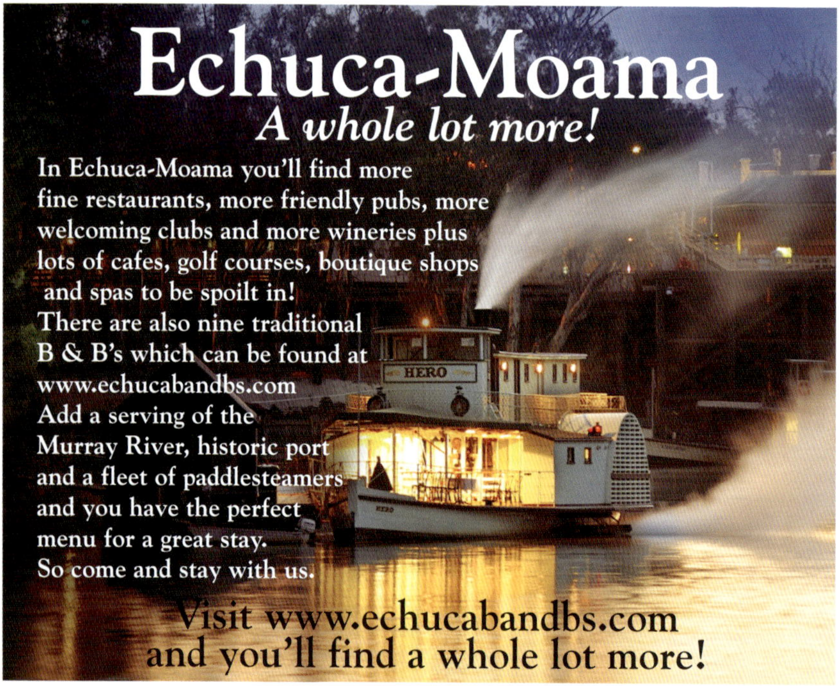

Echuca-Moama
A whole lot more!

In Echuca-Moama you'll find more fine restaurants, more friendly pubs, more welcoming clubs and more wineries plus lots of cafes, golf courses, boutique shops and spas to be spoilt in!
There are also nine traditional B & B's which can be found at www.echucabandbs.com
Add a serving of the Murray River, historic port and a fleet of paddlesteamers and you have the perfect menu for a great stay.
So come and stay with us.

Visit www.echucabandbs.com and you'll find a whole lot more!

Geelong

Avalon Airport just fifteen 15 kilometres north-east of Geelong is home to the Australian International Air Show, a popular and spectacular biennial event held in March. The city's waterfront is a hive of activity, with cafes, restaurants, yacht club, marina, antique carousel, art-deco promenade and swimming pavilion.
Nola Haines, Baywood B&B and Geelong Otway Tourism www.greatoceanroad.org.

Geelong
Baywoodbyne B&B

B&B
Nola Haines
41 The Esplanade
Geelong
Vic 3215
1.5 km N of Geelong

Tel (03) 5278 2658
baywoodbyne@bbbook.com.au
www.greatoceanroad.org

Double $120-$140
Single $110
Children Over 6 welcome
Full breakfast
Visa MC Eftpos accepted
2 Double 1 Twin (3 bdrm)
Bathrooms: 1 Ensuite 1 Private

Centrally located accommodation in a lovely 1921 California Bungalow style home. Superb view overlooking Corio Bay; a short stroll to city centre and colourful waterfront precinct. Warmth, comfort, convenience are yours, together with books and music. Offering: Ground floor, double bedroom with ensuite (extra bed available), sitting and dining room, open fire, picture window. First floor, two double bedrooms, sitting area and beautiful view. Tea/coffee making toaster, fridge. Off-street parking. Easy access to Melbourne, (train or car one hour) and the famous Great Ocean Road. Direct bus service to Geelong from Melbourne (Tullamarine and Avalon) airports. Local transport nearby to city, Lorne and Apollo Bay. Wildlife/birding tours can be arranged.

Victoria
Geelong
Ardara House

B&B
Owen & Maureen Sharkey
4 Aberdeen Street
Geelong
Vic 3218
0.5 km S of Geelong

Tel (03) 5229 6024
Fax (03) 5229 6180
ardara@bigpond.net.au
www.ardarahouse.com.au

Double $130-$160
Single $80-$110
Children $20
Continental breakfast
1 Queen 2 Double 2 Single (5 bdrm)
Bathrooms: 4 Ensuite 1 Guest share

   AAA Tourism
★★★★

Built in the Edwardian period (circa 1900) as a large family home, Ardara House offers the grace and homeliness of a bygone era. Guests can enjoy the relaxed and friendly atmosphere of fine Irish hospitality close to the heart of Geelong and on the beginning of the Great Ocean Road. Four spacious guest rooms feature luxurious beds and old world decor but with all the modern comforts and conveniences. Many of Geelong's finest restaurants, entertainment facilities as well as the shopping centre are only a stroll away.

Pets are welcome at many properties – contact hosts first to check on facilities available. Look for The Pets Welcome Logo

Gippsland – Nilma North

Experience the four seasons and indulge the five senses. Enjoy lush pastures, magnificent forests, spectacular views and rolling hills, renowned cool climate wines, world famous cheeses and fabulous food.
Kaye Greene, Springbank B&B, James Walshe Photography

Gippsland - Nilma North
Springbank B&B

B&B & Cottage
Kaye & Chris Greene
240 Williamsons Road
Nilma North
Vic 3821
8 km E of Warragul

Tel (03) 5627 8060 or 0437 350 243
Fax (03) 5627 8149
bookings@springbankbnb.com.au
www.springbankbnb.com.au

Double $155-$175
Single $125-$135, Full breakfast
Dinner & Massage by arrangement
Cottage: Double $135-$165 Single from $115
Visa MC Eftpos accepted
3 Queen (3 bdrm) Bathrooms: 3 Ensuite

AAA Tourism ★★★★☆

Springbank, a delightful 1890's Victorian Homestead offers luxury and boutique accommodation for a maximum of 3 couples set on 20 acres close to Warragul. Quiet, private & restful with extensive cottage gardens provides the perfect setting. Gourmet breakfasts, BBQ and outdoor cooking facilities, warm and friendly atmosphere. Open fires in the winter and reverse cycle airconditioning. Superb dining by arrangement.

Victoria

Gippsland - Sale

Sale is a great place to visit and stay and central to all of Gippsland's great historic & natural wonders. Whether your visit is for relaxation, sightseeing or adventure, we invite you to enjoy and experience the great diversity of our area.
Tim Dunnett, Bon Accord B&B

Gippsland - Sale
Bon Accord B&B

Luxury B&B & Self Contained Apartment
Tim Dunnett
153-155 Dawson Street
Sale
Vic 3850
2 km N of Sale Town Centre

Tel (03) 5144 5555
bonaccord-bookings@hotmail.com
www.bonaccordb-b.com.au

Double $155
Single $125, Full breakfast
Apartment from $175 per night without breakfast
Visa MC Eftpos accepted
1 King 3 Queen 2 Double 4 Single (6 bdrm)
Bathrooms: 4 Ensuite 1 Private

AAA Tourism
★★★★

Situated on two acres of gardens in Sale, Gippsland, Bon Accord is one of the city's oldest heritage properties dating from the early 1860's. Choose from three individual styled and fully renovated historic courtyard buildings or the beautifully restored Stables self contained apartment with 2 bedrooms. The main house at Bon Accord can also be made available for groups bookings. We are fully licensed and our luxury accommodation is available for honeymooners or those special wedding guests, as well as business and pleasure travellers.

Victoria

Grampians - Dunkeld
Royal Mail Hotel - Mt Sturgeon Estate

**Farmstay & Luxury Homestead
& Semi Self Contained Cottages**
Amy Peters
98 Parker Street, Dunkeld , Vic 3294
30 km E of Hamilton

Tel (03) 5577 2241
Fax (03) 5577 2577   relax@royalmail.com.au
www.royalmail.com.au

Double $220-$280
Single $220-$280, Children u/14 no charge,
Continental provisions , Restaurant, Bistro & Bar
available at hotel 3km away, Whole Homestead
$1380 pn, 2 b/r cottage $270-$315 pn,
Visa MC Amex Eftpos accepted
2 King 3 Queen 2 Single (6 bdrm)
Bathrooms: 1 Ensuite 3 Guest share

AAA Tourism
★★★★

Royal Mail Hotel's Mt Sturgeon Estate offers unique accommodation at the base of the Grampians Ranges with magnificent mountain views. The Estate's circular drive brings guests to the elegant 6 bedroom colonial Mt Sturgeon Homestead perfect for luxurious group getaways. The nearby bluestone shearers' cottages provide a rural sanctuary with open fires, Italian leather sofas and outdoor seating with bbq. Guests of the Estate have full access to hotel facilities such as swimming pool and the award winning Royal Mail Restaurant (The Age Good Food Guide 2009 Country Restaurant of the Year).

Grampians - Halls Gap
Mountain Grand Boutique Hotel

Guest House
Kay & Don Calvert
Main Road Town Centre
Halls Gap
Vic 3381
In Halls Gap

Tel (03) 5356 4232 or 1800 192 110
don@hallsgap.net
www.mountaingrand.com

Full breakfast
Dinner, B&B $206-$248
Indulgence Getaway (all meals) $248-$295
Visa MC Eftpos accepted
3 King 3 Queen 7 Double (13 bdrm) most rooms
can become twin/triple
Bathrooms: 12 Ensuite Spa Rooms available

AAA Tourism
★★★★

The Mountain Grand is a boutique hotel/guest-house/conference centre set amongst the picturesque Grampians mountains. Rooms have ensuites some with spas, suiting the era of the guesthouse. Guests may serenely relax in three lounge areas with a book or DVD. An al fresco courtyard, upstairs balcony and a mezzanine sundeck offer alternative places to be served afternoon teas or enjoy fine wines & beers from the club bar. "The Balconies" Restaurant provides a Delightful Dining experience. Cool Jazz musicians feature Saturday nights.

Victoria
Grampians - Wartook Valley
The Grelco Run

Self Contained Luxury Cottages & Homestead B&B
Graeme & Liz McDonald
520 Schmidts Road
Brimpaen, Vic 3401
30km E of Hamilton

Tel (03) 5383 9221
Fax (03) 5383 9221   grelco@skymesh.com.au
www.grampiansgrelcorun.com

Double $143
Single $71.50, Children $27.50,
Full breakfast provisions, Dinner $66,
Homestead: Single $110, Double $220 and
includes full breakfast, Visa MC accepted
2 King 3 Queen 2 Single (6 bdrm)
Bathrooms: 1 Ensuite 3 Guest share

The Grelco Run offers 2 self contained cottages set apart in natural bush, sleeping 6 in each, and a luxuriously appointed homestead with 3 guest bedrooms each with an ensuite. By prior arrangement we serve elegant hosted dinners in a convivial atmosphere. Our son Cameron operates the renowned Grampians Horse Riding Centre with escorted tours from the property. As we are adjacent to the National Park there are superb opportunities for bushwalking, 4WD driving, fishing, viewing abundant wildlife and wild flowers and visiting all major scenic attractions and nearby wineries.

Many properties offer activities onsite such as horse riding.
Look for The Onsite Activities Logo

Victoria

Heathcote

Once a gold mining region, Heathcote's new gold is Shiraz. Quickly becoming the Shiraz capital of Australia, winemakers and locals alike are keen to talk about the Cambrian soil and the big, beautiful red wines that come from grapes grown here.
Leslye Thies, Emeu Inn B&B, Restaurant and Wine Centre

Heathcote - Goldfields
Emeu Inn Bed & Breakfast, Restaurant & Wine Centre

Luxury B&B & Self Contained Cottage
Fred & Leslye Thies
187 High Street
Heathcote
Vic 3523
45 km SE of Bendigo

Tel (03) 5433 2668
Fax (03) 5433 4022
info@emeuinn.com.au
www.emeuinn.com.au

Double $180-$270
Single $150-$220, Children $40, Continental breakfast, Dinner Two-courses $50 pp, Cottage $420/couple: two nights, Extra person $40/nt, Visa MC Diners Amex Eftpos JCB accepted.
7 Queen (7 bdrm) Bathrooms: 7 Ensuite

Indulge yourself in luxury at the Award-winning Emeu Inn. Relax in the spacious suites with queen beds, private ensuites with spas or open fires and all the extras gourmet travellers expect. Dine in our Good Food Guide-recommended restaurant where international cuisine and local wines are standard fare. Our Wine Shop is stocked with local wines to take away! Enjoy some golf, Lake Eppalock, the forests, the shops or the wine! Part of the Goldfields, Heathcote's an easy weekend getaway!

Victoria
Horsham
Orange Grove B&B

B&B & Self Contained Cottage
Graeme and Nola Hill
123 Keatings Road
Horsham
Vic 3401
8 km NW of Horsham

Tel (03) 5382 0583 or 0427 536 346
Fax (03) 5382 7238
bookings@orangegrovebandb.com.au
www.orangegrovebandb.com.au

Double $150-$200
Single $100-$120
Full breakfast provisions
Pet-Friendly, Visa MC Eftpos accepted
2 Queen 1 Twin (3 bdrm)
Bathrooms: 1 Private

Conveniently located approximately halfway between Melbourne and Adelaide, Orange Grove offers luxury accommodation in a restored historic mudbrick homestead (early 1900s) located on 25 acres just minutes drive from Horsham. Enjoy a relaxed friendly welcome to a spacious quiet country setting with renovated gardens for your pleasure. The whole cottage is available exclusively, and features an open living area with cooking facilities and lounge with open fire (air-conditioning in summer). There is also a private enclosed outdoor courtyard with BBQ facilities. Pets are welcome.

Lakes Entrance
Kalimna Woods Cottages

Self Contained Cottages (8)
Cameron & Debbie Miller
30 Kalimna Jetty Road
Lakes Entrance
Vic 3909
2 km W of PO

Tel (03) 5155 1957
info@kalimnawoods.com.au
www.kalimnawoods.com.au

Double $115-$215
Single $115-$215, Children $15
Breakfast by arrangement
Extra adults $20 per night
Visa MC Eftpos accepted
8 Queen 8 Single (12 bdrm)
Bathrooms: 8 Private

AAA Tourism
★★★★

Romantic Spa and Woodfire Cottages set in a wonderful rainforest and garden setting on the edge of Australia's largest inland lake system. Bellbirds, King parrots and Lorikeets are just some of the abundant birdlife. At night watch the Sugar Gliders and Possums feed. Explore the lakes, see the Koalas at Raymond Island or visit the nearby Buchan Caves. Only 300 metres to the Kalimna Jetty and 2 km to the town centre. Kalimna Woods cottages are self catering. Breakfast hampers are available.

Victoria

Lorne
La Perouse B&B

Luxury B&B & Cottage Suite
Laurel & Sue
26A William Street
Lorne
Vic 3232
0.5 km E of Lorne

Tel 0418 534 422
email@laperouselorne.com.au
www.laperouselorne.com.au

Double $180-$300
Special French breakfast included in tariff
(we cater for gluten-free)
Visa MC Amex Eftpos accepted
1 King/Twin 3 Queen (4 bdrm)
Bathrooms: 4 Ensuite

Unrivalled luxury in the heart of Lorne, La Perouse enjoys sensational views of the Great Ocean Road, known for its rugged coastline. All four suites host Victorian period features, whilst allowing you to enjoy modern day comforts including en-suite bathrooms. Breakfast is served Parisian style in our cafe. Discover the nearby restaurants, stroll along the beach or relax in front of the fire. Peaceful elegance, romance and attention to detail surround you. Let us pamper you with our own special brand of hospitality.

Lorne - Aireys Inlet
Lorneview B&B

B&B & Separate Suite
Nola & Kevin Symes
677 Great Ocean Road
Eastern View
Vic 3231
14 km E of Lorne

Tel (03) 5289 6430
Fax (03) 5289 6735
lorneview@bigpond.com
www.lorneview.com.au

Double $130-$170
Single $120-$160
Continental breakfast
Visa MC accepted
2 Queen (2 bdrm)
Bathrooms: 2 Ensuite

AAA Tourism
★★★★

Lorneview has two spacious guest rooms, separate from main house, one overlooking the ocean and the other overlooking the bush. Each room has QS bed, ensuite, TV, CD/DVD player, heating, air conditioning, refrigerator, iron, ironing board, tea and coffee facilities. Delicious breakfast of fresh fruit, homemade muesli, muffins and croissants is served in your room or on balcony overlooking beach. Dinner unavailable, but many excellent restaurants nearby. Barbecue and Games Room provided. Enjoy walks along the beach and go to sleep listening to the waves.

Victoria

Lorne - Aireys Inlet
Qdos Treehouses

Luxury B&B & Cottage, no kitchen
Graeme & Glynis
35 Allenvale Road
Lorne
Vic 3232
1 km W of Lorne

Tel (03) 5289 1989
Fax (03) 5289 1983
qdos@iprimus.com.au
www.qdosarts.com

Double $180-$250
Full breakfast
Visa MC Diners Amex Eftpos accepted
1 Queen (1 bdrm) Japanese style
Japanese bath

This unique venue offers the visitor a fine art gallery that represents some of Australia's finest artist, sculpture garden with major works, a large ceramic studio and the great cafe where most thing are made in-house from seasonal produce from our gardens. The Qdos Treehouse accommodation is where aesthetics matters and tranquil set in the Great Otway National Park, yet only minutes from the Lorne main beach.

Lorne - Otway Ranges - Birregurra
Elliminook

Luxury B&B & Self Contained Apartment
Jill & Peter Falkiner
585 Warncoort - Birregurra Road
Birregurra
Vic 3242
38 km N of Lorne

Tel (03) 5236 2080
Fax (03) 5236 2423
enquiries@elliminook.com.au
www.elliminook.com.au

Double $160-$240
Single $140-$220
Full breakfast
Visa MC Amex accepted
4 Queen 2 Single (5 bdrm)
Bathrooms: 4 Ensuite

Award winning Elliminook c1865 is a beautifully restored and decorated National Trust classified homestead providing a great relaxing getaway. Guests will enjoy the historic garden, croquet, boules, tennis court, open fires, liquor service, sumptuous cooked breakfast, fresh flowers in your room, and welcoming hospitality. From Elliminook you can explore the Great Ocean Road, Twelve Apostles, Shipwreck Coast, Otway Fly Tree Top Walk, including Birregurra's historic walk, waterfalls and rain forest of the scenic Otway Ranges. For a unique accommodation experience be our welcome guest. Stay in our new self contained south wing with private entrance.

MELBOURNE'S BEST
BED & BREAKFASTS

- mouth watering breakfasts
- stunning surrounds
- great locations
- informative hosts

Present this advertisement on arrival to receive a complimentary bottle of Australian wine.

www.melbournesbest.com.au
PHONE (03) 9428 8104

Victoria

Melbourne
Apartment 401

CBD Apartment
Gayle Lamb
258 Flinders Lane
Melbourne
Vic 3000
In Melbourne

Tel (03) 9428 8104 or 0412 068 855
Fax (03) 9421 0956
email@apartment401.com.au
www.apartment401.com.au

Double $250-$350
Accommodation only
Visa MC Diners Eftpos accepted
1 Queen (1 bdrm)
Bathrooms: 1 Ensuite

Melbourne CBD apartment. Perfect for art lovers, foodies and shoppers, this stunning 1 bedroom apartment in the historic Majorca House building is located right in the heart of Melbourne's bustling, bohemian arts precinct, just one block from the Yarra river. The spacious, light filled lounge-dining room looks down on Degraves Street, famous for its coffee bars and eateries. The bedroom has a queen sized bed and a tiny, Parisian style Juliet balcony. There is a fully equipped, stylish kitchen and a large tiled bathroom complete with bathtub.

Melbourne
Robinsons in the City

B&B & Guest House
Tish Black & Paul Humphreys
405 Spencer Street (cnr Batman Street)
West Melbourne
Vic 3003
1 km NW of Melbourne

Tel (03) 9329 2552
Fax (03) 9329 3747
robinsons@robinsonsinthecity.com.au
www.ritc.com.au

Double $185-$345
Single $185-$345
Full breakfast
Off-street parking (limited)
1 King/Twin3 King 2 Queen (6 bdrm)
Bathrooms: 1 Ensuite 5 Private

AAA Tourism
★★★★

Robinsons in the City is Melbourne's smallest boutique hotel, located on the fringe of Melbourne's CBD, this 1850's property is stylish, different and thoroughly delightful. Ideally located close to; Southern Cross Railway & Bus Station, Etihad Stadium (formally Telstra Dome), Docklands (New Quay, Waterfront City and Harbour Town precincts), Queen Victoria Market and Melbourne's famous Parks and Gardens. This urban bed and breakfast is a rare find in the Melbourne CBD and offers something very different than that of larger traditional hotels.

Victoria

Melbourne - Brighton
Waratah Brighton Boutique B&B

Luxury B&B
Brigitte & Harry Orth
70 Roslyn Street
Brighton
Vic 3186
12 km SW of Melbourne

Tel (03) 9592 0501 or 0419 596 300
Fax (03) 9592 0414
stay@waratahbrighton.com.au
www.waratahbrighton.com.au

Double $185-$275
Single $165-$195
Full breakfast
Visa MC accepted
3 Queen 1 Double (4 bdrm)
Bathrooms: 4 Ensuite

Waratah Brighton is a gracious relaxed 1880's period home set on a beautiful allotment with tranquil private garden, large swimming pool and Hydro Spa house. Facilities include a spacious formal guest sitting room with a large dining table, gas log fire place, high ceilings, chandeliers, decorated with a delightfully eclectic European Haute Bohemia style, lovingly created to provide a refreshingly out of the ordinary experience. An informal sitting room with open fire place, leather lounges and Foxtel TV leads to a sun shaded outdoor entertainment area. The centre of Waratah Brighton B&B is the open style kitchen where you can have a conversation with the hosts.

Melbourne - Camberwell
Springfields

B&B
Robyn & Phillip Jordan
4 Springfield Avenue
Camberwell
Vic 3124
9 km E of Melbourne

Tel (03) 9809 1681 or 0434 353 750
Fax (03) 9809 1681
the.jordans@pacific.net.au
www.bbbook.com.au/springfields.html

Double $130
Single $90
Children welcome - contact us for prices
Full breakfast
1 King/Twin 1 Twin (2 bdrm)
Bathrooms: 1 Guest share 1 Private

"Springfields" is our attractive and spacious family home in a quiet avenue in one of Melbourne's finest suburbs. Guests comment on the quietness, and the fresh fruit salad at breakfast! Guests can enjoy the peace and privacy of their own lounge - or join us for a friendly chat. Public transport is nearby. Children are most welcome. Make our home your home when you next visit Melbourne.

BBBook.com.au

Victoria

Melbourne - Carnegie
Josephine's B&B

B&B
Jo & Ed Biggs
40 Rosanna Street
Carnegie
Vic 3163
12 km SE of Melbourne CBD

Tel (03) 9569 9386 or 0412 458 736
josephinesbb@optusnet.com.au
www.josephinesbb.com.au

Double $90-$110
Single $70-$95, Children $20, Continental breakfast, Family from $120-$150
Reduced tariffs for extended stays
Visa MC Eftpos accepted
1 Queen 1 Twin 1 Single (3 bdrm)
Bathrooms: 2 Private

Situated in a pleasant garden setting, Josephine's Bed & Breakfast in Carnegie is just 12km from the CBD. Serviced by rail, tram and bus and just off the Monash Freeway. We are perfectly suited for families or business travellers with three guest rooms. Each booking includes a private bathroom. Guests can enjoy a range of facilities, including a comfortable guest lounge with cable TV, DVD and VCR. A cot and high chair are also available. Enjoy a cooked or continental breakfast in the modern family room or alfresco in the garden. Close to parks, playgrounds and sporting facilities.

Melbourne - Fairfield
Fairfield Guest House

B&B & Self Contained Apartment & Guest House
Clare & Lindsay Nankivell
18 Station Street
Fairfield
Vic 3078
5 km N of Melbourne

Tel (03) 9482 2959 or 0438 891 817
Fax (03) 9482 1956
fairfieldguesthouse@hotmail.com
www.babs.com.au/fairfield

Double $90-$185
Single $75-$165, Continental provisions
Visa MC Eftpos accepted
5 Queen 1 Twin 1 Single (7 bdrm)
Bathrooms: 3 Ensuite 2 Guest share

AAA Tourism ★★★★

Fairfield Guest House offers seven rooms ranging between rooms with shared bathroom facilities to rooms with private bathrooms and lovely self contained suite with double spa bath and all the comforts of home. We are only ten minutes from Melbourne CBD a short stroll to all public transport and the beautiful Fairfield Park Boathouse offering the best Devonshire Teas in Melbourne overlooking the Yarra River. We cater for all budgets and we are pet friendly for those that love travelling with their animals.

Melbourne - Richmond
Villa Donati

B&B
Gayle Lamb & Trevor Finlayson
377 Church Street
Richmond
Vic 3121
2.5 km E of Melbourne CBD

Tel (03) 9428 8104 or 0412 068 855
Fax (03) 9421 0956
email@villadonati.com
www.villadonati.com

Double $205-$255
Single $185, Full breakfast, Visa MC Diners Amex Eftpos accepted
3 Queen 1 Double (4 bdrm)   Bathrooms: 4 Ensuite

  AAA Tourism ★★★★☆

Cool classic exterior, rich stylish interior - Villa Donati is a chic, inner city bed and breakfast. Previously home to distinguished architects, archbishops and the 'Moulin Rouge' massage parlour, Villa Donati has been restored to capture the essence of the European pensione.

Today, this historic and charming property is a stunning mix of contemporary and antique design. Each room has its own unique style and furnishings - fine bed linen, imported toiletries, antiques and original art works. The guest sitting room offers city views and the cafe style breakfast room is the perfect place for indulgent breakfasts.

Villa Donati is situated in cosmopolitan Richmond, only minutes from the CBD and Melbourne's main shopping, entertainment and sporting precincts.

From the Visitors' Book: More like staying at a friend's smart artefact-strewn pad than in a hotel. Light, high-ceilinged rooms are all individually furnished. Add freshly cooked breakfast and city skyline views and this is a very special find.

BBBook.com.au

Victoria

Melbourne - Richmond
Rotherwood

B&B Self Contained Apartment
Flossie Sturzaker
13 Rotherwood Street
Richmond, Melbourne
Vic 3121
1.5 km E of Melbourne Central

Tel (03) 9428 6758
Fax (03) 9428 6758
rotherwoodbb@bigpond.com
www.bbbook.com.au/rotherwood.html

Double $145-$185
Single $125-$175, Children Additional,
Special breakfast, S/C Apt includes breakfast,
Visa MC accepted
Separate Queen sized bedroom
Bathrooms: 1 Private

'On the Hill' in Richmond, 'Rotherwood' is at the heart of Melbourne's attractions. Walking distance of the MCG, Royal Botanic Gardens, National Tennis Centre, shops and caf√©s. 5 minute tram ride to City. Easy access to National Gallery, Concert Hall, Crown Casino, and Southbank. Private entrance to Victorian era apartment. Large sitting room leading to terraced garden. Bedroom, private bathroom, and separate dining room with cooking facilities. Special Breakfast provided. Extra fold-out bed. Airport transport available. TV and Wireless Internet. Short or long term stay.

Melbourne - Richmond
94 Highett B&B

B&B Suites
Jeff Cheffers & Lexie Rossiter
94 Highett Street
Richmond
Vic 3121
2.5 km E of Melbourne CBD

Tel (03) 9421 0248 or 0418 932 204
jeffcheffers@optusnet.com.au
www.bbbook.com.au/94HighettBB.html

Double $150-$180
Full breakfast
Additional guest $25 per night
Visa MC Eftpos accepted
3 Queen (3 bdrm)
Elegant suites with individual sitting rooms
Bathrooms: 2 Ensuite

94 Highett is a beautiful B&B accommodation in Richmond providing quality facilities with a more personal approach. Guests have a choice of two elegant suites each with private entrances and individual sitting rooms, ensuite with spa and can sleep 4 adults. Both suites have heating and individually controlled air-conditioning, bar fridges, tea and coffee making facilities, LCD TV's and wireless internet. The elevated deck provides stunning views of the city at night while the intimate courtyard is the perfect spot for an evening sundowner. A full breakfast is served in the dining room or courtyard weather permitting.

Victoria

Melbourne - St Kilda
Alrae Bed & Breakfast

B&B
Vivienne Wheeler
7 Hughenden Road
St Kilda East
Vic 3183
5 km SE of Melbourne

Tel (03) 9527 2033 or 0409 174 132
Fax (03) 9527 2044
alrae2@bigpond.com
www.visitvictoria.com/alrae

Double $165-$205
Single $99-$121, Children $33-$66,
Special breakfast, Dinner $44 B/A, Spare sofa
bed $66-$121, Visa MC Amex JCB accepted
1 Queen 1 Twin (2 bdrm)|
Bathrooms: 1 Ensuite 1 Private

Alrae, a well kept secret, is 5 km. from Melbourne CBD, handy public transport including daytime suburban airport shuttle bus, beach, shops, sports venues, restaurants and theatres. It features a Queen bedroom with ensuite, air-conditioning, fridge, private entrance. The Twin bedroom with a view has adjoining private bathroom with spa shower over bathtub, aircond. Air-conditioned guests' dining room cum lounge, specialty breakfasts and dietary variations. All rooms have TV/VCR, TV/DVD, clock radios, books etc. BBQ, OSP. Corporate, Seniors, Medical profession, Members Motor Organisations, Conditions apply.

Melbourne - Williamstown

Enjoy this unique historical peninsula with glorious parks, yacht clubs, spectacular city views, great walks, a protected swimming beach, galleries, museums, theatres, restaurants and a wonderful Sunday craft market. Only 15 minutes from the centre of Melbourne with the option of travel by ferry, train or car.
Melissa Meek, Captains Retreat B&B

Victoria
Melbourne - Williamstown
Captains Retreat B&B

Luxury B&B
Melissa Meek-Jacobs
2 Ferguson Street, Williamstown, Vic 3016
In Williamstown

Tel (03) 9397 0352 or 0438 358 823
Fax (03) 9397 0352   captainsretreat@bigpond.com
www.captainsretreat.com.au

Double $165-$225
Single $155-$215, Elegant small functions by arrangement
Full cooked breakfast or provisions left out for early birds
Visa MC Diners Amex Eftpos accepted
1 King 4 Queen 1 Single (6 bdrm)
Bathrooms: 5 Ensuite 1 Private

Being just one door from the water, and walking distance to restaurants, shops and yacht clubs, Captain's Retreat is a beautiful, recently refurbished Victorian in a fabulous location.

This charming old home with its somewhat chequered history, (including having been a convent and a brothel!), boasts beautiful decor, very comfortable beds, ensuite bathrooms (3 with spas) digital televisions gas fireplaces in most bedrooms and a large guest lounge with fire and guest balcony. Two suites even have their own private lounge rooms. It's a big house!

Your choice of continental or cooked breakfasts are served either in the downstairs kitchen, up in the guest lounge/dining or on the north facing rear balcony.'

This is a lovely place to just come and 'be' so it is no wonder that guests often return.

Mildura
Mildura's Linsley House

B&B & Homestay
Colin & Desley Rankin
PO Box 959
Mildura
Vic 3502
15 km E of Mildura at Trentham Cliffs

Tel (03) 5024 8487 or 0417 593 483
Fax (03) 5024 8914
linsleybb@bigpond.com
www.innhouse.com/linsley.html

Double $120
Single $80
Full breakfast
Visa MC accepted
2 Queen 2 Single (3 bdrm)
Bathrooms: 2 Ensuite

Linsley House B&B has a magnificent river view. Colin and Desley Rankin take pleasure in welcoming you to their charming and tranquil home which is situated in a quiet rural setting and has panoramic views of the garden and Murray River from the bedrooms. The large lounge/dining area includes: full kitchen facilities, TV, fridge, woodfire, air-conditioning and comfortable antiques. Mildura is renown for its oranges, dried fruits, wineries and Mediterranean weather.

**The difference between a hotel and a B&B.
You don't hug the hotel staff when you leave.**

Victoria

Mornington - Mount Eliza
Sartain's at Mornington

Cottage Stay
Sally Sartain
75 Oakbank Road
Mount Eliza
Vic 3930
5 km SW of Mount Eliza & 5 km E of Mornington

Tel (03) 5975 1014
Fax (03) 5975 1014
sally@sartains.com.au
www.sartains.com.au

Weekly minimum stay $750 per week
Breakfast provisions first night
Visa MC Eftpos accepted
1 Queen (1 bdrm)
Bathrooms: 1 Private

    AAA Tourism ★★★★

You are invited to share the Sartain's Experience. Stylishly renovated self-contained air-conditioned/heated cottage; TV with foxtel/DVD, radio, dining area, fully equipped kitchen, modern bathroom and laundry. Quality facilities set in private gardens including all-weather tennis court with entertainment pavilion and BBQ, and surrounds including horse paddocks. Close to beaches, shops, golf and wineries. As much or as little as you would like to do. All set in a relaxing country atmosphere.

Mornington Peninsula - Dromana
Lakeside Villas at Crittenden Estate

Self Contained Villas
Margaret Crittenden
25 Harrisons Road
Dromana
Vic 3936
6 km N of Dromana

Tel (03) 5987 3275 or 0417 329 626
Fax (03) 5981 0714
lakesidevillas@crittendenwines.com.au
www.lakesidevillas.com.au

Double $250-$280
Single $250-$280. Full breakfast provisions,
Onsite restaurant: open lunch daily, dinner weekends, Extra guest $50 pn,
Visa MC Eftpos accepted
3 King (3 bdrm) Bathrooms: 3 Ensuite

    AAA Tourism ★★★★☆

Perched overlooking the vineyards lake these contemporary villas are an oasis of tranquillity. Quality appointments throughout ensure your stay is an experience of relaxation. The open plan living and kitchen, which spills out onto your own private balcony over the lake, creates a feeling of spaciousness and warmth. Amenities include king size beds, double spa baths, open fire and your own laundry. Because Lakeside Villas are family owned and operated we offer the personal services of a small establishment without compromising on the necessary luxuries.

Phillip Island - Cowes
Glen Isla House

Luxury B&B & Hotel & Luxury Country House B&B
Madeleine & Ian Baker
230-232 Church Street, Cowes, Vic 3922
0.15 km W of Cowes

Tel (03) 5952 1882 or (03) 5952 3000
Fax (03) 5952 5028
infobbb@glenisla.com
www.glenisla.com

Double $265-$395
Not Suitable for children, Special Cooked Breakfasts,
Single Tariff POA, Visa MC Diners Amex Eftpos accepted
1 King 6 Queen 2 Twin (9 bdrm)
Bathrooms: 7 Ensuite 1 Guest share

   AAA Tourism ★★★★★

Set in the secluded heritage gardens of the historic and heritage classified Glen Isla homestead (c1870). Multi award- winning luxury country-house B&B offering elegant surroundings. Absolute privacy, 100 meters direct access to a pristine sandy beach.
"Arguably the island's best accommodation" - Melbourne Age. "The best address on the island" - Lonely Planet Guide 2009. Highly recommended Frommer's Guide 2007, 2008 & 2009.
Accommodations include the historic Anderson Heritage Suite cottage with four-poster king bed, log fire, spa, period furnishings and HD TV+DVD system ; Six purpose-architected Glen Isla "classic" rooms with walk-in robe/luggage room, private en-suite, LCD TV/DVD, superb garden vistas & separate entrances; the Gate Cottage - an elegant 2 bedroom - 2 storey cottage set under 2 x 100 year old oak trees in the heritage gardens.
Special cooked breakfasts served daily in the dining room at individual table settings with vistas of the heritage gardens dating back to the late 1800's.

Victoria

Phillip Island - Cowes
Abaleigh on Lovers Walk

Self Contained Apartments
Jenny Hudson
6 Roy Court
Cowes, Phillip Island
Vic 3922
0.4 km E of Cowes PO

Tel (03) 5952 5649
Fax (03) 5952 2549
info@abaleigh.com
www.abaleigh.com

Double $180-$270
Single $170-$260, Full breakfast provisions
Apartment from $230 dble
Visa MC accepted
2 King/Twin 1 King 2 Queen (5 bdrm)
Bathrooms: 5 Ensuite 5 Private

  AAA Tourism ★★★★☆

Abaleigh's FSC absolute beach frontage apartment and studios offer the finest accommodation. Featuring: spas, water views, Jetmaster log fires, double showers, breakfast-stocked kitchens, laundries, courtyards with barbecues for outdoor living, air conditioned, TV, DVD, stereo and more. Five minutes foreshore stroll to restaurants and central Cowes. Peaceful, private, ideal for couples or small groups of adults. Best Hosted Accommodation Regional Tourism Awards. AAA ****1/2, "In one word perfect." J&M, Malvern.

Phillip Island - Cowes
Genesta House

B&B & Guest House
Susan Handley
18 Steele Street
Cowes
Vic 3922
0.3 km E of Post Office

Tel (03) 5952 3616
genesta@nex.net.au
www.genesta.com.au

Double $160-$250
Special breakfast
Qualified Massage Therapist on property
(by appointment)
Visa MC Eftpos accepted
4 Queen (4 bdrm)
Bathrooms: 4 Ensuite

Historic guest house in the heart of Cowes, 5 minutes walk to front beach/pier and main street with cafés and restaurants. A Special breakfast is served in the Guest Lounge/breakfast room overlooking the outdoor spa and bbq area. Relax and unwind beside the trickle of the fountain in the ambience of Genesta House.

Victoria

Princetown

Twelve Apostles are majestic limestone rock formations in the Southern Ocean off the south west coast of Victoria. Thousands of visitors are intrigued and amazed at this unique natural wonder.
Lynne Boxshall, Arabella Country House

Princetown - Twelve Apostles
Arabella Country House

Luxury B&B & Homestay
Lynne & Neil Boxshall
7219 Great Ocean Road
Princetown
Vic 3269
6 km E of Princetown

Tel (03) 5598 8169
Fax (03) 5598 8186
arabellacountryhse@bigpond.com
www.innhouse.com.au/arabella.html

Double $155-$165
Single $85, Children $25 under 6 years old,
Full breakfast, Dinner $35 for 3 courses,
Visa MC Eftpos accepted
3 Queen 1 Double 2 Single (4 bdrm)
Bathrooms: 4 Ensuite

Arabella Country House is situated within sight of 12 Apostles, Port Campbell N.P. and Otway N.P. All are must see attractions for visitors to Victoria. Our promise is that our superior B&B experience will add to our guests' adventure along the Great Ocean Road. With comfortable relaxing surroundings, quality fittings and the freshest food, plus local knowledge make special memories. Together with our dogs, we really enjoy our guests' visit and hope to see you soon.

BBBook.com.au

Victoria

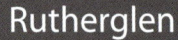

Rutherglen

Rutherglen is known throughout Australia as a place with great soul and home to some of the world's greatest wines. Rutherglen is also a place of country lanes, idyllic pastoral scenes, ancient River Red Gums and lush vineyards stretching off to the horizon.
Peter and Pauline Meade, Ready Cottage B&B

Rutherglen
Ready Cottage

B&B
Peter & Pauline Meade
92 High Street
Rutherglen
Vic 3685
0.4 km N of PO

Tel (02) 6032 7407
stay@readycottage.com.au
www.readycottage.com.au

Double $150-$165
Single $130-$145
Full breakfast
Visa MC accepted
3 Queen (3 bdrm)
Bathrooms: 3 Ensuite

AAA Tourism
★★★★

Enhance your visit to Rutherglen by staying at one of the town's original Victorian cottages. Ready Cottage blends stylish renovation with its old world charm and heritage. Enjoy traditional hosted Bed and Breakfast hospitality before setting out to explore the region's many attractions. After a day of wine tasting and touring, take time to relax in our private gardens before strolling to Main St to indulge yourself at the local restaurants, shops and hotels. All rooms include ensuites, queen size beds, TV and heating and cooling.

Rutherglen
Mount Ophir Estate

B&B & Homestead and Self Contained Cottages
Ruth Hennessy
168 Stillards Lane, Rutherglen, Vic 3685
5 km SE of Rutherglen

Tel (02) 6032 8920
mountophir@bigpond.com
www.mount-ophir.com.au

Double $170-$190
Full breakfast, Meals available on request, Rustic Function Centre,
Accommodation only available from $130 per couple,
Visa MC accepted
6 Queen (6 bdrm)
Bathrooms: 4 Ensuite 1 Guest share

Stay a few days and enjoy your organic farm retreat at Mount Ophir Estate, a beautifully restored historic winery estate in the heart of Victoria's prime wine growing district.

Choose B&B or Self Contained. The 1902 Homestead offers privacy, six comfortable bedrooms and a stunning country kitchen to indulge your cooking skills! The house is suitable for family groups and wedding parties as well as private retreats for couples.

The self contained Gatehouse is a pleasant fully renovated 3 bathroom Victorian farm house accommodating up to 12. 'Muscat Place' accommodating 6 is also available.

Mount Ophir Estate is a great place to view sunsets, stars while sipping a glass of Mount Ophir organic Shiraz!

Victoria
Sorrento - Mornington Peninsula
Tamasha House

B&B
Naomi & Peter Nicholson
699 Melbourne Road
Sorrento
Vic 3943
1 km E of Sorrento

Tel (03) 5984 2413
Fax (03) 5984 0452
tamasha@ozemail.com.au
www.peninsulapages.com/tamasha

Double $200
Single $120, Full breakfast
Dinner by arrangement
Visa MC Diners Amex JCB accepted
1 King/Twin 1 Double (2 bdrm)
Bathrooms: 2 Ensuite

Tamasha House, set in a beautiful garden, is situated between Ocean and Bay beaches and is a short distance from historic Sorrento. An ideal place to stay while exploring the Mornington Peninsula. Take the ferry to Queenscliff or go swimming with the dolphins, visit the wineries or discover the galleries and restaurants, all within a short distance. Your caring hosts offer a warm welcome, fine food and local knowledge.

When making an enquiry or booking, please tell your hosts,
"We saw you in the Bed & Breakfast Book!"

Victoria

Swan Hill - Lake Boga

Lake Boga - The hidden jewel in the heart of the Mallee 16km south of Swan Hill, offers unique recreational experiences, Sharlea Ultra Fine Wool tours, Catalina Flying Boat Museum and a natural wonderland for fishing, bird watching, wineries and horticulture.
Tricia & Bruce Pollard, Burrabliss B&B

Swan Hill - Lake Boga
Burrabliss Farms B&B

B&B & Separate Suite
Tricia & Bruce Pollard
169 Lakeside Drive
Lake Boga
Vic 3584
2 km S of Murray Valley Highway

Tel (03) 5037 2527 or 0427 346 942
info@burrabliss.com.au
www.burrabliss.com.au

Double $125-$180
Single $100-$150, Children $10,
Special breakfast, Country style breakfast included, Breakfast provisions in Villa, Dinner $45, Visa MC Amex Eftpos JCB accepted
2 King/Twin 1 King 2 Queen (5 bdrm)
Bathrooms: 3 Ensuite 1 Guest share

AAA Tourism
★★★★☆

After all you deserve it. Luxury accommodation at it's best: whether for your honeymoon, a romantic weekend or simply need to get away. Burrabliss is the idyllic location for a nature lover with 6 acres natural habitat. Suite Bliss offers stylish garden setting accommodation with king bed, spa, private lounge. Villa Bliss offers self contained. Traditional B&B also available. Enjoy yabbying, strolling through our country garden, exploring nearby wetlands with 68 bird species noted. Undercover BBQ facilities and car parking. Complimentary chocolates and wine. Burrabliss Farms offers complimentary guided tours of their Sharlea Ultra Fine Wool enterprise.

Victoria
Torquay

The Great Ocean Road is one of the major tourism icons in Australia. The Surf Coast region is home to some of the most spectacular scenery along this world renowned ocean drive, which includes Bells Beach, the home of Australian surfing.
Helen and Bob Bailey, Ocean Manor B&B

Torquay - Surf Coast
Ocean Manor B&B

Luxury B&B & Self Contained Suite
Helen & Bob Bailey
3 Glengarry Drive
Torquay
Vic 3228
17 km S of Geelong

Tel (03) 5261 3441 or 0407 597 100
Fax (03) 5261 9140
oceanmanor@bigpond.com
www.oceanmanor.com.au

Double $120-$180
Single $90-$100, Children $20, Extra adult $30
Continental breakfast , 2 bedroom suite $130-$200 , Visa MC Amex accepted
1 Queen 1 Twin (2 bdrm)
Bathrooms: 1 Ensuite 1 Guest share

AAA Tourism
★★★★

The 2 bedroom suite is situated upstairs to ensure privacy and take maximum advantage of the ocean view. The master bedroom features a queen sized bed, ensuite bathroom. Adjoining is a combined lounge and dining area which leads onto a decked balcony with sweeping ocean views. The air conditioned lounge has Foxtel, TV and DVDs. The mini kitchen with fridge and microwave leads to a second bedroom with separate toilet facilities and 2 single beds. A continental breakfast is included.

Victoria

Wangaratta

At the gateway to the Ovens and King Valleys, Wangaratta if famous for world class wines, gourmet food, spectacular golf courses and links to Ned Kelly. The Murray to Mountains rail trail and the Great Alpine Road both start at Wangaratta.
Margaret Blackshaw, The Pelican B&B

Wangaratta
The Pelican

B&B & Farmstay
Margaret & Bernie Blackshaw
606 Oxley Flats Road
Wangaratta
Vic 3678
6 km E of Wangaratta

Tel (03) 5727 3240 or 0413 082 758
pellcanblackshaw@hotmail.com
www.bbbook.com.au/thepelican.html

Double $120-$150
Single $75, Children $40
Full breakfast
Dinner $30 per person by arrangement
$40 extra person in double room
1 Queen 1 Twin 2 Single (3 bdrm)
Bathrooms: 1 Guest share 1 Private

AAA Tourism ★★★☆

The Pelican is a charming historic homestead set in parklike surroundings. Cattle and horses are raised on the 400 acres and early risers can go "trackside" to watch the harness horses at work. Guest rooms are in an upstairs wing of the home and have lovely country views where peacocks and pelicans are often spotted. The main bedroom has its own private balcony overlooking a lagoon fringed with giant red gums. Hearty breakfasts feature home grown produce and evening meals are available on request.

Victoria

Warrnambool

Nestled in the heart of the rugged Great Ocean Road region and surrounded by a lush hinterland of rural landscapes, Warrnambool offers a large range of cafes and restaurants, events and entertainment.

Pamela Beechey, Merton Manor Exclusive B&B and Flagstaff Hill Maritime Village

Warrnambool
Merton Manor Exclusive B&B

Luxury B&B & Separate Suites
Pamela & Ivan Beechey
62 Ardlie Street
Warrnambool
Vic 3280
1 km N of Warrnambool PO

Tel (03) 5562 0720 or 0417 314 304
Fax (03) 5561 1220
merton@ansonic.com.au
http://members.datafast.net.au/merton

Double $160-$180
Single $130-$150, Extra person $35
Full breakfast
Visa MC Diners Amex Eftpos JCB accepted
1 King/Twin 5 Queen 2 Single (6 bdrm)
Bathrooms: 6 Ensuite 6 double spas

AAA Tourism ★★★★☆

Merton Manor is a traditional B&B with mews style accommodation set within an historic Victorian villa. It features antiques, open fires, billiard and music rooms and grand dining room and is located mid way between Adelaide and Melbourne. All suites feature private entrances, climate control heating and air conditioning, private lounge rooms and ensuites with double spas. Merton Manor is situated close to the cultural attractions and restaurants of Warrnambool. The 12 Apostles, whale viewing, Tower Hill State Game Reserve and the Maritime Museum are all close by. AAAT 4 1/2 stars. Beach and Botanical Gardens nearby.

Victoria

Warrnambool
Quamby Homestead

B&B & Self Contained House
Julie & Karl Mischkulnig
3223 Caramut Road
Woolsthorpe, Vic 3276
32 km N of Warrnambool

Tel (03) 5569 2395
Fax (03) 5569 2244
quambyhomestead@bigpond.com
www.quambyhomestead.com.au

Double $145-$185
Single $125-$165, Children 3-12 $22, Baby cot provided FOC, Full breakfast, Dinner Available by prior arrangement, $33 per additional adult in Carriage House, Visa MC Diners Amex Eftpos JCB accepted. 1 King 5 Queen 1 Twin 2 Single (8 bdrm) Bathrooms: 7 Ensuite

AAA Tourism ★★★★

Located just 20mins inland from Great Ocean Road and Warrnambool, Quamby provides an ideal two night destination for exploring this fascinating region, which includes volcanic Tower Hill, historic Port Fairy and whale watching at Logan's Beach, Warrnambool, before travelling on to The Grampians, Ballarat Goldfields, Melbourne or Adelaide. Relax and enjoy local native wildlife (kangaroos, koalas, cockatoos, possums), watch cattle and horses graze in the paddocks, or take a stroll around the 2km property walk. Whatever your preference, come experience 'Quamby', Aboriginal for resting place.

Warrnambool - Allansford
Burnbrow Manor & Cottage

B&B & Self Contained Cottage
Beverley & Robert Burns
1 Hopetoun Street, Allansford, Vic 3277
In Allansford. 5 mins E of Warrnambool

Tel (03) 5565 1380 or 0418 346 305
Fax (03) 5565 1380
stay@burnbrowmanor.com.au
www.burnbrowmanor.com.au

Double $130-$160
Single $110-$140, Children over the age of 5, Special breakfast, Dinner vouchers for Allansford Hotel Bistro, Cottage 2-5 persons $130-$240, Extra person from $20 per night, Visa MC Eftpos accepted
2 Queen 1 Double 1 Twin 1 Single (4 bdrm) Bathrooms: 2 Ensuite 1 Guest share

AAA Tourism ★★★★

Environmentally Friendly 4 Star Traditional Bed & Breakfast at the western end of the Great Ocean Road. Upper floor dedicated to guests only, central lounge, kitchenette, dining area, CH, AC, Plasma TV, DVD, Austar, Wireless Internet, off street parking. 3.5 Star PET FRIENDLY 3 Bedroom Cottage accommodates 2-8. Ideal location to explore this fantastic region including local Beaches, volcanic Tower Hill, Hopkins River Falls, historic Port Fairy, the Grampians, Ballarat or midway stopover between Melbourne and Adelaide.

Victoria

Yarra Valley

Kalorama is set in the beautiful Dandenong Ranges near Olinda, where you can wander through picturesque walking trails and enjoy William Ricketts Sanctuary, Healesville Sanctuary, Puffing Billy, plus Yarra Valley Wineries. Indulge yourself with fine food and wine amongst the wide variety of local restaurants and cafes.
Loraine Potter, Holly Gate House and Andrew Chapman photographer

Yarra Valley - Dandenong Ranges
Holly Gate House B&B

Luxury B&B & Traditional
Loraine Potter
1308 Mt Dandenong Tourist Road
Kalorama
Vic 3766
5 km NE of Olinda

Tel (03) 9728 3218 or 0415 192 690
Fax (03) 9728 3218
reception@hollygatehouse.com.au
www.hollygatehouse.com.au

Double $160-$225
Single $160-$225, Full breakfast, Complimentary restaurant/function venue transfer, Visa MC Eftpos accepted
3 Queen (3 bdrm)
Bathrooms: 3 Ensuite 1 ensuite with spa bath

   AAA Tourism ★★★★

Luxury traditional accommodation in the romantic Dandenong Ranges, the gateway to the Yarra Valley. Three beautifully appointed Queen bedrooms all with private ensuite (one with spa). Pamper yourself or the one you love with a sauna and spa/hot tub package whilst staying in comfortable accommodation (two night bookings only). Package includes afternoon tea on arrival, fully cooked breakfast served in the guests' dining room. Sitting room with log fire. Outside solar heated pool in a pleasant garden setting. BBQ facilities. Complimentary transport to and from any local restaurant/function venue. Adult Retreat only/no pets. 45k from Melbourne. Melways Ref: Page52 J9.

Yarra Valley - Yarra Glen
The Gatehouse at Villa Raedward

Luxury Self Contained Apartment
John & Sandra Annison
26 Melba Highway
Yering
Vic 3770
7 km S of Yarra Glen

Tel (03) 9739 0822 or 0425 730 824
info@villaraedward.com.au
www.villaraedward.com.au

Double $220-$260
Single $220-$260
Full breakfast provisions
Visa MC Amex Eftpos accepted
1 Queen (2 bdrm)
Bathrooms: 2 Private
2 person spa, large shower in marble bathroom

  AAA Tourism ★★★★☆

Two architect-designed fully self contained units with undercover parking and private entrance and patio looking out over the Yarra Valley. Marble bathroom with large shower and two person spa overlooking a private courtyard garden. Fully equipped kitchen, reverse cycle air conditioning, DVD/TV. Complimentary bottle of Yarra Valley Bubbly, slippers, bathrobes, port, fresh coffee, sumptuous 3 course breakfast provisions, DVD library.

You can find great getaways in wine regions.
Some offer wine activities.
Look for The Wine Activities Logo

Bed & Breakfast, Farmstay and Accommodation Australia

There is a lot packed into Victoria, the smallest of the mainland States. Stately architecture from the nineteenth century goldrush days; mineral springs and spas; ocean and bay beaches; boutique and major wineries; vast eucalypt forests; alpine villages; gourmet trails; rolling farmlands and the majestic High Country. Historic paddle steamers still travel the Murray River at the border with New South Wales. The capital, Melbourne, is a vibrant city with fascinating laneways and arcades, restaurants, theatres, museums, galleries, great shopping and international sporting events.

BBFAA accommodation is ideal for short breaks, romantic getaways and special occasions, travelling with pets, family stays and group reunions.

Enjoy a warm welcome and true hospitality when you stay with a BBFAA member BBFAA brings you high quality places to stay throughout Australia that are as individual as you.

www.australianbedandbreakfast.com.au
1300 664 707

Recommended Accommodation - Victoria

Properties included below with a page reference are included in this chapter and with further details. We have also included recommended accommodation with information supplied by BBFAA. Contact the hosts by telephone number for further details and tell them, *"We found you in The B&B Book."*

Aireys Inlet	The Glen Farm Cotts	Old Coach Rd	Aireys Inlet	03 5289 6306	
Anglesea	Overboard Cottages	39C O'Donohues Rd	Anglesea	03 5289 7424	
Apollo Bay	Apollo Bay B&B	4 Murray St	Apollo Bay	03 5237 7153	
Apollo Bay	**Arcady Homestead**	**925 Barham River Rd**	**Apollo Bay**	**03 5237 6493**	*Page 201*
Apollo Bay	Cape Otway Cottages	615 Hordern Vale Rd	Apollo Bay	03 5237 9256	
Apollo Bay	Cape Otway Lightstation	Lighthouse Rd	Apollo Bay	03 5237 9240	
Apollo Bay	**Claerwen Retreat**	**480 Tuxion Rd**	**Apollo Bay**	**03 5237 7064**	*Page 203*
Apollo Bay	Glenoe Cottages	235 Tuxion Rd	Apollo Bay	03 5237 6555	
Apollo Bay	**Paradise Gardens**	**715 Barham River Rd**	**Apollo Bay**	**03 5237 6939**	*Page 201*
Apollo Bay	**Point of View**	**165 Tuxion Rd**	**Apollo Bay**	**0427 376 377**	*Page 202*
Apollo Bay	Shearwater Cottages	760 Lighthouse Rd	Apollo Bay	03 5237 9290	
Apollo Bay - Glenaire	Glenaire Cottages	3440 Great Ocean Rd	Glenaire	03 5237 9237	
Bacchus Marsh	Underbank Stud	Randwick Ave	Bacchus Marsh	03 5367 5300	
Bairnsdale	**Stringybark Cottages B&B**	**RMB 8915**	**Bairnsdale**	**03 5157 5245**	*Page 204*
Bairnsdale	**Tara House**	**37 Day St**	**Bairnsdale**	**03 5153 2253**	*Page 203*
Balliang	Ripley Park	90 Gilmores Rd	Balliang	03 5369 4222	
Balook	Tarra Bulga GH	1885 Grand Ridge Rd	Balook	03 5196 6141	
Beechworth	**Country Charm Swiss Cottages**	**22 Malakoff Rd**	**Beechworth**	**03 5728 2435**	*Page 205*
Beechworth	**Foxgloves**	**21 Loch St**	**Beechworth**	**03 5728 1224**	*Page 206*
Beechworth	**Freeman on Ford**	**97 Ford St**	**Beechworth**	**03 5728 2371**	*Page 206*
Benalla	Belmont B&B	80 Arundel St	Benalla	03 5762 6575	
Benalla	Benaway B&B	810 Anderson Inlet Rd	Benalla	03 5657 2268	
Benalla	**Rotherlea Lodge**	**PO Box 63**	**Benalla**	**03 5763 2262**	
Bendigo	Marlborough House	115 Wattle St	Bendigo	03 5441 4142	
Bright	Lavender Hue	20 Great Alpine Rd	Bright	03 5759 2588	
Buninyong	Graebern Lodge	602 Cathcart St	Buninyong	03 5341 3139	
Carisbrook	Lochinver Farm	245 Baringhup Rd	Carisbrook	03 5464 2356	
Chiltern	**The Mulberry Tree B&B**	**28 Conness St**	**Chiltern**	**03 5726 1277**	*Page 207*
Cobram	Tokemata Retreat	100 Cemetery Rd	Cobram	03 5873 5332	
Cosgrove Sth	Amarooka	2530 Midland Hwy	Cosgrove South	03 5828 9328	
Cudgewa - Corryong	**Elmstead Cottages**	**61 Ashstead Park Ln**	**Cudgewa**	**02 6077 4324**	*Page 207*
Dandenong Rngs - Emerald	**Fernglade on Menzies**	**11 Caroline Cres**	**Emerald**	**03 5968 2228**	*Page 209*
Dandenong Rngs - Gembrook	Brilynbrook Country Accom	3065 Launching Place Rd	Gembrook	03 5968 1938	
Dandenong Rngs - Kalorama	**Holly Gate House B&B**	**1308 Mt D'nong T'ist Rd**	**Kalorama**	**03 9728 3218**	*Page 244*
Dandenong Rngs - Olinda	**A Sunrise View**	**1 Beechwood Cl**	**Doncaster East**	**0412 621 259**	*Page 210*
Dandenong Rngs - Olinda	Arcadia Cottages	188-190 Falls Rd	Olinda	03 9751 1017	
Dandenong Rngs - Olinda	**Candlelight Cottages Retreat**	**7-9 Monash Ave**	**Olinda Village**	**03 9751 2464**	*Page 208*
Dandenong Rngs - Olinda	Folly Farm Rural Retreat	13 Cards Ln	Olinda	03 9751 2544	
Dandenong Rngs - Olinda	Mary Cards Coach House	1498 Mt D'ong T'st Rd	Olinda	03 9751 1301	
Dandenong Rngs - Research	Crestcastle B&B	24 Crest Rd	Research	03 9437 0603	
Dandenong Rngs - Sassafras	**Clarendon Cottages**	**11 Clarkmont Rd**	**Sassafras**	**03 9755 3288**	*Page 210*
Dandenong Rngs - Sassafras	Monreale Estate	81 The Cres	Sassafras	03 9755 1773	
Daylesford	Azidene House & Spa Apts	68 Central Springs Rd	Daylesford	03 5348 1140	
Daylesford	Balconies Daylesford	35 Perrins St	Daylesford	03 5348 1322	
Daylesford	Forget Me Not Garden Cotts	7-9 Stanhope St	Daylesford	03 5348 3507	
Daylesford	**Pendower House**	**10 Bridport St**	**Daylesford**	**03 5348 1535**	*Page 211*
Daylesford - Smeaton	**Tuki Retreat**	**60 Stoney Rises Rd**	**Smeaton**	**03 5345 6233**	*Page 211*

Victoria

Echuca	Ayr House B&B	62 Hare St	Echuca	03 5482 1973	Page 212
Echuca	Echuca B&Bs	50 Heygarth St	Echuca	03 5480 1200	
Echuca	Hodgson House	66 Wharparilla Dv	Echuca	03 5482 2128	
Euroa	Homelea on Clifton	12 Clifton St	Euroa	03 8812 2540	
Geelong	Ardara House	4 Aberdeen St	Geelong	03 5229 6024	Page 214
Geelong	Baywoodbyne B&B	41 The Esp	Geelong	03 5278 2658	Page 213
Geelong	Sabina on Little Myers	32 Sheridan St	Geelong	0427 785 404	
Gelantipy - Buchan	Karoonda Park	Gelantipy Rd	Gelantipy	03 5155 0220	
Gippsland - Nilma Nth	Springbank B&B	240 Williamsons Rd	Nilma North	03 5627 8060	Page 215
Gippsland - Sale	Bon Accord B&B	153-155 Dawson St	Sale	03 5144 5555	Page 216
Gisborne	Gisborne Park Stud B&B	1011 Bacchus Marsh Rd	Gisborne	03 5428 9374	
Glenlyon	Armley Park	1065 D'ford-M'bury Rd	Glenlyon	03 5348 7979	
Grampians - Apsley	Ardwick Homestead	1340 Wimmera Hwy	Apsley	03 5586 5255	
Grampians - Ararat	Crochan Country Rtrt	625 Ararat-Halls Gap Rd	Ararat	03 5352 4797	
Grampians - Black Range	Bellellen Homestead	17 Bellellen Rd	Black Range	03 5358 4800	
Grampians - Cavendish	South Mokanger Farm Cotts	728 Mokanger Rd	Cavendish	03 5574 2398	
Grampians - Dimboola	Riverside Host farm	150 Riverside Rd	Dimboola	03 5389 1550	
Grampians - Dunkeld	Royal Mail Hotel	Parker St	Dunkeld	03 5577 2241	Page 217
Grampians - Glenthompson	Cherrymount Retreat	60 Cherrymount Ln	Glenthompson	03 5577 4396	
Grampians - Halls Gap	M'tain Grand B'tique Hotel	Main Rd Town Centre	Halls Gap	03 5356 4232	Page 217
Grampians - Horsham	May Park Executive Apts	1 Darlot St	Horsham	03 5381 1966	
Grampians - Horsham	Sylvania Park Mohair Farm	Drung South Rd	Horsham	03 5382 2811	
Grampians - Laharum	Goonwinnow H'std	1212 N'thn Grampians Rd	Laharum	0425 713 044	
Grampians - Mirranatwa	Barrahead Cottage	149 Mirranatwa School Rd	Mirranatwa	03 5574 0204	
Grampians - Pomonal	Welch's on Wildflower	39 Wildflower Dv	Pomonal	03 5356 6311	
Grampians - Victoria Vly	Bona Vista	2521 Victoria Valley Rd	Victoria Valley	03 5574 0225	
Grampians - Wartook Vly	The Grelco Run	520 Schmidts Rd	Brimpaen	03 5383 9221	Page 218
Great Ocean Rd - Bambra	Countrywide Cottages	1205 Deans Marsh Rd	Bambra	03 5288 7399	
Great Ocean Rd - Barongarook	Wanawong B&B	950 Colac-Lavers Hill Rd	Barongarook	03 5233 8215	
Great Ocean Rd - Barwon Heads	King Tide Townhouse	20 Knox Dv	Barwon Heads	03 5254 1571	
Great Ocean Rd - Camperdown	Timboon House	320 Old Geelong Rd	Camperdown	03 5593 1003	
Great Ocean Rd - Freshwater	D'oro Tourist Farm	55 Brushfield Rd	Freshwater	03 5264 5130	
Great Ocean Rd - Jan Juc	Ocean Road Retreat	101 Sunset Strip	Jan Juc	03 5261 2971	
Great Ocean Rd - Johanna	Johanna River Cotts	420 Blue Johanna Rd	Johanna	03 5237 4219	
Great Ocean Rd - Johanna	Johanna Seaside Cotts	395 Red Rd	Johanna	03 5237 4242	
Great Ocean Rd - Moonlight Head	Moonlight Retreat	50 Parkers Access Rd	Wattle Hill	03 5237 5277	
Great Ocean Rd - Ocean Grove	Ti Tree Village	34 Orton St	Ocean Grove	03 5255 4433	
Heathcote	Emeu Inn B&B	187 High St	Heathcote	03 5433 2668	Page 219
Heathcote	Hut on the Hill	720 Dairy Flat Rd	Heathcote	03 5433 2329	
Hepburn Springs	65 Main	65 Main St	Hepburn Springs	03 5348 1826	
Horsham	Orange Grove B&B	123 Keatings Rd	Vectis	03 5382 0583	Page 220
Inverloch	South Kolora Cottages	1100 Kongwak Rd	Inverloch	03 5674 1305	
Jamieson	Emerald Park Holiday Farm	Licola Rd	Jamieson	03 5777 0569	
Katunga	Glenarron	14 Hutchin's Ln	Katunga	03 5864 6246	
Kingston	Heatherington Cottage	3832 Creswick-Newstead Rd	Kingston	03 5345 6167	
Kingston	Laurel Bank Cottages	79 Victoria Rd	Kingston	03 5345 7343	
Lakes Entrance	Kalimna Woods Cottages	30 Kalimna Jetty Rd	Lakes Entrance	03 5155 1957	Page 220
Lakes Entrance	Lakes Entrance Wav Hse Cotts	205 Palmers Rd	Lakes Entrance	03 5155 1257	
Lilydale	Murrindindi Exec Retreat	415 Ti-Tree Creek Rd	Yea	03 9735 3400	
Loch	Bellview Hill H'std	270 Soldiers Rd	Loch	03 5659 7285	
Longford	Frog Gully Cottages	Lot 2419 Rosedale Rd	Longford	03 5149 7242	

Victoria

Lorne	La Perouse B&B	26a William St	Lorne	0418 534 422	Page 221
Lorne	Qdos Treehouses	35 Allenvale Rd	Lorne	03 5289 1989	Page 222
Lorne - Aireys Inlet	Lorneview B&B	677 Great Ocean Rd	Eastern View	03 5289 6430	Page 221
Lorne - Otway Rngs	Elliminook	585 Warncoort Rd	Birregurra	03 5236 2080	Page 222
Macks Creek	The Barn at Glenwood Farm	Bulga Park Rd	Macks Creek	03 5186 1310	
Maldon	Nuggetty Cottage	30 Nuggetty Rd	Maldon	03 5475 2472	
Malmsbury	Malmsbury Oak B&B	31 Hunter St	Malmsbury	03 5423 2490	
Mansfield	Burnt Creek Cottages	68 O'Hanlons Rd	Mansfield	03 5775 3067	
Mansfield	Mansfield Spa Retreat	92 Malcolm St	Mansfield	03 5775 1531	
Mansfield	Wombat Hills Cottages	55 Lochiel Rd	Mansfield	03 5776 9507	
Maryborough	Fiorini's Guest House	35 Tuaggra St	Maryborough	03 5461 1054	
Melbourne - Brighton	Waratah Brighton Boutique B&B	70 Roslyn St	Brighton	03 9592 0501	Page 225
Melbourne - Camberwell	Springfields	4 Springfield Ave	Camberwell	03 9809 1681	Page 225
Melbourne - Carnegie	Josephine's B&B	40 Rosanna St	Carnegie	03 9569 9386	Page 226
Melbourne - Doncaster East	Blue Willow B&B	18 Maxia Rd	Doncaster East	03 9841 0264	
Melbourne - Eltham	Cantala B&B	62 Henry St	Eltham	03 9431 3374	
Melbourne - Eltham	Eltham South Lodge	58 Kent Hughes Rd	Eltham	03 9439 4933	
Melbourne - Fairfield	Fairfield Guest House	18 Station St	Fairfield	03 9482 2959	Page 226
Melbourne - Kooyong	Carlisle B&B	400 Glenferrie Rd	Kooyong	03 9822 4847	
Melbourne - Richmond	94 Highett B&B	94 Highett St	Richmond	03 9421 0248	Page 228
Melbourne - Richmond	Apartment 401	258 Flinders Ln	Melbourne	03 9428 8104	Page 224
Melbourne - Richmond	Rotherwood	13 Rotherwood St	Richmond	03 9428 6758	Page 228
Melbourne - Richmond	Villa Donati	377 Church St	Richmond	03 9428 8104	Page 227
Melbourne - St Kilda	Alrae B&B	7 Hughenden Rd	St Kilda East	03 9527 2033	Page 229
Melbourne - St Kilda East	Boutique Hotel St Marine	42 Marine Pde	St Kilda East	03 9534 1311	
Melbourne - West Melbourne	Robinsons in the City	405 Spencer St	West Melbourne	03 9329 2552	Page 224
Melbourne - Williamstown	Captains Retreat B&B	2 Ferguson St	Williamstown	03 9397 0352	Page 230
Melbourne - Williamstown	North Haven By the Sea	Merrett Dv	Williamstown	03 9399 8399	
Merrijig	Bluegum Ridge Cottages	434 Buttercup Rd	Merrijig	03 5777 5015	
Merrijig	Buttercup Cottage	271 Buttercup Rd	Merrijig	03 5777 5591	
Mildura	Mildura's Linsley House	PO Box 959	Mildura	03 5024 8487	Page 231
Mirboo Nth	Campbell Homestead B&B	295 Toomeys Rd	Mirboo North	03 5664 1282	
Moama	Morning Glory River Resort	Gilmour Rd	Moama	03 5869 3357	
Mornington	Petit Amour Cottage	York St	Mornington	03 5974 3286	
Mornington Pen - Arthurs Seat	Seahaze B&B	40 Seahaze St	Arthurs Seat	03 5987 2568	
Mornington Pen - Dromana	Lakeside Villas at Crittenden Estate	25 Harrisons Rd	Dromana	03 5987 3275	Page 232
Mornington Pen - Mt Eliza	Sartain's at Mornington	75 Oakbank Rd	Mt Eliza	03 5975 1014	Page 232
Mornington Pen - Mt Martha	Hideaway On Hinkler	28 Sheringham Dv	Mt Martha	03 9545 1015	
Mornington Pen - Rosebud	Nazaaray Beach House	266 Meakins Rd	Rosebud	03 5989 0126	
Mornington Pen - Rye	Blue Moon Cottages	12 Blakiston Grove	Rye	03 5985 8551	
Mornington Pen - Rye	Four Winds B&B	29 Ford St	Rye	03 5985 8939	
Mornington Pen - Rye	Plantation House	33 Maori St	Rye	03 5985 5926	
Mornington Pen - Rye	Rye Beach B&B	4 Alexandra Cres	Rye Beach	03 5985 1674	
Mornington Pen - Sorrento	A La Plage	1 Watson Rd	Sorrento	03 5984 1280	
Mornington Pen - Sorrento	Tamasha House	699 Melbourne Rd	Sorrento	03 5984 2413	Page 238
Mornington Pen - St Andrews Bch	Abode in Style	90 Serina Rd	St Andrews Beach	03 5988 6641	
Mornington Pen - Tootgarook	Truemans Cottage	14 Bona St	Tootgarook	03 5985 6279	
Mt Beauty	Braeview	4 Stewarts Rd	Mt Beauty	03 5754 4746	
Mt Dandenong	Adeline B&B	1462 Mt D'ong Tourist Rd	Mt Dandenong	03 9751 1116	
Mt Dandenong	Linden Gdns R'forest Rtrt	1383 Mt. D'ong Tourist Rd	Mt Dandenong	03 9751 1103	
Mt Dandenong	Observatory Cottages	8 Observatory Rd	Mt Dandenong	03 9751 2436	Page 209

Victoria

Murchison - Nagambie	Brecon House	55 Stevenson St	Murchison	03 5826 2003	
Musk	Barcaldine House	238 Dairy Flat Rd	Musk	03 5348 2741	
Musk	Musk Manor	10 School Rd	Musk, Daylesford	03 5348 4234	
Myrrhee	Casa Luna	1569 Boggy Creek Rd	Myrrhee	03 5729 7650	
Newborough	Brigadoon Cottages	108 Haunted Hills Rd	Newborough	03 5127 2656	
Newham	Rochford Road Th'breds	1190 Rochford Rd	Newham	0411 708 591	
Pakenham	Orchard Cottage	485 Toomuc Valley Rd	Pakenham	03 5942 7326	
Phillip Is - Cowes	**Abaleigh on Lovers Walk**	**6 Roy Court**	**Cowes**	**03 5952 5649**	*Page 240*
Phillip Is - Cowes	Farm Cottage	1165 Ventnor Beach Rd	Cowes	03 5956 8294	
Phillip Is - Cowes	**Genesta House**	**18 Steele St**	**Cowes**	**03 5952 3616**	*Page 234*
Phillip Is - Cowes	**Glen Isla House**	**230-232 Church St**	**Cowes**	**03 5952 1882**	*Page 233*
Phillip Is - Wonthaggi	Wonthaggi Cottage	22 Ballieu St East	Wonthaggi	03 5672 3346	
Princetown	**Arabella Country House**	**7219 Great Ocean Rd**	**Princetown**	**03 5598 8169**	*Page 235*
Princetown	Kangaroobie	Old Ocean Rd	Princetown	03 5598 8151	
Princetown	Macka's Farm	2310 Princetown Rd	Princetown	03 5598 8261	
Rockbank	932 Rockbank Ranch	932 Holden Rd	Rockbank	03 9746 1111	
Rutherglen	Cuddle Doon Cottages	12 Hunter St	Rutherglen	02 6032 7107	
Rutherglen	**Mount Ophir Estate**	**168 Stillards Ln**	**Rutherglen**	**02 6032 8920**	*Page 237*
Rutherglen	**Ready Cottage**	**92 High St**	**Rutherglen**	**02 6032 7407**	*Page 236*
Smeaton	Abergeldie B&B	3472 Creswick-N'tead Rd	Smeaton	03 5345 6223	
Swan Hill - Lake Boga	**Burrabliss Farms B&B**	**169 Lakeside Dv**	**Lake Boga**	**03 5037 2527**	*Page 239*
Tarnagulla	Rostrata Country House	RMB 1240, Dunolly Rd	Tarnagulla	03 5438 7254	
Torquay	An Oceanvista	48 Cowrie Rd	Torquay	03 5261 9826	
Torquay	**Ocean Manor B&B**	**3 Glengarry Dv**	**Torquay**	**03 5261 3441**	*Page 240*
Trentham	Studio 500	PO Box 160	Trentham	03 5424 8588	
Walkerville Sth	Bear Gully Coastal Cotts	33 Maitland Court	Walkerville South	03 5663 2364	
Wangaratta	**The Pelican**	**606 Oxley Flats Rd**	**Wangaratta**	**03 5727 3240**	*Page 241*
Waratah Nth	Prom Coast Holiday Ldge	1075 Waratah Rd	Waratah North	03 5684 1110	
Warragul West	Springwood Park H'std	420 Lardner Rd	Warragul West	03 5623 1396	
Warrnambool	**Merton Manor Exclusive B&B**	**62 Ardlie St**	**Warrnambool**	**03 5562 0720**	*Page 242*
Warrnambool	**Quamby Homestead**	**3223 Caramut Rd**	**Woolsthorpe**	**03 5569 2395**	*Page 243*
Warrnambool	Warrnambools No 1 Lux Apts	1/184 Timor St	Warrnambool	0439 447 725	
Warrnambool - Allansford	**Burnbrow Manor**	**1 Hopetoun St**	**Allansford**	**03 5565 1380**	*Page 243*
West Gippsland - Nar Nar Goon Nth	Serendipity Lavender Farm B&B	80 Croft Rd	Nar Nar Goon North	03 5942 9164	
Wongarra	Wongarra Heights Gst Hse	65 Sunnyside Rd	Wongarra	03 5237 0257	
Yarck	Glenfield Cottage	145 Middle Creek Rd	Yarck	03 5773 4304	
Yarra Vly - Dixons Creek	Amethyst Lodge B&B	139 Wills Rd	Dixons Creek	03 5965 2559	
Yarra Vly - Don Vly	Amarant Yarra Valley	1475 Don Rd	Don Valley	03 5967 3416	
Yarra Vly - Don Vly	Hill 'n' Dale Farm Cotts	1284 Don Rd	Don Valley	03 5967 3361	
Yarra Vly - Gladysdale	Deloraine Homestead	355 Tarrango Rd	Gladysdale	03 5967 1758	
Yarra Vly - Healesville	Myers Creek Cascades	269 Myers Creek Rd	Healesville	03 5962 3351	
Yarra Vly - Healesville	The Stables B&B	165 Donnelly's Wier Rd	Healesville	03 5962 1889	
Yarra Vly - Monbulk	Eagle Hammer Cottages	440 Old Emerald Rd	Monbulk	03 9756 7700	
Yarra Vly - Narbethong	Woodlands Rainforest Rtrt	137 Manby Rd	Narbethong	03 5963 7150	
Yarra Vly - Panton Hill	MossGlen on Panton Hill	30 Bakehouse Rd	Panton Hill	03 9719 7555	
Yarra Vly - Yarra Glen	**The Gatehouse at Villa Raedward**	**26 Melba Hwy**	**Yering**	**03 9739 0822**	*Page 245*
Yea	Cheviot Glen Cottages	175 Limestone Rd	Yea	03 5797 2617	
Yuulong	Wombalano Country Retreat	Great Ocean Rd	Yuulong	03 5237 5264	

Western Australia

Western Australia

Albany

During early June, Whales travel past Albany from the food-rich southern ocean to breeding grounds in the warm northern waters before returning late September. Experience, Albany's convict and whaling history, wild granite coastline, old taverns, settlers' cottages and grand National Trust homes in beautifully landscaped grounds.
Lew & Margaret Dowdell, Albany View St Lodge B&B/Art Studio & Gallery

Albany
Albany View St Lodge B&B/Art Studio & Gallery

B&B
Lew and Margaret Dowdell
35 View Street
Albany
WA 6330
1 km W of Town Hall

Tel (08) 9842 8820 or 0427 428 820
stay@albanyviewstbb.com.au
www.albanyviewstbb.com.au

Double $120-$130
Single $100-$105, Full breakfast
Discount for longer stays
Visa MC Eftpos accepted
3 Queen 1 Single (3 bdrm)
Bathrooms: 3 Ensuite

AAA Tourism
★★★★

Lew & Margaret welcome you to our lovely B&B. Reception is part of Margaret's Art Studio & Gallery. We offer quality accommodation just a short walk to shops, restaurants etc. We have 3 suites (2 with kitchenette-no cooker), fridge, microwave, tea/coffee making, TV, DVD, quality linen, crockery etc. Relax & enjoy breakfast upstairs with beautiful views of the harbour. Lovely gardens at rear with covered patio and BBQ. Guests are welcome to use our laundry. Off street parking and separate guest entrance. Free Wireless Internet connection.

Western Australia
Broome
Reflections B&B

B&B
Doug & Margaret Fong
69 Demco Drive
Broome
WA 6725
3 km S of Broome airport

Tel (08) 9192 6610 or 0419 955 245
Fax (08) 9192 6620
info@reflectionsbnb.com.au
www.reflectionsbnb.com.au

Double $120-$180
Single $120-$180, Full breakfast
Dinner $30/person b/a, Gourmet picnic b/a $35/couple, Rates include courtesy car from airport. 2 Queen (2 bdrm).
Bathrooms: 1 Ensuite 1 Private

Situated overlooking the turquoise waters of Roebuck Bay, this delightful 'home from home' offers a tranquil haven for guests wanting a peaceful break or, if you prefer, close enough to the holiday lifestyle of Broome. The gourmet breakfast, served whilst watching the ever changing scenes on the Bay, is renowned and the hosts Marg and Doug are always happy to share their first hand knowledge of Broome's history. The tropical garden setting abounds with birdlife and the sound of gently falling water over the water features completes the serenity.

The difference between a hotel and a B&B.
You don't hug the hotel staff when you leave.

Western Australia

Bunbury

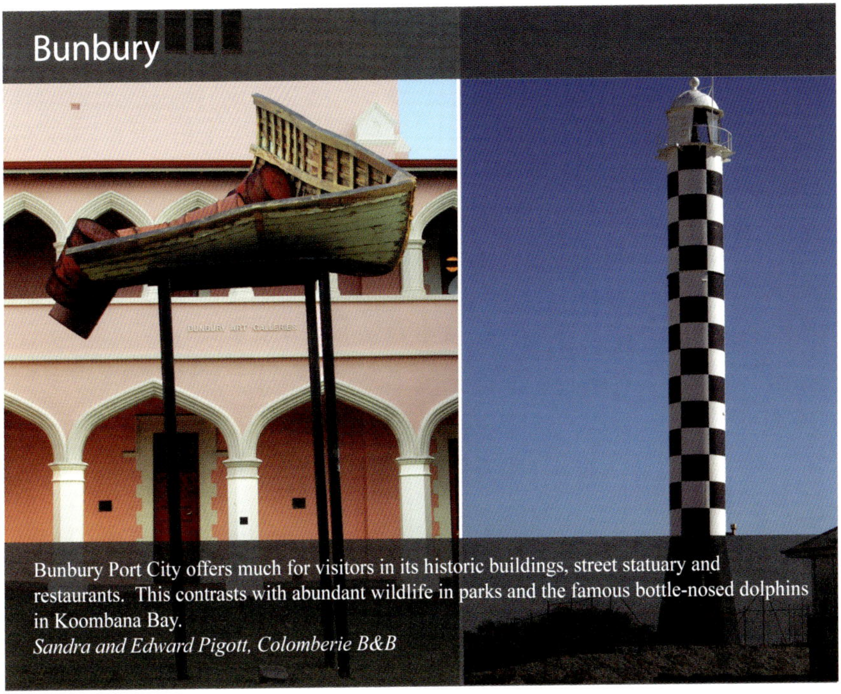

Bunbury Port City offers much for visitors in its historic buildings, street statuary and restaurants. This contrasts with abundant wildlife in parks and the famous bottle-nosed dolphins in Koombana Bay.
Sandra and Edward Pigott, Colomberie B&B

Bunbury
Colomberie B&B

B&B
Sandra & Edward Pigott
11 Duffield Place
Gelorup, Bunbury
WA 6230
7 km S of Bunbury

Tel (08) 9795 7734 or 0400 772 086
0417 913 398   Fax (08) 9795 7735
sp1@iinet.net.au
www.colomberie.com.au

Double $85-$110
Single $75-$85, Children on application by age,
Continental provisions, Dinner by arrangement,
Season rates apply High Oct-Dec
1 Queen 1 Double 2 Single (2 bdrm)
Bathrooms: 2 Ensuite

Colomberie B&B is an ideal location between Perth and the south-west. Two ensuite bedrooms with extra fold-out beds available. Guests' kitchenette and living/dining. Within easy driving distance of Capes and Margaret River regions with wineries, olive, lavender and berry farms, and of course, the many Busselton and Bunbury attractions including golf and swimming with dolphins. Non-smoking, children welcome, but the property is not suitable for children under five years. House is on one acre in a cul-de-sac surrounded by bushland and a beautiful garden.

Western Australia
Fremantle
Fothergills of Fremantle

Heritage Property, Luxury Accommodation
David Cooke, Suzy Llewellyn, Tasha Murrihy, Kwi Yeon Im
18-22 Ord Street
Fremantle
WA 6160
0.5 km N of Fremantle

Tel (08) 9335 6784
fothergills@iinet.net.au
www.fothergills.net.au

Double $170-$225
Children under 5 free, Cot available
Full breakfast , Visa MC accepted
1 King/Twin 6 Queen (7 bdrm)   Bathrooms: 5 Ensuite

AAA Tourism
★★★★

Our heritage-listed AAA four star B&B occupies three grand limestone Victorian homes built on the slope of Monument Hill overlooking Fremantle to the Indian Ocean beyond and with Rottnest Island on the horizon - and yet only a 6 minute stroll to the heart of Fremantle.

The elegant, air-conditioned spacious rooms are fitted with TV, DVD & Bose CD. Our mini fridge offers complimentary welcome snack, mineral water and soft drinks. Enjoy our luxury toiletries and climb into a bed dressed with luxury high thread count linen.

In the morning tuck into a wonderful breakfast - cooked and continental - all included as part of Fothergills unique service.

Our flowered courtyards are furnished with seating for your use and the whole property is filled with a rich collection of work by local, national and international artists. Of particular interest is the iconic series of stunning bronze statues, Iris, depicting human life evolving like a beautiful flower.

Western Australia

Fremantle
Terrace Central B&B

B&B & Hotel
Barry White
79-85 South Terrace, Fremantle, WA 6160
12 km S of Perth

Tel (08) 9335 6600 or 0428 969 859
Fax (08) 9336 7600
info@terracecentral.com.au
www.terracecentral.com.au

Double $165-$250
Single $165-$250, Children $50, Continental breakfast,
2 night min. weekends, Visa MC Diners Amex Eftpos JCB accepted
10 Queen 6 Double 2 Twin 2 Single (18 bdrm)
Bathrooms: 16 Ensuite

  AAA Tourism ★★★★

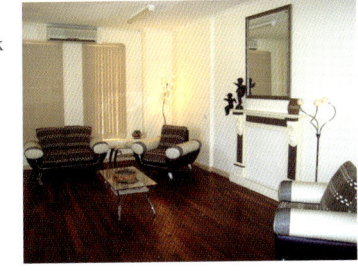

Heritage Boutique style B&B Hotel in the city centre of Fremantle with 18 air-conditioned en-suite bedrooms and 5 apartments. Close to rail and bus service. 3 minutes walk to Markets, shops. Close to all tourist attractions and ferry to Rottnest Island.

All rooms air-conditioned, en-suite bathroom. Free wireless broadband, TV & DVD Player, tea and coffee, fridge. Free parking.

Western Australia
Kalbarri
Gecko Lodge

Luxury B&B
Sharyn & Graham Geikie
9 Glass Street
Kalbarri
WA 6536
0.3 km SW of Kalbarri

Tel (08) 9937 1900 or (08) 9937 1922
0439 968 305   Fax (08) 9937 1899
stay@geckolodgekalbarri.com.au
www.geckolodgekalbarri.com.au

Double $200-$250
Single $160, Full breakfast, Seasonal tariffs,
Discounts for extended stays,
Visa MC Eftpos accepted
1 King 3 Queen (4 bdrm)
Bathrooms: 4 Ensuite

   AAA Tourism ★★★★☆

Gecko Lodge is a luxury, romantically appointed purpose built Bed & Breakfast Lodge designed for couples. Located only a stone's throw from the beach, river mouth, shops and cafes, Gecko Lodge provides an ideal base from which to explore Kalbarri's attractions (yet benefits from total seclusion and privacy). Enjoy well appointed ensuite rooms (2 with spas, 2 with double showers), afternoon tea and evening Port and chocolates. Enjoy our high standards of service and comfort in this beautiful part of the world.

Mandurah - North Yunderup - Pinjarra
Nautica Lodge

Luxury B&B
Glenda & Roger Lingard
203 Culeenup Road
North Yunderup
WA 6208
9 km E of Mandurah

Tel (08) 9537 8000 or 0419 944 627
info@nauticalodge.com
www.nauticalodge.com

Double $115-$175
Continental breakfast
Visa MC accepted
1 King/Twin 1 King 1 Queen 1 Twin
3 Single (2 bdrm) Luxury air-con suites
with LCD TV, en-suite and WIR
Bathrooms: 2 Ensuite

      AAA Tourism ★★★★

Situated in a unique and idyllic riverfront location on the beautiful Murray River 10 mins east of Mandurah. You can sit back on your terrace and appreciate an arm chair view of the river through the gum trees. It is an ideal place to relax while on holiday or unwind and/or entertain if on business. An exclusive guest lounge, dining, kitchenette and terrace overlook the river. The lounge has free Internet access, plasma HD TV, DVD, wine cellar, refrigerator, microwave, toaster and 24/7 tea & coffee.

Western Australia

Mandurah - Peel

The Peel region is so diverse with water sports of all kinds, estuary and canal cruises, dolphin encounters, surfing, sailing, canoeing, boat & fishing charters and crabbing. There are walking and bike tracks, sky diving, white water rafting and horse riding, historic tours, golfing and wine tasting.
Una Hird, Port Mandurah Canal B&B

Mandurah - Peel Region
Port Mandurah Canal B&B

Luxury B&B
Una Hird
3 Reverie Mews
Mandurah
WA 6210
1 km W of CBD

Tel (08) 9535 2252 or 0438 444 707
uhird@iprimus.com.au
www.babs.com.au/portmandurah

Double $100-$190
Full breakfast
Single rates on request
Long Stay Specials
2 Queen (2 bdrm)
Bathrooms: 2 Ensuite
Spa in Master Bedroom

Situated on the canals of Port Mandurah, Port Mandurah Canal Bed & Breakfast is the perfect place for a weekend get-away or that long hard earned break. Relax in a home away from home atmosphere and enjoy pure relaxation or hidden romance. Our luxury retreat offers two air conditioned suites with private facilities, including lounge room and balcony in beautiful surroundings overlooking the waters of Mandurah's famous canals. Dolphins are regular visitors to the canals. Catch your crabs from your own jetty. Walk to beaches. Mandurah's stunning waterfront which is full of Restaurants and Cafes, is just minutes away. Will pick up from station.

BBBook.com.au

Western Australia
Mandurah - Wannanup
Port Bouvard B&B

B&B
David & Diane
17 Voyager Close
Wannanup
WA 6210
10 km S of Mandurah

Tel 0418 948 273
contact@portbouvardbandb.com.au
www.portbouvardbandb.com.au

Double $160-$200
Full breakfast
Delicious dinners are available on request
10% discount offered for three nights or more
Visa MC accepted
2 King (2 bdrm) Sensational views from suites
Bathrooms: 2 Ensuite with baths

Port Bouvard B&B

We are located 90kms south of Perth on a clear canal, metres from the Indian Ocean with our own private jetty and absolutely amazing water views. Where else would you have dolphins frolicking in your backyard? Your private lounge and dining room forms part of the upstairs guest wing of the house with two immaculate suites, comfortable king beds, private ensuites with baths, LCD TV's and DVD's. Our resident Chef Dave has a career spanning more than 40 years, including working at the Dorchester Hotel in London. He's sure to tempt your taste buds with his mouth-watering menus.

Some properties have restaurants attached or offer meals on request.

Western Australia

Margaret River Wine Region

Margaret River region is an intricate tapestry of premium wineries, pristine beaches, awe-inspiring natural wonders, spectacular forests, fine restaurants and world-class arts and crafts. It has a unique warmth and charm that is an experience of its own and one not to be missed.
Donna Carter, The Noble Grape Guesthouse and Brookwood Estate www.Brookwood.com.au

Margaret River
The Noble Grape

Luxury B&B & Guest House
Rodney & Donna Carter
29 Bussell Highway
Cowaramup
WA 6284
12 km N of Margaret River

Tel (08) 9755 5538 or 0418 931 721
Fax (08) 9755 5538
stay@noblegrape.com.au
www.noblegrape.com.au

Double $135-$185
Single $120-$150, Children $30,
Continental breakfast , Extra adult $30
Visa MC Amex Eftpos accepted
1 King/Twin2 King 3 Queen 3 Single (6 bdrm)
Bathrooms: 6 Ensuite

AAA Tourism ★★★★

The Noble Grape is a cosy Guesthouse in the heart of the Margaret River Wine Region. Colonial style charm with quaint antiques nestled in an English cottage garden. Vineyards, beaches, galleries, chocolate and cheese factories minutes away. Enjoy a leisurely breakfast in our dining room overlooking the garden while watching the native birdlife. Spacious country style rooms with ensuite & hairdryer, r.c. air-conditioning, TV, DVD, refrigerator, microwave, tea/coffee, comfortable arm chairs and private courtyard. Guest barbecue. Wireless Internet. Room with universal access. Smoking outside only.

Western Australia
Margaret River
Rosewood Guesthouse

Luxury B&B & Separate Suite
Jane & Keith Purdie
54 Wallcliffe Road
Margaret River
WA 6285
1 km W of Post Office

Tel (08) 9757 2845 or 0427 772 911
Fax (08) 9757 3509
info@rosewoodguesthouse.com.au
www.rosewoodguesthouse.com.au

Double $189-$250
Single $179-$250, Full breakfast,
Suite $220-$275 double, Extra guests from $49,
Max 4, Visa MC Amex Eftpos accepted
2 King/Twin 4 King 1 Queen (6 bdrm)
Bathrooms: 6 Ensuite

   AAA Tourism ★★★★☆

Rosewood Guesthouse is an award winning B&B which provides a warm & friendly atmosphere, welcoming guests from all parts of the globe. Beautifully appointed rooms with modern en-suites. Log fire in the lounge with complimentary port, Rosewood breakfasts feature fantastic daily specials for variety. Just a 700 metre walk to the main street restaurants, 4 minute drive to wineries, Rosewood is the ideal base to explore the region and Jane & Keith will be happy to help plan your itinerary.

"We received the greatest hospitality...
Slept in the most wonderful bed...
Enjoyed the best breakfast...
We will return!"

Western Australia

Perth

Take a ferry down the Swan River to Fremantle, our historic port. Continue to Rottnest Island and enjoy a swim in a magnificent peaceful bay or watch for whales and dolphins. Visit the Swan Valley vineyards for wines, cheeses and other fresh products or wander into the hills to experience the wildflowers.
Jack Tucker, Caesia House.

Perth
Pension of Perth

B&B
Hoon & Steve Hall
3 Throssell Street
Perth
WA 6000
1 km N of Perth

Tel (08) 9228 9049 or 0421 739 103
Fax (08) 9228 9290
stay@pensionperth.com.au
www.pensionperth.com.au

Double $150
Single $120-$130, Full breakfast,
Extra person $30, Discounts for long stays,
Visa MC Eftpos accepted
2 King 2 Queen (5 bdrm) 1 family room
Bathrooms: 4 Ensuite 1 Private

The Pension of Perth is the perfect choice for couples looking for a special place to stay or business travellers wanting somewhere that is value for money, sophisticated, homely and private. It has the amenities of a fine hotel. The luxurious refurbishment reflects the elegance and comfort of its origins in 1897. It overlooks Hyde Park. Within walking distance from the centre of Perth. Our A-la-carte breakfast menu will make your stay memorable.

BBBook.com.au

Western Australia
Perth - Cottesloe
Rosemoore B&B

B&B
Shelley Rose
2 Winifred Street
Mosman Park
WA 6012
1.5 km S of Cottesloe

Tel (08) 9384 8214
rosemoore@bigpond.com
www.rosemoore.com.au

Double $150
Single $99
Continental breakfast
10% discount 2 nights or more
Visa MC Eftpos accepted
3 Queen 1 Single (3 bdrm)
Bathrooms: 3 Ensuite

Rosemoore is conveniently located just off Stirling Highway between Perth and Fremantle, Cottesloe Beach and The Swan River. Double and Twin rooms have their own bathrooms and reverse cycle air conditioning. A refrigerator and microwave are available on the verandah. The rooms have their own private access off the verandah to the off-street parking. The railway station, restaurants and shops are a short stroll away. Within two minutes drive of Rosemoore you can enjoy the beautiful view of Mosman Bay on the Swan River or take a dip at Cottesloe beach on the Indian Ocean.

Perth - Nedlands
Caesia House Apartment Nedlands

B&B & Self Contained Apartment
Jane & David Tucker
32 Thomas Street
Nedlands, Perth
WA 6009
5 km W of Perth Central City

Tel (08) 9389 8174 or 1800 008 206
Fax (08) 9389 8173
tuckers@iinet.net.au
www.caesiahouse.com

Double $145-$180
Single $140-$175, Breakfast by arrangement
Visa MC accepted
1 King/Twin 1 King (1 bdrm)
Bathrooms: 1 Ensuite
Studio bed and second ensuite available

A quiet serene oasis in the city, only 7 minutes from Perth city centre and Kings Park, within walking distance to numerous cafes, or wonderful riverside BBQ/picnic spots. Close to shops UWA, SirCharles Gardiner and Hollywood Hospitals bus to historic Fremantle, and beaches or Perth City centre. Convenient base for tours to scenic Rottnest Island, savour those wines in the Swan Valley or wildflowers in Hills. Off street parking, ground floor apartment including spacious ensuite bedroom with garden outlook, lounge area and dining/kitchen. BBQ and outdoor area.

Western Australia

Perth - Perth Hills

From the escarpment of Gooseberry Hill you can enjoy city and ocean views and some of the most wonderful sunsets you will ever see. Be enchanted by local wildlife including kangaroos and kookaburras. Enjoy wandering through the specialty arts and craft shops in neighbouring Kalamunda.
Geoff Telford, Grandview B&B

Perth - Perth Hills
Grandview B&B

B&B
Geoff Telford
30 Girrawheen Drive
Gooseberry Hill
WA 6076
3 km E of Kalamunda

Tel (08) 9293 2518 or 0418 908 341
Fax (08) 9293 2518
geoff@grandviewbandb.com.au
www.grandviewbandb.com.au

Double $140-$165
Special breakfast
1 Queen 1 Double (2 bdrm)
Bathrooms: 1 Ensuite 1 Private

Grandview B&B is nestled on the escarpment overlooking Perth city just 15 minutes from both the international and domestic airports & transfers can be arranged. At Grandview you can expect immaculate executive style accommodation within beautiful bush surroundings. The house is in a tranquil location offering the opportunity to relax and enjoy the most wonderful sunsets. Guests facilities include executive style room with Queen sized bed, Choice of firm or soft pillows, Ensuite Bathroom, Climate control air-conditioning, Dual control electric blanket, Television/DVD/Foxtel, , wireless broadband internet, Pool, Barbeque, Large jarrah deck and Outdoor 'rooms'.

Western Australia
Perth - Sorrento
Sorrento Beach B&B

B&B
Alan & Clodagh Tolley
30 Hood Terrace
Sorrento
WA 6020
1 km N of Sorrento

Tel (08) 94474871
clodagh@tolley.biz
www.sorrentobeachbb.com.au

Double $130-$170
Full breakfast
Visa MC accepted
1 King/Twin 1 Queen (2 bdrm)
Spacious bedrooms
Bathrooms: 1 Private

Sorrento Beach B&B is a classy new establishment located in the northern Perth coastal suburb of Sorrento a short stroll to beautiful Sorrento beach. Two spacious bedrooms, one queen and one with two king size singles, are suitable for a couple on their own or a group of four. Facilities include a large guest bathroom with spa, a cosy private sitting room with a large LCD TV, DVD player. Tea and coffee making facilities and a refrigerator are available. You may also take a drink on the balcony and enjoy the treetops. All guest areas include reverse cycle air conditioning.

Pets are welcome at many properties – contact hosts first to check on facilities available. Look for The Pets Welcome Logo

Western Australia

Perth - Trigg – Scarborough

Exquisite beaches and walking/bike riding paths. Excellent beachside cafes/restaurants. Enjoy Hillarys Marina and AQWA underwater world or ferry to Rottnest.
Sue Stein, Trigg Retreat B&B

Perth - Trigg - Scarborough - North Beach
Trigg Retreat Bed and Breakfast

B&B
Sue Stein
59 Kitchener Street
Trigg
WA 6029
15 km N of Perth

Tel (08) 9447 6726 or 0417 911 048
Fax (08) 9447 6525
sue@triggretreat.com
www.triggretreat.com

Double $150-$180
Single $150-$160, Gourmet continental breakfast or optional hot menu
Visa MC Eftpos accepted
1 King/Twin 3 Queen (4 bdrm)
Bathrooms: 4 Ensuite

AAA Tourism
★★★★☆

An affordable indulgence! 4 1/2 star tastefully furnished two-storey home. Four bedrooms with ensuite, A/C, luxurious queen or twin beds, TV, DVD, fridge, tea/coffee, free broadband wireless access, bedside treats. A gourmet, continental breakfast, served in guest dining room or garden courtyard. Optional hot selection available from enticing menu. A computer and unlimited access to the internet provided free. 'Stroll to the beach', exquisite WA coastline, walking, riding paths and cafes. Airport - 30 min direct route. Guest and owners facilities are separate. Prepare to be pampered!

Western Australia

Pinjarra – Peel Region

Established in 1834, Pinjarra is one of the oldest towns in Western Australia and has many interesting historic sights to see. Located south of Perth on the banks of the Murray River, Pinjarra is a small historic town a short drive from Mandurah and Rockingham..
Liz Nicholas, Lazy River Boutique B&B and Pinjarra Visitor Centre

Pinjarra - Peel Region
Lazy River Boutique Bed & Breakfast

Luxury B&B
Liz and Steve Nicholas
34 Wilson Road
Pinjarra
WA 6208
1 km W of Pinjarra

Tel (08) 9531 4550 or 0417 922 457
unwind@lazyriver.com.au
www.lazyriver.com.au

Double up to $350
Single up to $300
Full breakfast
Visa MC Eftpos accepted
1 King/Twin 3 Queen (4 bdrm) Luxury suites opening onto big verandahs with great views
Bathrooms: 4 Ensuite

      AAA Tourism ★★★★☆

Lazy River is a hideaway luxury boutique hotel in Pinjarra, just one hour South of Perth. This 4.5 star gourmet paradise, which is set apart from the hosts homestead, offers 4 spacious spa suites with big verandahs. We emphasise exquisite cuisine, with dinners prepared by Steve, a Swiss trained chef, and served in your suite. All this set in 5 acres of landscaped gardens on the Murray River. Activities include tennis, fishing, kayaking and croquet. Massages can be arranged by appointment.

Western Australia

Toodyay - Avon Valley
Pecan Hill B&B

B&B
Craig & Suzanne Lomax
99 Beaufort Street
Toodyay
WA 6566
4 km W of Toodyay

Tel (08) 9574 2636 or 1300 766 721
Fax (08) 9574 2367
info@pecanhill.com.au
www.pecanhill.com.au

Double $105-$115
Continental breakfast, Dinner $25 pp by arrangement, Full breakfast additional $12 pp
Visa MC Diners Amex Eftpos JCB accepted
1 King/Twin 3 Queen (4 bdrm)
Bathrooms: 4 Ensuite

   AAA Tourism ★★★★

Pecan Hill offers a true country experience with peace and tranquillity. Four tastefully furnished rooms with ensuites look out into natural woodland filled with native birds, Alpacas and Sheep. All rooms have glass sliding doors that access the wide verandah, carpet, reverse cycle air-conditioning, overhead fan, electric blankets and tea/coffee making facilities. The guest lounge has TV/VCR/DVD, library, log fire and air-conditioning. The pool is surrounded by gardens, paved areas and a pergola. As an adults retreat we do not cater for children or pets.

Many properties offer activities onsite such as horse riding.
Look for The Onsite Activities Logo

Western Australia

Bed & Breakfast, Farmstay and Accommodation Australia

From the tropical north to the temperate south, Western Australia is a destination for all seasons. Discover beaches with perfect white sand, coral reefs and turquoise water where dolphins come to the waters edge. Explore tall timber forests, amazing rock formations in The Kimberly such as the Bungle Bungles, rich farmlands and fine wine producing regions. The state capital, Perth blends a laid-back lifestyle with a range of eateries, galleries, entertainment, sports and great shopping. The neighbouring port city of Fremantle is renowned for its nineteenth century streetscape, alfresco dining and colourful markets.

BBFAA accommodation is ideal for short breaks, romantic getaways and special occasions, travelling with pets, family stays and group reunions.

Enjoy a warm welcome and true hospitality when you stay with a BBFAA member. BBFAA brings you over five hundred, high quality places to stay throughout Australia that are as individual as you.

www.australianbedandbreakfast.com.au
1300 664 707

Recommended Accommodation - Western Australia

Properties included below with a page reference are included in this chapter and with further details. We have also included recommended accommodation with information supplied by BBFAA. Contact the hosts by telephone number for further details and tell them, *"We found you in The B&B Book."*

Ajana	Riverside Sanctuary	442 Coolcalalya Rd	Ajana	08 9936 1021	
Albany	**Albany View Street Lodge B&B/Art Studio**	**35 View St**	**Albany**	**08 9842 8820**	*Page 253*
Albany	Mia Amore	44 Sanderson Rd	Albany	08 92913720	
Bridgetown	Glenlynn Cottages	Lot 12 Press Rd	Bridgetown	08 9761 2246	
Bridgetown	Lucieville Farm Chalets	RMB 390 South West Hwy	Bridgetown	08 9761 1733	
Bridgetown	Maranup Ford	Maranup Ford Rd	Bridgetown	08 9761 1200	
Bridgetown	Sunnyhurst Chalets	Lot 15 Doust St	Bridgetown	08 9761 1081	
Bridgetown	Windy Hollow B&B	Henderson Rd	Bridgetown	08 9761 2523	
Broome	Amsara Luxury Retreat	Coconut Wall	Broome	08 9192 7761	
Broome	Broome Oasis B&B	19/544 Broome Hwys	Broome	08 9192 2311	
Broome	BroomeTown B&B	15 Stewart St	Broome	08 9192 2006	
Broome	Cable Court B&B	4 Phillips Court	Cable Beach	08 9192 2392	
Broome	Divers Bell B&B	22 Piggott Way	Broome	08 9192 5548	
Broome	Ochre Moon B&B	13 Goodwit Cres	Broome	08 9192 7109	
Broome	**Reflections B&B**	**69 Demco Dv**	**Broome**	**08 9192 6610**	*Page 254*
Broome	The Bungalow	3 McKenzie Rd	Broome	08 9193 6393	
Bunbury	**Colomberie B&B**	**11 Duffield Place**	**Gelorup**	**08 9795 7734**	*Page 255*
Burekup	Evedon Park Bush Resort	Lennard Rd	Burekup	08 9726 3012	
Busselton	Baudins of Busselton	87 Busselton Hwy	Busselton	08 9751 5576	
Cowaramup	Taunton Farm Holiday Park	Bussell Hwy	Cowaramup	08 9755 5334	
Cowaramup	The Tasty Olive	233 North Treeton Rd	Cowaramup	08 9755 5658	
Dongara	The Old Rectory B&B	19 Waldeck St	Dongara	08 9927 2252	
Donnybrook	Boronia Farm	47 Williams Rd	Donnybrook	08 9731 7154	
Donnybrook	Jarragon B&B	9 Collins St	Donnybrook	08 9731 1930	
Dunsborough	Newberry Manor	16 Newberry Rd	Dunsborough	08 9756 7542	
Dunsborough	Toby Inlet B&B	2 Backwater Retreat	Dunsborough	08 9756 7653	
Esperance	Esperance B&B by the Sea	Lot 34 Stewart St	Esperance	08 9071 5640	
Forest Grove	Margaret River Stone Cotts	67 Rowcliffe Rd	Forest Grove	08 9757 7544	
Fremantle	**Fothergills of Fremantle**	**18-22 Ord St**	**Fremantle**	**08 9335 6784**	*Page 256*
Fremantle	Kilkelly's B&B	82 Marine Terr	Fremantle	08 9336 1744	
Fremantle	Port Mill B&B	3/17 Essex St	Fremantle	08 9433 3832	
Fremantle	Portside Villa Accom	Unit 6/6 Ord St	Fremantle	08 9336 1021	
Fremantle	**Terrace Central B&B**	**79-85 South Terr**	**Fremantle**	**08 9335 6600**	*Page 257*
Fremantle	The Painted Fish	37 Hulbert St	South Fremantle	08 9335 4886	
Harvey	Bluehills Farmstay	Lot 303 Weir Rd	Harvey	0439 313 898	
Harvey	Harvey Hills Farmstay Chls	Weir Rd	Harvey	08 9729 1434	
Hazelvale	Che Sara Sara Chalets	92 Nunn Rd	Hazelvale	08 9840 8004	
Kalbarri	**Gecko Lodge**	**9 Glass St**	**Kalbarri**	**08 9937 1900**	*Page 258*
Kendelup	Melaleuca Wey B&B	498 Beattie Rd	Kendelup	08 9851 4365	
Leschenault	Paradise Found	3 Thomas Court	Leschenault	08 9797 0933	
Mandurah	Bellavista B&B	22 Anniston Loop	Mandurah	08 9583 4849	
Mandurah	**Port Mandurah Canal B&B**	**3 Reverie Mews**	**Mandurah**	**08 9535 2252**	*Page 259*
Mandurah - Nth Yunderup	**Nautica Lodge**	**203 Culeenup Rd**	**North Yunderup**	**08 9537 8000**	*Page 258*

Western Australia

Mandurah - Wannanup	Port Bouvard B&B	17 Voyager Cl	Wannanup	08 9534 5205	*Page 260*
Manjimup	Karri Rose B&B	14 Karri St	Manjimup	08 9772 4240	
Margaret River	Llewellins Guesthouse	64 Yates Rd	Margaret River	08 9757 9516	
Margaret River	Margaret River GH	22 Valley Rd	Margaret River	08 97572349	
Margaret River	Rosewood Guesthouse	54 Wallcliffe Rd	Margaret River	08 9757 2845	*Page 262*
Margaret River	The Noble Grape	Lot 18 Bussell Hwy	Cowaramup	08 9755 5538	*Page 261*
Moresby	Bluntisham B&B	21 Sexton Dv	Moresby	08 9938 1448	
Mukinbudin	Watson's Way Country Stay	1487 Cunderin Rd	Mukinbudin	08 9047 0014	
Nannup	Crabapple Lane B&B	Lot 500 Barrabup Rd	Nannup	08 9756 0017	
Narrogin	Chuckem Farm	1481 Tarwonga Rd	Narrogin	08 9881 1188	
Narrogin	Gumnut Cottage	4087 Williams Kondinin Rd	Narrogin	08 9882 4030	
Perth	Pension of Perth	3 Throssell St	Perth	08 9228 9049	*Page 263*
Perth - Ardross	Mount Pleasant Apts	27 Collier St	Ardross	08 9316 9818	
Perth - Armadale	Armadale Cottage B&B	3161 Albany Hwy	Armadale	08 9497 1663	
Perth - Baldivis	The Pavilion B&B	26 Peverett Loop	Baldivis	08 95231420	
Perth - Beaconsfield	Morris B&B	13 Morris St	Beaconsfield	08 9337 3572	
Perth - Bolgart	Boshack Eco Springs	Wattering Springs Rd	Bolgart	08 9368 2747	
Perth - Brigadoon	Stocks Country Retreat	26 Boulonnais Dv	Brigadoon	08 9296 1945	
Perth - City Bch	City Beach B&B	11 Helston Ave	City Beach	08 9385 8824	
Perth - Claremont	Peartree Cottage	3D Scott St	Claremont	0407 388 307	
Perth - Como	Como B&B	2A Bickley Cres	Como	08 9450 1442	
Perth - Coogee	Coogee Beach Accom	16 Toulon Grove	Coogee	08 9434 1691	
Perth - Cottesloe	Rosemoore B&B	2 Winifred St	Mosman Park	08 9384 8214	*Page 264*
Perth - Gidgegannup	Kwaba Maya Country Rtrt	48 Inthanoona Rd	Gidgegannup	08 9574 6823	
Perth - Gidgegannup	Lakeview Lodge B&B	131 Lakeview Dv	Gidgegannup	08 9578 3009	
Perth - Gilgering	Lavendale Farm	5895 Great Southern Hwy	Gilgering via York	08 9641 4131	
Perth - Gingin	The Runner's Rest	182 Cockram Rd	Gingin	08 9575 1414	
Perth - Gosnells	Southern River B&B	20b Greenhood Court	Gosnells	08 9490 8229	
Perth - Halls Head	St Andrews B&B	1 St Andrews Court	Halls Head	08 9581 1824	
Perth - Henley Brook	The River Retreat	10070 West Swan Rd	Henley Brook	08 9296 1007	
Perth - Lesmurdie	Anapana Ridge	38 Gilchrist Rd	Lesmurdie	08 9291 7997	
Perth - Lesmurdie	Falls Retreat B&B	45 Falls Rd	Lesmurdie	08 9291 7609	
Perth - Lesmurdie	Greenways Hills Rtrt	38 Cagney Way	Lesmurdie	08 9291 8232	
Perth - Lesmurdie	The Good Life B&B	64 George Rd	Lesmurdie	08 92913106	
Perth - Morangup	Talleringa B&B	135 Redbrook Circle	Morangup	08 9572 9393	
Perth - Mt Helena	Catton Hall Country H'std	Wilkins Rd	Mt Helena	08 9572 1375	
Perth - Mt Lawley	Durack House B&B	7 Almondbury Rd	Mt Lawley Perth	08 9370 4305	
Perth - Muchea	Enderslie House B&B	15 Peters Rd	Muchea	08 9571 0595	
Perth - Mullalloo	Ocean Sunset B&B	119 Mullaloo Dv	Mullalloo	08 9307 7334	
Perth - Mullaroo	Lazing Lizard	11 Bearing Pde	Mullaloo	0421 359 477	
Perth - Nedlands	Bedfords B&B	75 Bruce St	Nedlands	0417 907978	
Perth - Nedlands	Caesia House Apartment	32 Thomas St	Nedlands	08 9389 8174	*Page 264*
Perth - Nedlands	Exley House B&B	2 Bedford St	Nedlands	08 9386 4452	
Perth - Neerabup	Dales B&B	79 Wildflower Dv	Neerabup	08 9405 4472	
Perth - Nth Perth	Above Bored B&B	14 Norham St	North Perth	08 9444 5455	
Perth - Perth Hills	Grandview B&B	30 Girrawheen Dv	Gooseberry Hill	08 9293 2518	*Page 265*
Perth - Quinns Rocks	Camira B&B	52 Camira Way	Quinns Rocks	08 9406 8284	
Perth - Safety Bay	Pelican's Landing	352 Safety Bay Rd	Safety Bay	08 9592 3058	

Tell hosts you found them in the Bed & Breakfast Book

Western Australia

Perth - Safety Bay	Robe Manor	110 Penguin Rd	Safety Bay	08 9528 2726	
Perth - Safety Bay	Xscapes B&B	39 Janet Rd	Safety Bay	08 9592 4038	
Perth - Scarborough	Oupa's B&B	92 Stanley St	Scarborough	08 9341 6905	
Perth - Shoalwater	Golfers Retreat	16 Sao Jorge Green	Secret Harbour	08 9524 7210	
Perth - Shoalwater	Manuel Towers	32a Arcadia Dv	Shoalwater	08 9592 2698	
Perth - Sorrento	Albacore B&B	18 Albacore Dv	Sorrento	08 94482238	
Perth - Sorrento	**Sorrento Beach B&B**	**30 Hood Terr**	**Sorrento**	**08 94474871**	*Page 266*
Perth - Trigg	Guadalupe Hill	12-20 Diego Court	Trigg	0400 292 100	
Perth - Trigg	**Trigg Retreat B&B**	**59 Kitchener St**	**Trigg**	**08 9447 6726**	*Page 267*
Perth - Victoria Park	Durham Lodge B&B	165 Shepperton Rd	Victoria Park	08 9361 8000	
Perth - West Swan	Settlers Rest Farmstay	90 George St	West Swan	08 9250 4540	
Perth - Woodridge	Woollybush Guest House	205 Woollybush Loop	Woodridge	08 9577 1909	
Pinjarra	**Lazy River Boutique B&B**	**34 Wilson Rd**	**Pinjarra**	**08 9531 4550**	*Page 268*
Porongurup	Bolganup Homestead	1957 Porongurup Rd	Porongurup	08 9853 1049	
Sth Porongurup	Jilba Cottage	338 Millinup Rd	South Porongurup	08 9853 1038	
Toodyay	**Pecan Hill B&B**	**Lot 59 Beaufort St**	**Toodyay**	**08 9574 2636**	*Page 269*

Index

94 Highett B&B 228

A

Abaleigh on Lovers Walk 234
Above Wollongong at
    Pleasant Heights B&B 112
Albany View St Lodge B&B/Art Studio
    & Gallery 253
Alexander Lakeside B&B 147
Alice's Cottages and Spa Hideaways 192
Alrae Bed & Breakfast 229
Amani B&B 31
Amble at Hahndorf 170
AnDaCer Boutique B&B 42
An Oasis In The City 88
Apartment 401 224
Apartments on Star 191
Aquarelle Bed & Breakfast 110
Arabella Country House 235
Arcadian Retreat 65
Arcady Homestead 201
Ardara House 214
Argyll House 36
Armidale Boutique Accommodation 25
Arrowee House B&B 56
A Sunrise View 210
Auntie Ann's B&B 84
Ayr House B&B 212

B

B&B on the Beach 179
Bank B&B 57
Barefoot Springs 30
Barossa Shiraz Estate 172
Bayview House B&B 138
Baywoodbyne B&B 213
Beale's Bedfish & Breakfast 127
Bed & Breakfast Sydney Central 87
Bed and Breakfast @ Kiama 68
Bed and Views Kiama 69
Bella Vista 71
Bellescapes 173
Bellevue Terrace 90
Bellingen Heritage Cottages 29
Benbellen Country Retreat 82
Bethany Manor Bed & Breakfast 35
Billabong B&B 140
Bimblegumbie 107
Birkdale Bed & Breakfast 136
Blue Mountains Lakeside 38
Boambee Palms B&B 44
Bon Accord B&B 216
Botanica Lodge 41
Bowerbank Mill B&B 187
Braeside 39
Bronte Guesthouse 61
Broomelea 33
Bumblebrook Farm Motel 41
Burnbrow Manor & Cottage 243
Burrabliss Farms B&B 239

C

Caesia House Apartment Nedlands 264
Callistemon Cottage 178
Camerons Farmstay 76
Candlelight Cottages Retreat 208
Capers Guest House and Cottage 64
Cape Trib Exotic Fruit Farm 143
Captains Retreat B&B 230
Cardwell B&B 142
Carinya B&B and Mackays' Rest 111
Cathie Lesslie B&B 91
Chalet Swisse Spa 27
Chamel Fields Farmstay 178
Chelsea Park & Arcadia House 86
Cherry Tree Cottage 83
Chorleywood B&B 86
Claerwen Retreat 203
Clarendon Cottages 210
Clovelly Bed & Breakfast 88
Cocora Cottage 53
Colomberie B&B 255
Corinda's Cottages 189
Country Charm Swiss Cottages 205
Cow Bay Homestay 144
Craigmhor Mountain Retreat 58
Cruickshanks Farmstay B&B 26
Cudgerie Homestead B&B 152

D

Derwent Bridge Chalets & Studios 188
Dolphin Sands Jervis Bay 66
Dunn's B&B 111

E

Eboracum 89
Eco Queenslander 149
Eden at Fogg Dam 126
Edenholme Grange 192
Elfin Hill 62
Elizabeth's Manor 22
Elizas on the Murray 109
Elliminook 222
Elmstead Cottages 207
Emeu Inn Bed & Breakfast 219
Encounter Hideaway Cottages 179
Engadine B&B 89
Erldunda Station B&B 125
Eskdale Bed & Breakfast 137
Eumarella Shores Lake Retreat 150

F

Fairfield Guest House 226
Ferguson's Hunter Valley Getaway 58
Fernbrook Lodge 49
Fernglade on Menzies 209
Fothergills of Fremantle 256
Foxgloves 206
Freeman on Ford 206

Tell hosts you found them in the Bed & Breakfast Book

G

Galvin's Edge Hill B&B 139
Gecko Lodge 258
Genesta House 234
Giba Gunyah Country Cottages 28
Glen Isla House 233
Grande Vue 189
Grandview B&B 265
Greenacres B&B 43
Green Gables 108
Green Mango Hideaway 40
Greenwich B&B 92
Grevillea Lodge 15

H

Hamilton Heritage 78
Hampton Homestead 32
Harborne Bed & Breakfast 98
Harolden 91
Harts 97
Hazel Cottage 152
Headlands Beach Guest House 46
Hillcrest Mountain View Retreat 73
Hill Top Country Guest House 60
Holly Gate House B&B 244
Holman Estate Pokolbin 63
Homestay Brighton 169
Honeysuckle Cottages
    & The Rocks Restaurant 154
Hume's Hovell 24

I

Inglebrae 137
Interludes at Bawley 28

J

Jacaranda Country Lodge 74
Jan's Forestville B&B 90
Jemby-Rinjah Eco Lodge 31
Jenny's B&B 139
Jireh 153
Josephine's B&B 226

K

Kadina B&B 80
Kalimna Woods Cottages 220
Kathy's Place B&B 124
Kerrowgair 113
Kirkendale 167

L

Lakeside Villas at Crittenden Estate 232
Lake Weyba Cottages 151
Landfall 27
La Perouse B&B 221
Lazy River Boutique Bed & Breakfast 268
Leura's Magical Manderley 34
Lillypilly's Country Cottages 155
Lilybank 141
Lisnagarvey Cottage 50
Lochinvar House 60
Lorneview B&B 221

M

Magnolia House B&B 93
Majic Views B&B 36
Maleny Country Cottages 155
Manly Harbour Loft 95
Markdale Homestead 48
Meadowlake Lodge 72
Melba House 33
Merewether Beach B&B 77
Merton Manor Exclusive B&B 242
Metro on Alexander 176
Michaela's Place 96
Mildura's Linsley House 231
Millamolong 47
Montrave House B&B Home & Pet Stay 147
Mooloolah Valley Holidays 156
Morpeth Convent Guest House
    & St Bede's Cottage 62
Mountain Grand Boutique Hotel 217
Mountain Jewel B&B 38
Mount Ophir Estate 237
Mulberry Cottage B&B 194

N

Naracoopa B&B 136
Narrabundah B&B 15
Nautica Lodge 258
Newcomen B&B 77
Ninderry House 154
Noosa Valley Manor Luxury B&B 151
Norfolk Bay Convict Station 193
Nthaba Cottage B&B 123

O

Oakhampton Homestead
    & Country Holidays 103
Observatory Cottages 209
Ocean Manor B&B 240
Ohanez Holiday House 174
Old Nubba Schoolhouse 114
Orana House 190
Orange Grove B&B 220

P

Paddington B&B 98
Paradise Gardens 201
Pecan Hill B&B 269
Pendower House 211
Penlan Cottage 83
Pension of Perth 263
Pepper Tree B&B 96
Pericoe Retreat B&B 50
PJ's 70
Point of View 202
Pomona Spa Cottages 186
Pompei B&B 92
Port Bouvard B&B 260
Port Mandurah Canal B&B 259
Possums Rest B&B 167
Pub Hill Farm 75

Q

Qdos Treehouses 222
Quamby Homestead 243

R

Ready Cottage 236
Redbank Gums B&B 52
Reflections B&B 254
Restaurant & Wine Centre 219
Reynella Homestead 21
Rivendell 29
Riviera Bed & Breakfast 145
Robinsons in the City 224
Robyn's Nest Guest House 71
Rock-Al-Roy B&B 148
Rooftops B&B 57
Rosemoore B&B 264
Roseneath B&B 190
Rose Villa 168
Rosewood Guesthouse 262
Rotherwood 228
Royal Mail Hotel - Mt Sturgeon Estate 217
Rumbalara B&B 145

S

Sandholme Guesthouse 67
Sartain's at Mornington 232
Saunders Gorge Sanctuary 171
Schouten House 195
Scotland Island Lodge 102
Seapod B&B 169
Seascape Lodge on Emu Bay 175
Seashells Kiama 69
Secrets on the Lake 156
Shoal Bay B&B 85
Silent Grove Farmstay B&B 55
Simpsons of Potts Point Boutique Hotel 100
Snug Cove B&B 54
Solitary Islands Lodge 45
Sonja's B&B 70
Sorrento Beach B&B 266
Springbank B&B 215
Springfields 225
Stringybark Cottages B&B 204
Surveyor's Hill Winery and B&B 13
Syl's Sydney Homestay 101

T

Talinga 106
Tallowood Ridge 104
Tamasha House 238
Tantarra B&B 78
Tara House 203
Terrace Central B&B 257
Terra Nova House 94
The Bank Guesthouse 105
The Chamomile B&B 146
The Gatehouse at Villa Raedward 245
The Greens of Leura 35
The Grelco Run 218
The Hideaway 124
The Mulberry Tree B&B & Tea Rooms 207
The Noble Grape 261
The Old George and Dragon Guesthouse 59
The Old Parkes Convent 81
The Old School 114
The Pelican 241
The Pittwater Bed & Breakfast 97
The Two Story B&B 43
Time and Tide Beach Apartment 170
Tinaroo Haven Holiday Lodge 140
Tomah Mountain Lodge 37
Trigg Retreat Bed and Breakfast 267
Troldhaugen Lodge 67
Tuki Retreat 211

U

Undine Colonial Accommodation 191

V

Victoria's Byron Bay 39
Victoria Court Sydney 99
Villa Donati 227

W

Walls Court B&B 51
Waratah Brighton Boutique B&B 225
Water Bay Villa B&B 168
While Away B&B 157
Whitby on Wallis B&B 79
Whitsunday Heritage Cane Cutters Cottage 135
Whitsunday Lodge B&B 135
Whitsunday Moorings B&B 134
Willowbrook Cottages B&B's 177
Wombat Hill B&B 30
Woodlands B&B 81